Foundation Flash 8 Video

Tom Green
Jordan Chilcott

friendsof
DESIGNER TO DESIGNER™
an Apress® company

Foundation Flash 8 Video

ISBN-13 (pbk): 978-1-59059-651-7

ISBN-10 (pbk): 1-59059-651-X

Printed and bound in China 9 8 7 6 5 4 3 2 1

Distributed to the book trade worldwide by Springer-Verlag New York, Inc., 233 Spring Street, 6th Floor, New York, NY 10013. Phone 1-800-SPRINGER, fax 201-348-4505, e-mail orders-ny@springer-sbm.com, or visit www.springeronline.com.

For information on translations, please contact Apress directly at 2560 Ninth Street, Suite 219, Berkeley, CA 94710. Phone 510-549-5930, fax 510-549-5939, e-mail info@apress.com, or visit www.apress.com.

The source code for this book is freely available to readers at www.friendsofed.com in the Downloads section.

Credits

Lead Editors Chris Mills and Charles E. Brown	**Assistant Production Director** Kari Brooks-Copony
Technical Reviewer Tim Diacon	**Production Editor** Katie Stence
Editorial Board Steve Anglin, Dan Appleman, Ewan Buckingham, Gary Cornell, Jason Gilmore, Jonathan Hassell, James Huddleston, Chris Mills, Matthew Moodie, Dominic Shakeshaft, Jim Sumser, Matt Wade	**Compositor** Dina Quan
	Artist Kinetic Publishing Services, LLC
	Proofreader Nancy Sixsmith
Project Manager Denise Santoro Lincoln	**Indexer** Lucie Haskins
Copy Edit Manager Nicole LeClerc	**Cover Image Designer** Corné van Dooren
Copy Editor Liz Welch	**Interior and Cover Designer** Kurt Krames
Manufacturing Director Tom Debolski	

To Gary Lima, mentor and friend, who makes it clear to anyone who will listen that everything he learned about management, he learned in a rock and roll band.

Tom

This book is dedicated to my children, Margot, Henry, Jack, Joshua, and Dina, her husband Wayne and their daughter Cassidy Helen. You all are the reason I ever wanted a video camera in the first place.

Jordan

CONTENTS AT A GLANCE

CONTENTS

CONTENTS

FOREWORD

"If it ain't broke, don't fix it."

I couldn't disagree more. I distinctly remember a manager in big new media company I worked at giving one of the designers a hard time for working up a neat volume slider for a website. The manager couldn't understand why the designer wanted to waste time designing a new means of adjusting volume when the existing standard design did the job fine. His argument isn't without merit under some circumstances. This book, for example, will show you how to use components to deliver video quickly and efficiently. Components are valuable timesavers that allow you to use standard, off-the-shelf controls.

But, imagine if James Dyson had listened to the people who laughed at him when he said he was going to invent a better vacuum cleaner? He accepted that Hoover, among others, produced a good product that worked well, but he looked for a better way, and in the process invented the world's best vacuum cleaner. I'm sure it's the acceptance of the accepted that is the reason my car's engine is not powered by water, there is no cure for the common cold, and that red wine gives me a sore head the next day.

There are two types of people who are going to get the most out of this book. First there are those of us who enthusiastically embraced Flash video when it first became available and have been using it effectively on and off ever since. We're old school, we know our stuff, and we clearly don't need a book like this. But go on, give it a read. Flick through it for a bit.

It's easy to become complacent with what you know when what you know works. Fortunately for us, the good people at Macromedia/Adobe have been anything but complacent and have continued to focus on developing video within Flash. The way we used to work with Flash video still works, so why fix it? Because there are newer, better ways of working. A lot of people are still embedding video into the timeline and using workarounds for hassles like synchronizing frame rates. If this sounds like you, then I suggest that you set some time aside to spend reading this book and discover a better way.

The other type of person for whom this book is perfect is the video virgin. This whole thing might seem a bit daunting—but don't worry, it's not. Video is too often perceived as a black art, but once you get your head around a few simple concepts, you'll be asking yourself why it's taken until now for you to give it a shot.

I'd like to take this opportunity to salute the authors specifically for the first chapter. You're going to be thrown in at the deep end before you know how to swim. You'll not have time to let your fear of the water get in the way and within a few minutes you'll be treading water, laughing at how easy it is. This approach to learning is nothing short of genius.

As a video virgin, you will start to hear the same kind of comment again and again from those advising you—whether they be classroom tutors, web tutorials, or indeed authors of books like this. Developments in recent years really have made life better for people looking to broadcast digital video, especially over the Internet—so much so that anyone who has been using video for more than a couple of years will be found preaching to you about how easy you've got it these days, and how difficult life used to be. I'm no exception—there never has been a better time to get into video for the first time, and here's why:

1. The creation tools are simpler and cheaper with both Apple and Microsoft's recent operating systems coming preloaded with worthwhile video capture and editing software. If you do have some extra budget available, then Adobe's latest tools (such as After Effects 7) give you a feature set previously reserved for very expensive specialist video editing suites.

2. Flash Player as the delivery mechanism makes worrying about whether end users have the right video plug-in a thing of the past. In the bad old days, the variety of video formats and incompatibilities between platforms put most clients off using video in their projects.

3. Even my mum's got broadband! We've finally gotten to the point where modem users have to admit to being the second-class citizens that they are. Okay, that's a bit harsh, but when you surf using a modem there is an acceptance that you're not going to fully appreciate everything that is out there. Your modem is enough to get your email, do your online banking. and sell your unwanted Christmas presents on eBay. Modem users have fallen to the position of lowest-common denominator.

It's okay to deliver video over the Internet now. It really is.

Come on in, the water's warm.

Hoss Gifford, 2006

Hoss Gifford is a Flash video guru based in Scotland.
For more on his work, visit `hossgifford.com`.

ABOUT THE AUTHORS

Tom Green is Professor of Interactive Media in the School of Media Studies at the Humber Institute of Technology and Applied Learning in Toronto. When not in class, Tom is a partner at CommunityMX and has written several articles for the Macromedia Developer Center. He is also a member of Team Macromedia, one of the founding members of FlashinTO, the largest Macromedia User Group in the world, a certified Macromedia Dreamweaver Developer, and has spoken at many web development, Flash, and distance-learning conferences throughout the world. His website can be found at www.tomontheweb.ca.

Jordan L. Chilcott, born and raised in Toronto and now a resident of Guelph, Ontario, graduated from Radio College of Canada's Electronic Engineering Technology program in 1983, only to discover that he had a passion for computer programming. Spending his days working as a service technician, Jordan invested many sleepless nights teaching himself Assembly Language. He published his first program in 1985 and started learning higher-level languages such as C and C++.

Jordan cofounded The Computer Software Specialists, now known as Interactivity Unlimited, and eventually left the computer hardware industry to focus on his passion for programming. Today, Jordan has written various web and kiosk applications for various industries, including the automotive and airline industry and programs in various languages, including ActionScript, ColdFusion, Java/J2EE, and C/C++/Objective C. When not programming or administering the Dreamweaver-Talk list, he spends time with his wife Joelle and five children, Margot, Dina, Henry, Jack, and Joshua (he has also recently become a grandfather). Jordan also loves to compose, produce, and record music, helping upcoming artists as well as producing movie soundtracks; he is a wedding photographer with Joelle; and he now holds a Black Belt in Goju Ryu Karate.

ABOUT THE TECHNICAL REVIEWER

Tim Diacon lives and works in Brighton, England. Having studied graphic design at Brighton University, he briefly worked as a freelance web designer before joining Crush Design and Art Direction, where he has worked as a print and web designer for the past three years, creating Flash-based applications for clients such as Disney, Heineken International, and Diageo.

ABOUT THE COVER IMAGE DESIGNER

Corné van Dooren designed the front cover image for this book. Having been given a brief by friends of ED to create a new design for the Foundation series, he was inspired to create this new setup combining technology and organic forms.

With a colorful background as an avid cartoonist, Corné discovered the infinite world of multimedia at the age of 17—a journey of discovery that hasn't stopped since. His mantra has always been "The only limit to multimedia is the imagination," a mantra that is keeping him moving forward constantly.

After enjoying success after success over the past years—working for many international clients, as well as being featured in multimedia magazines, testing software, and working on many other friends of ED books—Corné decided it was time to take another step in his career by launching his own company, *Project 79*, in March 2005.

You can see more of his work and contact him through www.cornevandooren.com or www.project79.com.

If you like his work, be sure to check out his chapter in *New Masters of Photoshop: Volume 2*, also by friends of ED (ISBN: 1590593154).

ACKNOWLEDGMENTS

The path to this book has been a "long, strange trip" that started over hamburgers a couple years back when Mike Downey, the Flash product manager, showed a group of us the pre-alpha version of Flash 8. He demoed a video using the FLV Playback component and the new On2 VP6 codec, and to say jaws were hitting the table would be an understatement. When Flash 8 was released in late 2005, the web video revolution kicked off and I have been writing about it ever since.

This book itself actually started over coffee with my editor, Chris Mills, at a Starbucks in New York. Since that conversation, Chris has pushed, prodded, and, on occasion, laid a swift kick into my pants as this book moved from concept to the final product. Along the way I discovered that Chris and I share the same fascination for this technology and that we have become good friends along the way. It is also odd to see Charles Brown appear on the team for this book. It was Charles who first introduced me to Chris in New York, and it was Charles who also wrangled many of the code explanations in this book into coherence. Thanks, buddy.

I would also like to thank Denise Santoro Lincoln, our project manager, who has the amazing ability to actually get a writer to meet a deadline.

This is the fourth book where Jord and I have shared the cover. We have an amazing professional relationship and have also developed a great friendship.

Finally, I want to acknowledge the support and understanding of my wife, Keltie, and my two children, Lindsay and Robert. The three of them have gotten used to me being in a "writing mood" and holing myself up in my home office for inordinate amounts of time. It will be nice to see them again.

Tom

INTRODUCTION

This book actually has its genesis back in the early 1990s when the Internet was about to arrive. Apple pulled a bunch of Humber College faculty together in one of the classrooms on campus and demonstrated a thing they called "QuickTime." The video they showed was only 180 by 120 and the sound was pretty crappy, but it was at that point that I realized videotape was an endangered technology and that computers could actually play video.

For the next few years, like any emerging technology, Digital Video underwent a rather intense phase of competing technologies, players, formats, and so on. Just when the dust settled around the QuickTime standard, the Internet hit and another round of competing technologies and players for web video was launched.

Up until a couple of years ago, web video was something you "paid for." If it was streaming technology, you paid for proprietary hardware and software. Consumers paid for it emotionally. Long download times, especially with dial-up modems, were the norm and the odds were pretty good that the viewer didn't have the plug-in to view the video. Even Flash was struggling. The best we could do was drop the entire video on the timeline and pray that the viewer was as hooked on "cool" as we were and was prepared for a long wait as the SWF loaded.

In September 2003 I had an insight that, at least for me, was the equivalent to whatever happened to St. Paul on the road to Damascus. I had just finished writing a book about the Macromedia Studio and decided I really wanted to get a handle on video delivery through the Web. I wondered how to play with it in Flash MX 2004. I created the FLV and ran it through the FLV Media Controller component. What happened next is the event that caused the straight line to the book you currently have in your hands.

I dropped the SWF into a Dreamweaver page and, through the magic of CSS, ran the text around the video much like text running around an image in a print magazine. I uploaded the page to my server to test it, and when I opened the page in a browser it suddenly occurred to me that something profound was going on. First, the video played like a dream and the text ran around the image. It occurred to me as soon as I saw the page that I was looking at the future of web video.

There was no plug-in. The delay was minimal. The video played perfectly, and it was a part of the content in the page, not separate from it. I mulled this over, played with it, and on October 14, 2003, wrote an article for Community MX titled "Bye Bye QuickTime." The start of the piece went this way:

> *The other day I was sitting in the office of one of my colleagues at the college where I teach and we were discussing some rather broad web issues. He teaches the hardcore coding side of the equation and I handle the hardcore design issues. Together we are the poster boys for a "Geeks and Freaks" project team. We were talking about an upcoming presentation around the Studio MX 2004 products that I am about to do for the faculty and I casually let slip I was coming to the conclusion that "QuickTime, Windows Media Player and RealPlayer/RealAudio are dead web technologies." His reaction was similar to someone who has just experienced a 20,000-volt cattle prod jolt to the armpit.*
>
> *Now that I have your attention, as well, let me explain.*
>
> *Why do we need the QuickTime, Windows Media and Real Players when it comes to video and audio on the web? I, for one, am seriously tired of Apple's persistent begging for me to upgrade to Pro when I launch their player. I am absolutely frustrated with Windows Media Player and its inability to either find a codec or to tell me which flipping codec is missing. Real, to me is a litterbug, strewing my desktop with RAM files. Not only that, I have absolutely no guarantee the users even have the plug-ins and can see the content.*
>
> *The other issue is purely selfish. If I control the web turf why am I ceding a piece of the interface to a third party?*
>
> *Which brings me to that Trojan Horse known as the Flash Player 7. . .*

This article still resonates today. As I was writing this Introduction my email client just dinged and the following from a "time challenged" Community MX subscriber arrived in my In basket:

> *Title—Bye Bye QuickTme*
>
> *Feedback—I ran into this tutorial, and it impressed me to see how almost a year earlier you had foreseen what I came to dream of 7 mo ago. And yet this is my problem . . .*

I didn't include that note to prove how clever or "ahead of the curve" that I am. I couldn't care less, but it is so typical of why this book has been written. Macromedia—now Adobe—has sparked a web video revolution with Flash Professional 8. Tie that in with Adobe's video products, especially After Effects 7, and we are about to see uses for web video that we never thought of even three years ago. We are like kids in a candy store with web video. The creative and practical uses of this technology are immense, and, like all emerging technologies that are instant web standards, we are all in the same boat trying to figure out what we can do with this stuff.

This book is not the definitive answer to that question. In many respects it is Jord and me saying "Hey, here is what we have figured out you can do. Now go drive a truck through it." As you work your way through the various chapters and exercises, you will be presented with techniques and ideas that range from the dead simple to the rather complex. You will see some rather cool video techniques that live in a code-free zone and techniques that fill a blank stage with eye-popping effects driven solely by ActionScript. You will build videos that have a commercial application and others that fall squarely into the "art/experimental" zone. Regardless of complexity or use, the subliminal message behind every exercise in this book is "Here is what you can do."

This book is also the start of a dialogue between us. We aren't going to claim we are experts in the field simply because the field is too new. We are all making it up as we go along and learning where the edge of the video envelope is on the Web. As such, as you go through the code you may find yourself saying, "That ain't the way I would do it." By all means contact me at tom@tomontheweb.ca and tell me how you would do it. If you have a technique you have discovered or "have driven a truck" through one of the techniques in the book, by all means let me know. I am just as eager to learn from you. This book, in many respects, is the start of a journey we are taking, together, as we come to grips with Flash video.

Like all journeys, we start at the beginning and explain how to create an FLV file and get it playing in Flash. From there you learn how to create a video using iMovie and MovieMaker. Chapter 3 starts the exploration of Flash video by looking at alternative FLV creation tools. Adobe doesn't own the market for FLV creation; Sorenson Squeeze and On2's Flix are explored, contrasted, and compared and. . . darned if it isn't a draw. If all you need to know is how to create a video for Flash and create the video, then you close the book at this point and move on.

The creative exploration of video starts in the next chapter—Chapter 4—which shows you how to use the video UI components that are new to Flash 8 and how to deliver video without using the FLV Playback component.

If there is any one aspect of Flash video that has the design community just "gaga," it is the ability to use an alpha channel. In this chapter we not only show you how to create the alpha channel video in Premier, After Effects, and Final Cut Pro, but we then show you some rather slick things you can do with it, with techniques ranging from "video-on-video" to placing the FLV on an HTML page.

We must admit that the addition of the filters and blend effects to Flash is in the realm of "ultra-cool," and we have a whole chapter showing you how to use them singly and in combination with each other to create video effects that move way beyond cool. Staying with the "cool" factor, the next chapter shows you how to implement some rather fascinating masking effects, from placing a video in a phone to creating and adding masks to the video at runtime.

The next three chapters push the creative exploration of video even further and show you a number of techniques that will push your Flash skills to the next level. Chapter 8 shows you how to build video walls and incorporate motion graphics created in After Effects into Flash. The next chapter demonstrates a number of ways to play multiple videos using techniques that range from the simple to the complex. Chapter 10 is where you get to kick back and have a bit of fun using a webcam in ways you may not have considered.

Everything to this point in the book is stuff you can build for your clients. Chapter 11 is just for you. This chapter is devoted to creating a small project that lets you see how a video will look if you change the color, add a blur or glow filter, apply a blend mode, or apply all of these effects. In many respects, this chapter is designed to introduce you to adding the filters and blends using ActionScript.

The book ends with a number of entry-level Motion graphics techniques created in After Effects 7 and placed into Flash. These two applications were made for each other, and this chapter just scratches the surface of what will become a powerful web video production combination over the next few years.

We hope you learn something from this book and, most important of all, that you have the same amount of fun Jord and I had as we embarked upon this exploration of Flash video. In many respects, "fun" is the key word. Playing what-if games and having fun with this technology is what will drive it forward over the next several years.

Tom Green
February, 2006

Layout conventions

To keep this book as clear and easy to follow as possible, the following text conventions are used throughout.

Important words or concepts are normally highlighted on the first appearance in **bold type**.

Code is presented in `fixed-width font`.

New or changed code is normally presented in **`bold fixed-width font`**.

Pseudocode and variable input are written in *`italic fixed-width font`*.

Menu commands are written in the form Menu ➤ Submenu ➤ Submenu.

Where I want to draw your attention to something, we've highlighted it like this:

> *Ahem, don't say I didn't warn you.*

Sometimes code won't fit on a single line in a book. Where this happens, we use an arrow like this: ➥.

```
This is a very, very long section of code that should be written all ➥
on the same line without a break.
```

1 CREATING AN FLV USING THE VIDEO WIZARD AND THE FLASH 8 VIDEO ENCODER

Let's start this book in an odd place. Let's learn how to swim.

There is a school of thought around learning to swim that claims the best way is to jump into the deep end and figure it out. That is sort of where we are starting this book. We are going to dive right into the deep end of creating a video for Flash Professional 8 but we will be there helping you along every step of the way.

Before you step off the pool deck and into the deep end, here are a few things you need to know:

- You are not *creating* a video. You are *encoding* a video. This means you will be simply converting a QuickTime video from one format—MOV—to another—FLV. This conversion process is referred to as encoding.

- FLV files can be encoded using the Video Import Wizard built into Flash Professional 8. The "Wizard" is really nothing more than a series of panels that carefully walk you through the process of creating the FLV.

- FLV files can also be encoded using the standalone Flash 8 Video Encoder. When you installed Flash Professional 8 on your computer, you also installed a separate application called the Flash 8 Video Encoder. You can find it on your PC by going to `Program Files\ Macromedia\Flash 8 Video Encoder` or `Applications/Macromedia/Flash 8 Video Encoder` on a Macintosh.

- With two encoding choices, you may be wondering which way to go. Either one is acceptable, but if you are new to using the video features of Flash Professional 8 we suggest you start with the Wizard. Once you start moving into more complex video use and special effects, the standalone Video Encoder will become your tool of choice.

We'll start with the Video Import Wizard built into Flash Professional 8, but first you need to know a bit about the file that is being encoded.

Before you import

Flash can only import video if you have either QuickTime 7, QuickTime 6.5, or for you Windows users, DirectX 9 installed on your computer. If you don't have them, things may not work as expected, so you may need to visit the Microsoft or Apple websites to download and install the software.

If you have QuickTime on your Mac or PC, you can import the following file formats:

- **Audio Video Interleave (AVI)**: The AVI format is very common on Windows systems.
- **Digital Video (DV)**: This is the format, DV, used by your camcorder.
- **Motion Pictures Experts Group (MPEG)**: This is the organization that devised the MPG or MPEG standard.
- **QuickTime (MOV)**: This standard, developed by Apple in the early 1990s, is the one used by most video professionals.

If you are a Windows user and have DirectX 9 installed, you can also use these formats:

- **Windows Media File (WMF or ASF)**: This is the format—WMV or ASF—commonly used by the Windows Media Player.
- **Audio Video Interleave (AVI)**
- **Motion Picture Experts Group**

Knowing the formats you can use makes life easier all around. If you are creating the video, then you know what file format to use, and if someone else is producing the video file for you, you can tell them what format to use to create the video.

> *Throughout this book we will be using the terms* video *or* digital video. *Both refer to a document using one of the formats listed earlier. If we are referring directly to a file produced by a video camera, we will refer to it as a* **DV** *file.*

The other thing you need to do is make sure the video you are using is as uncompressed as possible. That may sound odd but it really has a lot to do with the quality of the final product. The encoders used by Flash actually compress the file. Video that is compressed has already lost some information, which is why video compressors are called "lossy." If you compress an already-compressed file you are going to lose a lot more information, and that will have a direct impact on the quality of the finished product. The thing that does the compression job is called a codec, which is short for enCOder-DECoder or COmpressor-DECompressor, depending on who you are talking to.

Importing a video with the Flash Video Import Wizard

The source video for this exercise is a music video named "Tortoise." It is a QuickTime video that is one minute long and has a file size of 9.2 MB, which puts it in the realm of really big web files. You can download the ZIP version of this file from www.friendsofed.com or, if you have some footage you would rather use, feel free to substitute.

When importing video it is important that you closely match the frame rate—fps, or frames per second—and physical dimensions of the source video. These two values are easily obtained by opening the video in QuickTime and selecting Window ➤ Info (PC) or Window ➤ Show Movie Info (Mac). The Info window will open to display all of the information you need, as shown in Figure 1-1. Matching the values here will ensure smooth playback later on.

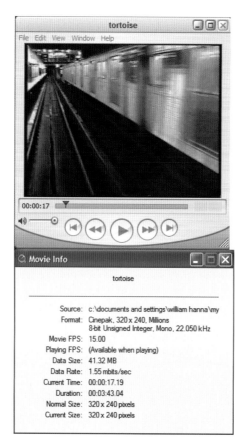

Figure 1-1. The sample video is opened in QuickTime and the Info window is displayed.

Now that we know what we are working with, let's go swimming:

1. Open Flash Professional 8 and create a new document; be sure to save it to the same folder as the location for the FLV (more about why in a moment). The first thing to check is the frame rate of the Flash movie. It should closely match that of the video, which, in our case, is 15 fps. If the video is shot using the North American NTSC standard, you obviously are not going the have Flash play at 29.97 fps. In this situation, setting the Flash frame rate to 24 will work.

2. The next step in the process is to select Import ➤ Import Video. This will open the Video Import Wizard.

   The Video Import Wizard is a rather clever series of screens that walk you through the entire video encoding process, starting from locating the video to actually placing it on the stage and having it ready to play. You will be asked some rather interesting questions along the way, such as "Is the video to be played from your web server?" and "What style of video controls would you like to use?"

3. The first screen that opens—Select Video—simply asks you to locate the video to be encoded (see Figure 1-2). There are only two places where the video can be located. The first is in a folder on your computer. The second location is on an actual server used to stream media. This means you either have a Flash Media Server, Flash Communication Server (FlashComm), or a FlashComm account with an Internet service provider. The other server location is a Flash Video Streaming Service (FVSS). These are companies that charge you a monthly fee to store and deploy Flash video on the Web.

Click the Browse button and when the Open dialog box appears, navigate to the folder containing the video to be encoded. Click on it and then click the OK button. If you have a FlashComm or FVSS account, you only need to enter the URL where the video file is located. Click the Next button.

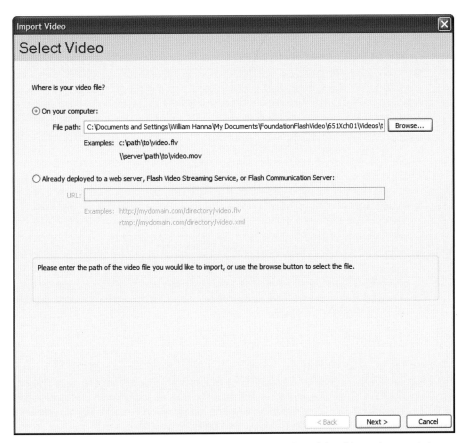

Figure 1-2. Use the Select Video panel to navigate to the location of the video to be encoded.

4. Now that Flash knows where the video is located, you need to tell it where it will be sent for playback. The next screen you see, Deployment, determines how the FLV file will be created (see Figure 1-3). Your choices are

- Progressive download from a web server: This option assumes the FLV file will be sitting in a directory on your web server and playing from that server. When you select this option, Flash understands that the video data must be streamed into the SWF in a slightly different manner than if you were to use FlashComm or FVSS. This "slightly different manner" is called a progressive download. What happens is that enough data is "streamed" into the SWF to enable it to play smoothly from start to finish. When that point is reached, the video starts to play. This means there may be, depending on the size and length of the video, a very slight delay before the video starts to play.

- Stream from Flash Video Streaming Service: This option assumes you have an account with one of these companies.

- Stream from Flash Communication Server: This option assumes the FLV will be located in your FlashComm account.

- Embed Video in SWF and play in timeline: Essentially this option will move the FLV into the Flash library and put the video on the main timeline or, if the video is in a movie clip, on the movie clip's timeline. In many respects this is not recommended. When a video is placed on a Flash timeline, the timeline will expand to include one Flash frame for each frame in the video. For example, a 60-second video may require 720 frames to play if it were to be imported directly to the timeline. That may not seem like much, but when a SWF loads in a web page, it won't start playing until every frame in the movie, including the 720 frames in the imported video and its audio, have loaded. The other nasty aspect of this option is a corresponding increase in the size of the SWF to accommodate the video. Still, if the video is short—5 to 10 seconds—or you want to play with it in some manner, this option works.

- Linked QuickTime video for publishing to QuickTime: In the early pre-video days of Flash—Flash Player 5 and lower—you could actually convert the Flash movie to a QuickTime video. The upshot of this was total loss of interactivity. This feature is rarely, if ever used, these days, though animators who prepare Flash for broadcast do make use of it.

Select the Progressive download option and click the Next button.

So what is the difference between a stream and a progressive download? The difference lies in how the video is delivered to the Flash Player from the server. The first thing to understand is that a stream, in very basic terms, is the flow of information. In the case of a video, it is the information that actually plays the video in the Flash Player on your web page. The difference comes down to when the video starts to play.

If you choose one of the two streaming options, the FLV is sitting on a server designed to stream video into the Flash Player. This server is a Flash Media Server, and FLV files arriving in your Flash Player start to play as soon as the first bit of information hits the Player. The Flash Media Server, in many respects, controls the flow of the information into the Player.

A progressive download doesn't use a media server. It uses your web server to start the flow of information into the Player. When the FLV is "called" by the Player, the FLV information starts flowing into the Player. The Player waits for enough information to arrive so it can start playing the FLV to ensure the video doesn't stop when it starts playing. For example, the Player may sit around waiting for 10 percent of the information in the FLV to accumulate before it starts playing the video in the Player. It may only take 1 second for this to happen.

So the difference comes down to time. If you are using a Flash Media Server, the video starts playing right away and "Play means Play." If you use a progressive download, there will be a very short delay before the video starts to play.

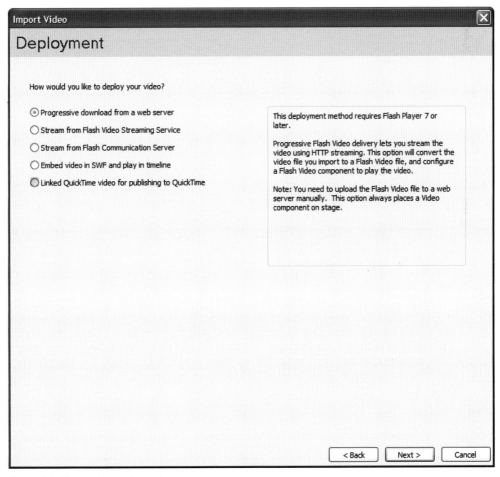

Figure 1-3. The Deployment panel

5. The next screen to open is the Encoding panel (see Figure 1-4). This is where you will have to decide what codec will be used to create the FLV, the streaming rate, the frame rate, and a number of other choices that will have an impact on playback. The decisions you make here will have a direct impact on your viewer's experience, so let's spend some time here looking at this panel.

Figure 1-4. The Encoding panel

The first thing you see is the default encoding profile. If you click the drop-down menu you will see seven presets, each targeted at either the Flash 7 or Flash 8 Player. If you select a preset, the settings are outlined in the information area directly below your choice. Essentially, the choice of Flash Player comes down to a choice of codec. The Flash Player 7 only uses the Sorenson codec and the new On2 VP6 codec can only be used in the Flash Player 8.

The default you are looking at essentially says the video will only be playable in the Flash 8 Player. It is encoded using the Flash 8–only On2 VP6 codec, which explains why it can only be played in the Flash 8 Player. The rest of the information tells you the video will stream at a rate of 400 kilobits per second (kbps) and that the sound in the video will be converted to an MP3 stereo format and streamed out at 96 kbps.

Over on the right side of the screen you see the first frame of the video and under it are three sliders. The top slider lets you move forward and backward in the video. The two sliders under it set the *in* and *out* points.

The top slider is commonly called a *jog control,* and if you move it to the right you will see that you can advance through the video. The other important thing that happens is the time under the image changes to show you exactly where you are in the video. This time measurement is quite precise—hours: minutes: seconds: milliseconds. This measurement will come in very handy later on in this book when you create a movie that triggers events based on the current time of the video.

The in and out points are also quite useful. They establish the start and the end of the video and can be used to remove unwanted footage at the start or the end of the video or even to extract a short piece in the middle of the video. Using the in and out sliders to remove footage also has the pleasant side effect of reducing the final size of the FLV file.

The final feature of this panel is the Show Advanced Settings button. Click this button and the panel fills with a number of settings, sliders, and so on that allow you to precisely control many of the streaming values and other properties used when a video is encoded. We'll dig deeper into this area later on in this chapter when we use the Flash 8 Video Encoder.

> **6.** Click the Next button to advance to the Skinning panel. Select the SteelExternalAll.swf option from the drop-down list.

The Skinning panel has a rather confusing name. In this panel you actually determine if you will add playback controls to the video. Previous versions of Flash treated skinning in much the way Henry Ford treated the color of Model T cars: *"They can have any color they want as long as it is black."* Previous versions of Flash let you use any skin you wished as long as it was the "Halo" skin used to determine the look and feel of Flash components.

Flash Professional 8 offers you 33 different controller styles or skins that come in a variety of colors (see Figure 1-5). In addition, you can even create a custom skin—put your client's logo in the controller or whatever—and use it. When you select a skin style you can see what it looks like in the preview area of the panel. The various skins appear in one of two areas: over the video or under the video. You can't place them at the top or on the sides of the video.

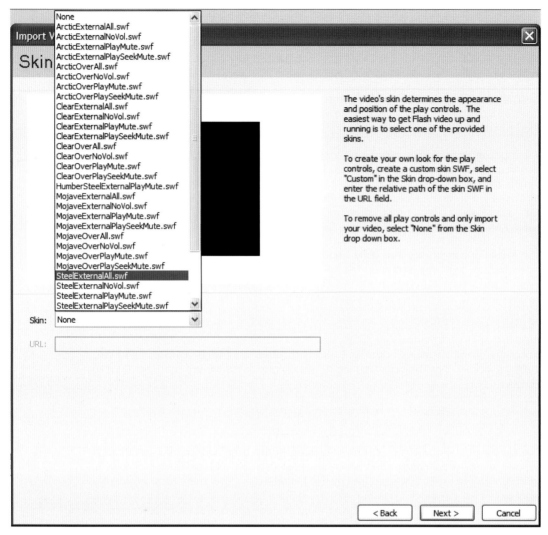

Figure 1-5. The Skinning panel with the various skin (or control) options shown

7. Click the Next button to open the Finish Video Import panel. Carefully read the instructions and click Finish.

The first thing that will happen is you will be prompted to save your Flash file. Navigate to the folder where this file is to be saved, name the file, and click OK. The window will close and you will be shown the progress of the video encoding process as well as a review of the options chosen in the Encoding panel (see Figure 1-6).

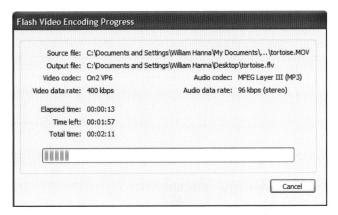

Figure 1-6. You will be shown the progress of the encoding process.

The encoding process actually does two things. It creates the FLV used in Flash and places it in the same folder as the Flash file you just saved. The second thing it does is place a copy of the `SteelExternalAll.swf` skin in that folder as well.

8. When the Encoding process finishes, you are returned to the Flash stage and the video is placed on the stage. Press Ctrl+Enter (PC) or Cmd+Return (Mac) to preview the video through the Flash Player on your computer (see Figure 1-7).

Figure 1-7. Playing back the video that has been imported into Flash

Congratulations and welcome to Flash video. You have just encoded a video, chosen the skin, put it on the Flash stage, and played the video. All of this in eight rather simple steps. If you have used previous versions of Flash, you will see that Macromedia has pulled off a rather interesting feat. They made what was a rather complicated process even more complex but easier to use. If you have never used Flash video, created an FLV, or regarded the entire video in Flash "thing" as being a bit over your head... welcome to the shallow end of the pool.

Now towel yourself off because we are going back to the deep end of the pool. Now you will learn how to use the new Flash 8 Video Encoder application.

Using the Flash 8 Video Encoder

The Video Encoder and the Video Encoding Wizard are somewhat the same but also completely different. The purpose of the Encoder is to create the FLV file and nothing more. Skins and so on are added in Flash. The Encoder is available in both Macintosh and PC versions of the application.

One of the more common uses for the Encoder is for batch-processing files. This means you can add, for example, six videos to the Encoder and convert all six videos to FLV with the click of a button (see Figure 1-8).

Figure 1-8. The Flash 8 Video Encoder icon

1. Navigate to the Flash 8 Video Encoder. The Encoder is found in ...\Programs\Macromedia\Flash 8 Video Encoder on the PC and in .../Applications/Macromedia/Macromedia Flash 8 Video Encoder on the Mac.

2. The first screen that opens is where you add the video to be encoded (see Figure 1-9). Click the Add button and navigate to the folder containing the video you will be using. If you are using the materials supplied by this book, navigate to the Tortoise.mov file and click Open. When your video appears in the dialog box, click the Settings button to open the Encoding Settings panel.

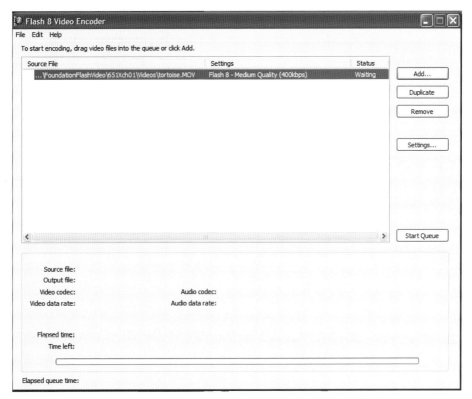

Figure 1-9. The first screen of the Flash Video Encoder is used to locate the video to be encoded.

You don't have to use the Add *button to navigate to videos in the Encoder. When the Encoder opens, you can open the folder containing the video or videos and simply drag them into the* Source File *area. Notice the use of the word* videos. *This handy little application can be used to batch-process the encoding of any number of videos.*

3. The first reaction you will have to the Encoding Settings panel is "Hey, haven't I seen this before?" You have. It is the same panel used by the Flash Video Wizard you used earlier to encode an FLV. Click the Show Advanced Settings button to open the advanced settings area at the bottom of the panel (see Figure 1-10). Just go with the defaults for now and click the OK button.

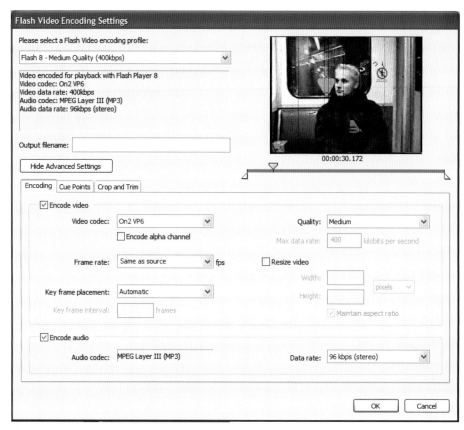

Figure 1-10. The advanced encoding settings

The advanced settings give you a tremendous amount of control over the video encoding process and even what the viewer sees.

The first thing you can do is name the file. This is a great way, for example, of creating a video targeted at a variety of bandwidth situations. You could have a copy of this video named `TortoiseLow` aimed at users who have dial-up and limited bandwidth and another aimed at the high-speed user named `TortoiseHi`.

The three tabs—Encoding, Cue Points, and Crop and Trim—quite succinctly state their purpose. The default selection is, of course, Encoding.

> In this chapter we are just going to stay with this area of the Encoder. We'll use the Cue Points and the Crop and Trim features later on in this book.

The encoding area divides the panel into two distinct sections. The top section contains the settings used for the video portion of the file. Here's what each one does:

- Video codec: This pop-down menu allows you to choose between the Sorenson Spark or On2 VP6 codecs. If your movie is targeted at the Flash Player 7 or lower, you must use the Sorenson Spark codec. If you have a "talking head" video containing an alpha mask, select Encode alpha channel. This feature only works with the Flash 8 Player and the On2 VP6 codec. If you select Sorenson Spark, this selection will be grayed out.

> *Chapter 5 is devoted to creating and using video containing alpha channels.*

- Frame rate: This choice gives you seven selections. The frame rate determines how fast—frames per second—the video will play. A good rule to follow is this: match the frame rate of the FLV to the FLA. If your FLA has a frame rate of 12 fps, then use that number as the frame rate for the FLV. In fact, Macromedia makes this easy because the default value is just that.

- Key frame placement: Key frames in video, in many respects, are similar to key frames in Flash. In video, a key frame contains all of the data in that frame—where they part company is in what happens between the key frames. In video, the frames between the key frames are called difference frames or, if you are really "techie," delta frames. Difference frames have the stuff that doesn't change between key frames removed. This means the file size is reduced. Now let's be very careful here because a bad decision can ruin your work.

  If you were stand at the side of a major city intersection and film cars and people walking by, there is going to be a lot of change and very few difference frames. Now take your camera into a farmer's field and shoot some footage of a tree. There won't be a lot of change and thus not a lot of difference frames. This explains why a 30-second video of a Formula One race is a lot larger in file size than that of a 30-second video of a tree in a field. Fewer difference frames means larger file size. The problem is, if you spread out the key frames in the Formula One video, the image quality degrades and looks blurry. We wish we could say to you there is a hard-and-fast rule about key frame frequency, but there isn't. Before you encode the video, watch the video and see if there is a lot of movement both in the video and with the camera. This will determine the key frame frequency. If you are at all unsure of what to do, select Automatic from the pop-down and let the software do the work for you.

- Quality: This drop-down has absolutely nothing to do with the "quality" of the final output. It has everything to do with the quality of the user's experience. This is where you set the data rate for the video stream into the user's computer (see Figure 1-11).

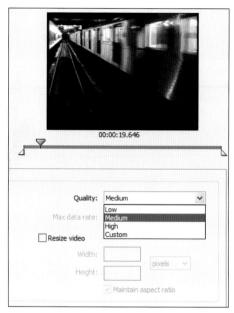

Figure 1-11. The four quality options available to you

If you select one of the three presets, the Max data rate value in the grayed-out dialog box below the Quality choice will show either 150, 400, or 700 kbps. What this means is that a video using the High Quality setting will be fed into the computer at the rate of 700,000 bits per second. This is great for T1 or high-speed Internet connections but fatal for the dial-up user. If you can form a mental image of trying to push a grape through a common garden worm, you can see what your user is in for. The modem simply won't be able to keep pace and the video will start, stop, start, stop, and so on. The result is one seriously upset user. If you select Custom, you can enter your own value in the Max data rate text box (see Figure 1-12). We tend to use a data rate of 300 kbps for most situations but use a relatively low number—100 to 125 kbps—for dial-up.

Figure 1-12. Setting a custom quality/data rate value

- Resize video: Ignore this area. Changing the dimensions of a video will only make it really fuzzy if you make the dimensions larger and less fuzzy if you reduce the dimensions. The most common dimensions for video are 320×240, 240×180 and 180×120. This uses the standard 4:3 aspect ratio established by Apple when they unleashed QuickTime on an unsuspecting world. If you must resize a video, then make sure to always have the Maintain aspect ratio check box selected. We highly recommend that, if you must resize a video, do it in a video-editing application, not here. We'll show you how to do that in the next chapter.

- Encode audio: Video is composed of two tracks. One is a video track, which we just dealt with, and the other is the audio track. This area (see Figure 1-13) allows you to manage the encoding of the audio track. Actually, not really. All audio in an FLV is converted to the MP3 format. All you can do is manage the audio stream.

Figure 1-13. Setting the data rate for the audio track

- Data rate: You get quite a few choices here; the bottom line is the larger the data rate, the larger the final file size. The choice you make here is added to the video rate for a total data rate for the FLV. For example, if you select the 400 kbps rate for the video and 256 kbps for the audio, the total data rate for the FLV will be 656 kbps, which, for many users, will result in a "grape through the worm" experience. Unless there is a compelling need for stereo—okay, the train rumbling from one speaker to the next or the high-quality soundtrack are very cool effects but are they really necessary?—you can knock the audio back to 64 kbps mono and the user will never know the difference.

4. When you click OK, you are returned to the main Video Encoder window. Click the Start Queue button.

Next, the video encoding progress bar and the video itself will appear. You will also be shown the location of the source file, the location of the encoded file, and the settings chosen in the Encoder (see Figure 1-14).

Figure 1-14. The video is encoding and you will see a preview.

The other thing that happens is that the name of the Start Queue button changes to a Stop Queue button. If you have made a mistake, click the button and a dialog box appears asking if you want to finish encoding the current file. If you click the No button, the process stops and an Errors dialog box will appear (see Figure 1-15). Don't get upset. You didn't make a mistake. All this dialog box does is to show you your settings and inform you that you interrupted the process.

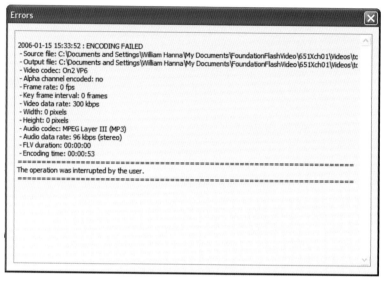

Figure 1-15. The Errors dialog box

When you click the Close box in the Errors dialog box, you are returned to the Encoder.

What you can't do at this point is say, "Well, I didn't mean to do that" and then select the video and click the Start Queue button. Nothing will happen. If you check the Status column you will see your encoding status has been changed to Skipped.

5. Select Edit ➤ Reset Status (see Figure 1-16).

When you release the mouse, the status will change to Waiting. At this point you can return to the Encoder and change the settings or click the Start Queue button. When the encoding process is finished, close the Encoder by clicking the Close button.

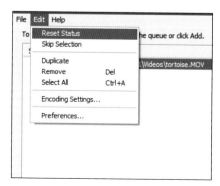

Figure 1-16. Restart the encoding process by selecting Reset Status.

Playing an FLV file in Flash Professional 8

The first thing to understand about the FLV file you just created is that you really can't play it anywhere but through the Flash 8 Player. In fact, you really can't play any FLV file in a web page unless it is played through a Flash SWF.

Flash Professional 8 makes the addition of video to a Flash movie even easier and more intuitive than in the past. This is accomplished through the use of the new FLV Playback component found in the FLV Playback – Player 8 component list.

1. Open a new document in Flash Professional 8. When Flash finishes opening, select Window ➤ Components (Ctrl+F7 on a PC or Cmd+F7 on a Mac).

2. Open the FLV Playback – Player 8 component category and drag a copy of the FLV Playback component onto the stage (see Figure 1-17).

When you release the mouse, depending on what you have done, you may or may not see a skin. Don't worry about that. The important thing here is to notice that the component resembles the FLV Player created using the Video Wizard. The major difference is that the Wizard knows where the FLV is located and what skin to use. This component needs to be given that information.

> The FLV Playback component will not work with Flash Player 7 or lower. If you are targeting this player, use the MediaPlayer component in the Media Player 6 – 7 components section.

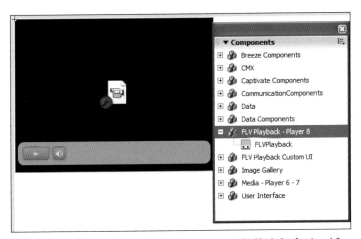

Figure 1-17. Selecting the FLV Playback component in Flash Professional 8

3. Select the component on the stage and, in the Property Inspector, select the Parameters tab to open the component's parameters. You can also select the component and open the Component Inspector (see Figure 1-18) by selecting Window ➤ Component Inspector. Regardless of which method you choose, the information required by either one is identical.

> We will be using the Component Inspector only because we can show you the values in a single screen shot. The Parameters pane on the Property Inspector can't be expanded. You have to scroll to get at some of the areas needed.

Figure 1-18. There are two methods of accessing the FLV Playback component's parameters.

4. Click once in the autoPlay parameter and select False from the drop-down menu. This ensures the movie doesn't start playing as soon as it loads.

5. Click once in the contentPath area. When you see the magnifying glass—it is a browse button—click it to open the Content Path dialog box and navigate to the folder where you saved the encoded video. Before you close this dialog box by clicking OK, be sure to click the Match source FLV dimensions check box (see Figure 1-19). This ensures the component matches the exact dimensions of the encoded video.

It is important that you save the FLA file to the same folder as the FLV before setting a contentPath. If the FLV is in one folder and the FLA is in another, the contentPath will consist of an absolute address, which gets embedded into the SWF. If the Flash file is saved to the same folder as the FLV, a relative path (see Figure 1-19) containing just the name of the FLV file will appear. If you have an absolute address, it will get compiled into the SWF, and when the user tries to play the video nothing will happen—the user sees a blank screen in the video area—because the Flash Player will look for the address on your computer to locate the FLV. Not being able to find your computer, it will essentially ignore the fact there is a video to play.

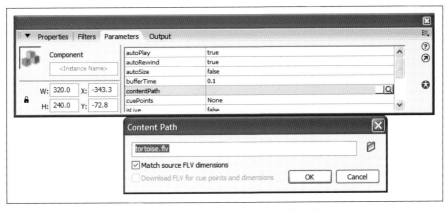

Figure 1-19. The contentPath Parameter and the Content Path dialog box

6. Click the Skin parameter and click the magnifying glass to open the Select Skin dialog box (Figure 1-20). Select SteelExternalAll.swf and click OK.

Figure 1-20. The Select Skin dialog box

21

7. You now have all of the information necessary for Flash to play the video (see Figure 1-21). Close the Component Inspector.

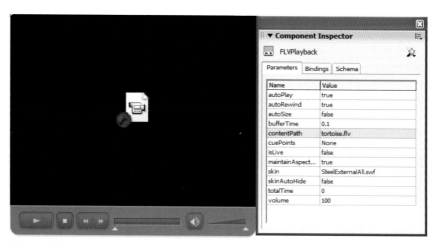

Figure 1-21. Our completed FLV Playback component parameters

If you set the skinAutoHide *value to* true, *the controls will only appear when the user rolls over the video on the web page.*

For you Actionscript junkies: yes you can control all of these parameters using ActionScript. We'll get to how this is done later in the book.

If you now press Ctrl+Enter (PC) or Cmd+Return (Mac), you can test the movie in the Flash Player.

Obviously, there is a bit of an issue here. There is a lot of wasted space on the stage, and that space uses bandwidth. Close the preview and let's fix that right now.

8. Click once on the stage and click the Size button in the Property Inspector to open the Document Properties dialog box.

The Document Properties dialog box in Flash Professional 8 has been seriously improved over earlier versions of the application. In fact, it is new. The Title and Description areas of the dialog box now allow you to enter metadata into the SWF (see Figure 1-22). This means your Flash content is now searchable by web search engines—they can now find your Flash work.

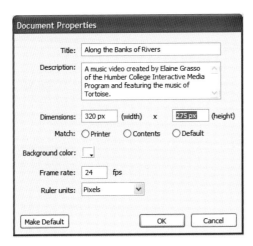

Figure 1-22. Use the Document Properties dialog box to remove the wasted space on the stage, to add metadata, and to set the Flash movie's frame rate to closely match that of the video.

Set the width of the document to 320 pixels, which matches the width of the video. Set the height value to 275. This allows for the height of the video—240 pixels—and leaves room on the stage for the Playback controls (see Figure 1-23). Click OK to close the Document Properties dialog box and test the movie.

If you publish the movie, just be aware that the FLV, SWF, and controller SWF should all be in the same directory before you upload to your website.

Figure 1-23. The video, with skin, playing in the FLV Playback component

Summary

Okay, get out of the pool and grab a towel. You are now able to swim with Flash video. In this chapter we covered a lot of ground, but you have also seen just how easy it can be to add video to Flash Professional 8. Whether you choose to use the Video Import Wizard or the Flash 8 Video Encoder to create the FLV file is really irrelevant because they both use the Encoder. The only difference between the two methods is that the Flash 8 Video Encoder only creates the FLV. The skin and so on need to be entered using the FLV Playback component's parameters if you create the video using the Encoder.

One other major advantage is file size. The original QuickTime movie was 42 MB in size. The FLV, thanks to the On2 VP6 compression, weighs in at 10.9 MB.

In the next chapter we show you how to create your own video using video-editing software.

2 EDITING VIDEO FOR FLASH

Before we dive into creating Flash video, it is important that you understand where the content you will use comes from and how the video being encoded and used in Flash is created.

Video is prepared in an editing program of some sort. Among the more popular professional video-editing tools are

- Premiere Pro 2 (Adobe)
- After Effects 7 (Adobe)
- Final Cut Pro (Apple)

They are industrial strength and come with an industrial-strength price tag. In fact, each one of them has quite a number of books dedicated specifically to the application or effects that can be produced by them.

For the rest of us, two tools are available—and free—and come with practically every computer on the market these days. They are

- Windows Movie Maker
- Apple iMovie

By the time you reach Chapter 6 you will have been exposed to all five of these applications.

We will start with the last two—Movie Maker and iMovie—because we are going to work with some rather simple source footage that doesn't require a lot of power under the hood.

> You should download the files used in this chapter from www.friendsofed.com before you get going.

Before we start, we have created a separate tutorial for each of the applications. Let's face it: we don't know which platform you use so we are covering all the bases. Although we don't recommend skipping exercises, in this case feel free to go to the app you are going to use. In either case, it is a relatively simple three-step process:

1. Capture video from a camera or import footage.
2. Edit the footage.
3. Export the footage in a format that can be encoded for Flash.

The footage we will use for this section was shot by our assistant, Alex Guhlushkin, who is more affectionately known as "Tom and Jord's Little Helper." Alex, a multimedia student in Toronto, was asked to grab a video camera and shoot some clubbing footage for this chapter. We were handed a bunch a short clips, and after trying to figure out what Alex had given us, suddenly saw a trend (see Figure 2-1) and went to work.

Figure 2-1. Let's go to a club.

Before we get going, here's a quick bit of background.

Nonlinear editing

Maybe this makes me sound like an old fart, but you have it easy these days. If you have never had the pleasure of using an analog video-editing system, you aren't missing much. Analog editing involves using X-Acto knives and razor blades to cut and splice tape. It was an exacting process that required an enormous degree of organization and patience. Editing video on a computer, a process called **nonlinear editing (NLE)**, can be done quickly and, because it is nondestructive—razor blades and X-Acto knives are things of the past—it is also very forgiving.

In fact, most video production today is done using the NLE process and the footage shot is captured by everything from cell phones to professional-grade cameras. That footage, ranging from your child's birthday party to earthquakes in Pakistan, is saved in a format—usually digital video (DV)—that can be easily placed in an NLE system, edited, and then put on the Web, sometimes in less than an hour. In many respects, anyone with a DV camera and a computer can make a video.

Windows Movie Maker

Movie Maker is a small nonlinear editing application that is installed when you install Windows XP. If you are an advanced video developer or have quite a bit of experience with Premiere or Final Cut Pro, for example, you are going to find this application a bit rudimentary. Even so, it does give the average user the tools necessary to create and export a video.

Getting started is not at all difficult. Select Start ➤ All Programs ➤ Accessories ➤ Windows Movie Maker. Double-click the application and you will see the window shown in Figure 2-2.

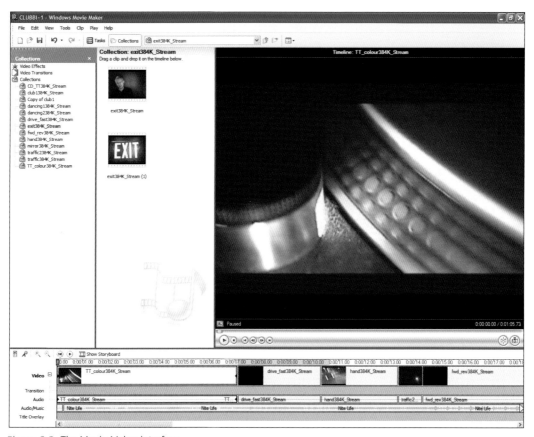

Figure 2-2. The Movie Maker interface

As you can see, there isn't much complexity to this application; it is designed for ease of use and quick editing. Rather than get into how to use the features of the application, we'll explain many of the important aspects as we move through this exercise.

Though Movie Maker allows you to capture video directly from your camera, we are going to focus on creating a video compiled from a series of clips. This is probably the most common way you will work with the application because you will be bringing in footage for use in the application. In addition, you can import images and audio files into Movie Maker.

1. Open Movie Maker and click the Import Video link in the Tasks pane to open the Import File dialog box. Navigate to the Exercise folder for this chapter and open the MovieMaker folder (see Figure 2-3). The video clips inside the folder will be visible. If you press the Shift key and click on the first and the last clip, you will select them all. Click the Import button and the clips will be added to the Clip library, which is called a collection (see Figure 2-4).

This is a Microsoft product we are dealing with here. This means Movie Maker will not be able to import a QuickTime movie that contains the .mov *extension. If you are going to be using a bunch of QuickTime clips, they will have to be converted to a WMV, AVI, or even MPEG-4 format before they can be brought into Movie Maker.*

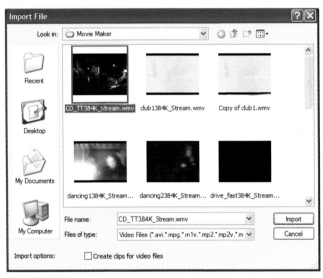

Figure 2-3. Clips are imported into Movie Maker.

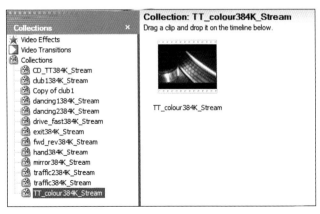

Figure 2-4. All clips are added to a collection.

29

2. Click on a clip and it will appear in the central pane.

3. Once you are happy with your collection, select File ➤ Save Project and save the project to your Chapter 2 Exercise folder or some other location on your hard drive.

This video also has a soundtrack attached to it. You will need to bring the audio file into Movie Maker as well. Here's how:

4. Click the Tasks button to open the Movie Maker Tasks pane and click the Import audio or music link.

5. Navigate to the Chapter 2 Exercise folder and import the Nite Life.mp3 file. When you click the Import button, a progress bar will appear showing you the progress of your import. When it is finished, the file will appear in the central pane.

Working with clips

You never get exactly the shot you need. Usually it is a little ways into the clip, or there is a section of the clip that should be used. Movie Maker lets you split and combine clips. Here's how:

1. Select a clip and move the playback head in the preview area to the point where you want to split the clip.

2. Click the Split Clip button on the controller (see Figure 2-5). If you look at your central pane, you will see you now have two clips (see Figure 2-6).

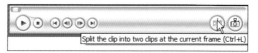

Figure 2-5. Splitting a clip

Figure 2-6. A split clip

So what if you make a mistake and split the clip in the wrong place? No problem.

3. Select both of the clips and right-click to open the context menu.

4. Select Combine (see Figure 2-7) and the clip will be restored.

30

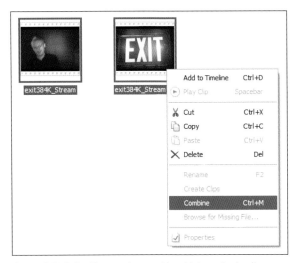

Figure 2-7. Split clips can be combined into a single clip.

Editing in Movie Maker

Editing your movie in this application is as simple as dragging and dropping. You drag a clip from the clip pane and drop it into place when you release the mouse.

The arrangement of the clips on the timeline can be done in one of two ways: storyboard and timeline. Though they are both different, they are both extremely useful. You can switch between them at any time by clicking the Show Storyboard or Show Timeline button.

Let's start with the Storyboard mode, shown in Figure 2-8.

Figure 2-8. The Movie Maker Storyboard view

Storyboard allows you to arrange the clips in the video in chronological order; the movie will run from left to right. The arrows between the clips allow you to add transitions and other special effects between the clips.

This view is great for just getting the clips in some semblance of order. To add them to the timeline, simply drag them from the clip pane and release them into the frames. Once you have done that, click the Play button in the controller and review your work.

Though it is useful, using Storyboard mode is much like fishing with hand grenades. You just don't have the precision in timing and trimming offered by the Timeline mode.

The Timeline mode is where the "heavy lifting" is done with Movie Maker. When you are looking at this mode (see Figure 2-9), the timeline changes to a number of channels—Video, Transition, Audio, Audio/Music, Title Overlay—and each clip can be trimmed.

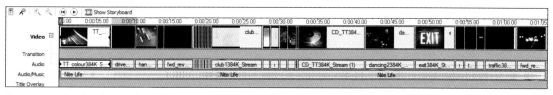

Figure 2-9. The Timeline mode is where the "heavy lifting" is done.

As you can see, the clips are arranged on the timeline. The neat thing about adding clips here is they are "butted" right up against the end of the preceding clip. You can then fine-tune them by dragging them to different positions on the timeline. If you want precision, click the zoom buttons—magnifying glasses with a + or – symbol—to get a closer look at your editing decisions and transitions.

Rather than get into an overly long "how to" regarding the video to be created, let's just hone our basic skills. Once you have those basic skills in place, you can open the Chapter 2 Movie Maker exercise file—Clubbing.MSWMM—and build your own version using the clips and audio in the folder.

1. With your Movie Maker file open, drag the audio file from the clip pane onto the audio track in the timeline.

2. With the collection open, click the TT_colour384_Stream file and drag the clip onto the video channel.

3. Click once on the drive _ fast384_Stream file and drag it from the clip pane onto the timeline (see Figure 2-10).

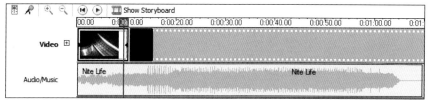

Figure 2-10. Two clips and the audio track are on the timeline.

4. So what does it look like? Click the Rewind button above the timeline and then click the Play button.

The Turntable clip and the Drive Fast clip are a bit long, which gives us a good excuse to show you two ways of shortening a clip. The process of shortening a clip is called *trimming*.

5. Click the Zoom tool and click on the Turntable clip on the timeline.

6. Switch to the Timeline mode and click once on the Turntable clip in the timeline. When you select it, you will notice that a small tool tip appears that gives you the clip's duration. Two small arrows, pointing in, appear on the right and left edges of the clip. These are the trim handles. Place the cursor over the handle on the right edge of the clip and the cursor changes to a red double arrow. Click and drag that edge toward the left edge of the clip (see Figure 2-11). As you drag, the time inside the tool tip will change. When the time reaches 0:07:00—7.0 seconds—release the mouse. You have just trimmed 3.5 seconds off of the end of the clip and reduced its duration to 7 seconds.

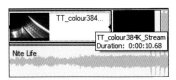

Figure 2-11. Trim a clip by dragging a handle.

Clicking and dragging is a rather inexact science, but it does work. Another way of trimming a clip is to use the preview as your guide. In this next example, you are going to remove the bit of black at the start of the Drive Fast clip and change its duration to 3.2 seconds.

7. Drag the playback head to the start of the Drive Fast clip on the timeline. Click the Next Frame button on the controller in the preview window. Keep clicking it until you are beyond the black area of the clip and can see the street. This should be at about the 7:40 mark in the controller. Click once on the clip and select Clip ➤ Set Start Trim Point. Now that you have trimmed off the start of the clip, you can now concentrate on setting the duration of the clip.

Remember, the clip is to last for 3.2 seconds. The one in front of it is 7 seconds. This means all you need to do is to trim off the end of the clip.

8. Using the Next Frame button, keep clicking until the duration reached 10.20 seconds in the preview window (see Figure 2-12). Select the clip and select Clip ➤ Set End Trim Point. The clip shortens to 3.2 seconds.

Figure 2-12. Use the time code on the controller to precisely set when a trim occurs.

Exporting

Once everything is in place and working to your satisfaction, you can export the movie.

1. Select File ➤ Save Movie File to open the Save Movie Wizard.

2. In the first screen, select My Computer as the location for the file and click Next.

3. When the next screen appears, name the file and save it to a folder on your computer. Click Next to open the Movie Setting dialog box (see Figure 2-13). The Setting details are important. You need to make sure you are exporting a file that is 320×240 with a 30 fps frame rate. Click Next and the movie will be converted to a WMV file.

Figure 2-13. The format for the video is determined in this screen.

You aren't limited to one format for output. In the Movie Setting dialog box, select Show more choices. Click the Other settings pop-down (see Figure 2-14) and you can output the video to everything from PocketPC to television.

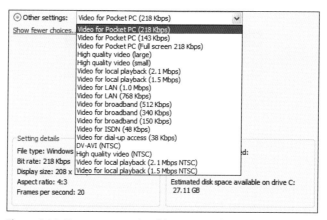

Figure 2-14. You can output the video to a number of formats and uses.

Apple iMovie

Since the introduction of QuickTime and then the addition of FireWire to the Mac, Apple has been at the vanguard of video technologies on the computer. With the release of iMovie a few years back, Apple reestablished its predominance as a producer of easy-to-use and even easier-to-learn software. Along the way, iMovie rekindled the video revolution whose path, if you really think about it, led you to this section of the book.

The current iteration of iMovie is iMovieHD or iMovie 6. In an effort to remain current—at least until Apple releases a new version—we will be using that version here. Finally, the creative process and the decisions you make are the same regardless as to whether you use MovieMaker, iMovie, or another video application. This exercise, therefore, should be regarded more as a "how to" than anything else.

Getting started with iMovie is not terribly difficult. The application can be found in the `Macintosh HD/ Applications/TRA Apple Applications` folder. Double-click the iMovie icon and you will be presented with the interface shown in Figure 2-15.

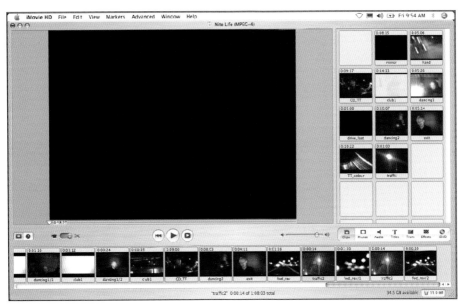

Figure 2-15. The iMovie interface

The neat thing about video applications is that if you have used one, you can pretty well use them all. For example, this interface and that of Movie Maker aren't terribly different from each other when you look at their fundamentals. Both have a timeline and a storyboard view. Both contain an area where clips are stored and dragged onto the timeline. Both contain a controller and zoom-in and zoom-out controls for precise clip positioning.

Though you can capture video directly to iMovie, we are going to concentrate on using a series of clips that are brought into iMovie and assembled to construct the same movie as in the previous exercise. We have also included the completed project files in the `Chapter 2/Complete/iMovie` folder. Feel free to open it up and examine how we created the "Clubbing" video.

To get started, you need to create a project and import the clips you will be using.

1. Select File ➤ New Project to open the Create Project dialog box. Enter a name in the Project box. Now click the Video format drop-down arrow. This will open a list of video formats used by iMovie. Select MPEG-4 (see Figure 2-16) and click the Create button.

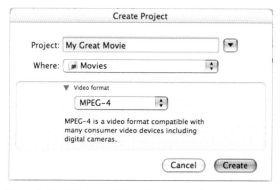

Figure 2-16. All iMovie videos start as a project.

2. When you are returned to the interface, select File ➤ Import and when the Import window opens, navigate to the Videos folder located in `Chapter 2/Exercises/ iMovie/Videos`. Select all of the movies and click the Open button. You will be shown the progress of the import process, and when it is finished the clips will all appear in the clip window (see Figure 2-17).

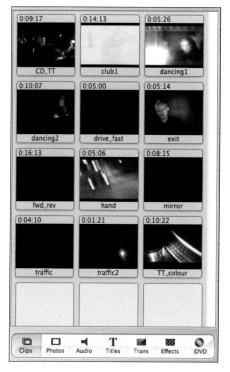

Figure 2-17. The clips are imported and ready to be added to the video.

3. Select File ➤ Import and navigate to the audio folder. Select the `NiteLife.mp3` file and click the Import button. This is where iMovie and Movie Maker part company. The audio track is placed right on the timeline.

Clicking the Audio button in the clip window will open iTunes. This means you can also use any music you may own as the soundtrack for your work. In this case you would select the song or audio clip from the Song list and drag it onto the timeline. You can also move the playback head to the point on the timeline where the song is to be placed and click the Place at Playhead button (see Figure 2-18). The song will appear at that point on the timeline.

Figure 2-18. Your iTunes library can be used to add audio to your videos.

The iMovie editing modes

Like Movie Maker, iMovie contains two editing modes: Timeline and Clip Viewer.

The buttons to control these views are found just above the timeline. The button that looks like a clock switches to the Timeline mode and the one that looks like a slide switches to Clip Viewer mode.

Clip Viewer mode shows you individual icons for each clip. The information shown on the clip is the clip's duration (in the upper-left corner) and the name of the clip. This is a handy visual reference as to what clip is where and how long it lasts.

As you drag clips from the clip pane to the timeline, they will all be placed against each other in the order in which they are placed. If you want to rearrange the order, simply move the clip to the new position and the timeline will adjust to accommodate the clip (see Figure 2-19).

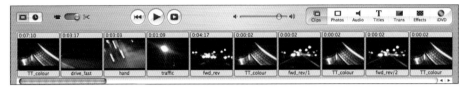

Figure 2-19. The Clip Viewer

The Timeline mode is the workhorse of the application. Here you can trim clips, add transitions between clips, and even adjust the volume of a section of the audio track associated with the clip (see Figure 2-20).

When you click the clock icon, the timeline changes to this mode. The line you see running through each clip is the audio track. If you click on the line, you will add a handle that can be used to adjust the volume of the clip. Though we don't recommend this for obvious reasons, it is a handy feature if used judiciously.

> *Let me guess. You just read that paragraph, clicked on the line, and now you have a handle on the clip. How do you get rid of it? Just drag the handle down to the original line level and it will disappear.*

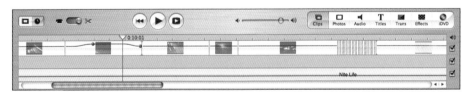

Figure 2-20. The Timeline view

Working with iMovie clips

Now that you are familiar with the interface and how to add your content, let's turn our attention to adding the content to a video.

1. Click on the TT_colour clip in the clip pane. When you do this, the clip will appear in the preview window.

This is the place where the true power of iMovie comes to the surface. In this pane you can:

- Preview a clip or "scrub" it by dragging the playback head to the right or the left.
- Play the clip in the window or even full screen.
- Trim the clip by using crop markers for the video.

It is this last technique that is of most concern to us. This is how clips are edited and the extraneous pieces in the clip can be removed.

2. Drag the playback head to the 7:00-second mark. Notice how, when you place the cursor on the preview window, two little white "half arrows" will appear under the clip. These are the crop markers. Drag the right marker all the way to the end of the video. Drag the left marker until you see 7:00 in the time code above the marker. When you release the mouse, you will notice the Scrubber bar is blue and yellow. Press the Delete key and the portion of the video—the yellow section—between the crop markers will be removed (see Figure 2-21).

> If you are going to do this, work on a copy of the original clip. A quick way of doing this is to select the clip in the clip pane, hold down the Option key, and click/drag the clip to an empty slot in the pane.

> You don't have to press the Delete key. You can also select Edit ➤ Crop to remove a selection.

Figure 2-21. Video can be cropped.

A less invasive way of trimming out unwanted content is to split the clip. If you remember, the Drive Fast clip has a bit of black at the start of the clip. It needs to be removed. There are two ways of doing that:

3. Drag a copy of the Drive Fast clip to the timeline. Drag the playback head until you see 0:07:14 in the time code on the Scrubber bar.

4. Select Edit ➤ Split Video Clip at Playhead or press Cmd+T. The clip will be split on the timeline into two clips (see Figure 2-22).

> *If you do split a clip on the timeline, be sure to drag the clip you don't need from the timeline into the clip pane. You never know when you might need it.*

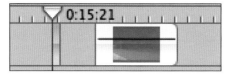

Figure 2-22. Video can be split.

Another way of splitting a clip is to... well ...split the clip.

5. Click a clip in the clip pane.

6. Drag the playback head to the point where the split is to be made. If you are looking for real precision, use the arrow keys on your keyboard to move the playback head forward or backward.

7. Select Edit ➤ Split Video Clip at Playhead and the clip will become two clips in the clip pane.

Exporting your movie

Once you have a video that meets your objectives, you can export it so that it can be placed into Flash by using the FLV encoder.

1. Open the iMovie folder in your Chapter 2 Exercise folder and open the `NiteLife` iMovie file.

2. Select File ➤ Share. The Share dialog box that opens is quite complete. As you can see, you can prepare your video for a number of uses, ranging from an email attachment to a QuickTime video.

3. In the Compress movie for drop-down menu, select Full Quality (see Figure 2-23). You are going to be encoding the video for Flash, so file size is not a primary concern at this stage of the process.

4. Click the Share button and the movie will be compressed into a QuickTime format with the `.mov` extension (see Figure 2-24).

Figure 2-23. The QuickTime movie is about to be created.

If you are a real control freak and own a copy of QuickTime Pro, you can select Expert Settings *in the* Compress movie for *drop-down menu. This will open the QuickTime Export Settings dialog box and from here you choose a variety of codecs and other compression settings.*

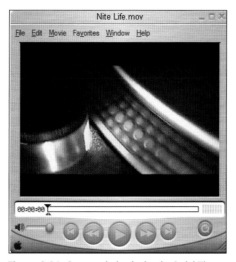

Figure 2-24. Our movie is playing in QuickTime and is ready to be converted to an FLV.

41

Summary

Now that you have had a chance to use the editing features of Movie Maker and iMovieHD, start playing with them to create your own videos. See what ideas you can bring to life and what you can do with these applications. You will soon discover that the amount of fun you can have with them should be illegal and that your only constraint will be that which you place on your creativity. In the next chapter, we are going to look at a couple of products that don't use the FLV Encoder or Flash to create the FLV.

3 ALTERNATIVE FLV CREATION TOOLS

Up to this point you have been creating video, encoding it, and playing it through Flash. If the previous two chapters have whetted your appetite to really get into using Flash video, then you will eventually encounter the products offered by ON2 and Sorenson Media. Though their codecs are integral features of the Flash 8 Video Encoder, they offer commercial FLV creation tools—ON2 Flix and Sorenson Squeeze—which offer even more features and control than the Flash 8 Video Encoder.

An obvious question is *"Why should I purchase these applications if I already have them in Flash?"* First off, we are not here to sell their products but if you are going to be creating and using a lot of Flash video, these applications will make your life easier. For example, both offer 2-pass variable bit rate encoding options. We'll get deeper into what that means later on in this chapter, but for now, know that the advantage is usually a smaller FLV with no loss of quality. Another feature offered by both applications is batch processing. Instead of encoding videos individually, both allow you to encode an entire folder of videos at once.

Before we dig into these tools, now would be a good time to take a small break and explain data rate. You will be asked to set this value in both applications, and a bad choice can have a profound impact on both the quality of the FLV and the user's experience.

Data rate

One of the fundamental maxims of working with digital video is this: Data rate controls quality. Bandwidth controls the user experience.

Regardless of which computer platform is used, bandwidth, or "the pipe," is your prime consideration. When it comes to creating and playing Flash video, always keep an eye on the pipe.

The pipe can make or break the user's experience. If users have a lot of bandwidth, such as a T1 line in a corporation or high-speed Internet into their home, they can view full-length movies with little or no disruption. If they are in a remote or rural situation, the odds are very good they have a dial-up modem, meaning their bandwidth is limited. To wrap your mind around the differences, think of a highway tunnel that goes under a lake. If the tunnel is part of an eight-lane highway, thousands of cars simply approach the tunnel and zip through it at the posted speed. This is because the tunnel's entrance is the same width as the highway.

Now abruptly reduce the diameter of the tunnel from four lanes to one lane each way. We have all experienced how infuriating the delay can be as thousands of cars squeeze into one lane of traffic and reduce their speed to a crawl as they approach the tunnel's entrance and proceed into the tunnel. The cars in this example are data and how fast they move is the data rate. Think of a T1 line as the tunnel for the four-lane expressway, the single-lane tunnel as a dial-up service, the highway as the server, and the user as the poor guy behind the steering wheel in the car.

It goes without saying that when you plan to deliver video you need to have a solid bandwidth strategy in place for the user, the server, and the video. The server bandwidth strategy must take into account the maximum number of users that can access the video at any one time. The last thing you need is for your user to get into the middle of a traffic jam waiting to download and view the video.

When it comes to the user, you need to be aware of the width of the tunnel up ahead. You must leave enough room for the data stream but also other Internet activities. Not doing this is similar to having a transport truck sitting at the side of the road and jutting out into traffic. Things will stop or seriously slow down as the cars reduce their speed to avoid driving into the back of the truck. In a dial-up situation, a user with a 56.6 K connection can drive along the highway at 56.6 Kbps. When it comes to video, a target data rate of 40 Kbps is normal, which leaves room for other activities.

So what is data rate? Data rate is simply the amount of data (cars on a highway) transferred per second to the user's computer. This, in turn, determines the bandwidth required to play the video. The data rate calculation is

Data rate = (w×h×color depth×frames per second) / compression

Let's do the data rate calculation for the `Tortoise` video used in this chapter. The video's values are

- Width = 320
- Height = 240
- Color depth = 24
- Frames per second = 15
- Compression = 60 (The benchmark compression ratio for both Flix and Squeeze is 60:1.)

Data rate = (320×240×24×15) / 60

Data rate = (27,648,000) / 60

Data rate = 460,800

The data rate for the video at 15 fps is 460,800 bps, or 461 kbps. The second line of the calculation is there for a deliberate reason. If you were to apply no compression to the video, you would use a data rate of about 27.6 million bps. To deliver that video, you would need an Internet connection the size of a tunnel between Britain and France. Toss in the compression, and the video can safely be delivered to most users.

> *The Flash Player supports a maximum data rate of 4 mbps.*

Other factors that could impact the user experience are frame rate and key frame placement.

Frame rate is the speed at which a video plays. One of the more common frame rates for digital video is 29 or 30 fps, which matches the North American video standard of 29.97 fps. Another common frame rate is 24 fps. Regardless of which one you have been handed, there will be occasions where you may wish to reduce the rate, such as in low-bandwidth situations. If you want to lower the frame rate, you should use equal divisions of the source frame rate. For 30 fps, use 15 fps; for 10 fps, use 7.5 fps; and so on. For 24 fps, use 12 fps, 8 fps, 6 fps, and so on.

In Chapter 1, we explained how key frames work. By spreading out the key frames, you can have quite a positive impact upon the final size of the FLV. What you don't want to do is to think all video is created equally. If there is a lot of motion—a Formula One race—you will need more key frames. If it is a low-motion video—a tree in a field—you can get away with fewer key frames. The bottom line is, this decision is up to you but it is the prudent developer who reviews the entire video prior to converting the file to an FLV.

One final consideration in regard to data rate is that the number shown in the compression applications is a bit disingenuous. In Chapter 1, you set the data rate of a video to 300 kbps. This is not the final data rate. Remember, video is composed of both an audio track and a video track. The number you set affected just the video track. If you look at the data rate for the audio track, it was set to 96 kbps (see Figure 3-1). This means the data rate for the video is 396 kbps.

Figure 3-1. Add the data rate values for both the audio and the video tracks to determine the total data rate for your FLV.

Regardless of whether you use Flash Professional 8, Flix Pro, or Sorenson Squeeze 4.3 to create the video, they are all going to ask you the following questions:

- What bit rate will be used to stream the video?
- What frame size will be used to present the video?
- What frame interval should be used for the key frames?

To help you answer those questions, Tables 3-1 and 3-2 provide some suggested values.

Table 3-1. High-motion video

Type	Video bit rate	Audio bit rate	Frame size	Frame rate	Key frames
Small	188 K	32 K mono	240×180	15 or 12 fps	8 seconds
Medium	336 K	64 K mono	320×240	30 or 24 fps	8 seconds
Large	850 K	96 K stereo	480×360	30 or 24 fps	8 seconds
Full screen	1304 K	96 K stereo	640×480	30 or 24 fps	8 seconds

> If you are targeting a 56 K modem, you must keep the rate under 40 K, and don't use less than 16 K for the audio.
>
> The key frame number is an approximation. Start there and work backward.

Table 3-2. Low-motion video

Type	Video bit rate	Audio bit rate	Frame size	Frame rate	Key frames
Small	68 K	32 K mono	240 ×180	15 or 12 fps	8 seconds
Medium	132 K	48 K mono	320 ×240	30 or 24 fps	8 seconds
Large	286 K	64 K stereo	480 ×360	30 or 24 fps	8 seconds
Full screen	504 K	96 K stereo	640 ×480	30 or 24 fps	8 seconds

Using Flix Pro

Flix Pro for Macromedia Flash (the current version is 8 and is available for both the Macintosh and the PC) from ON2 Technologies is a standalone application that encodes high-quality video for Flash Professional 8. Though it uses the same FLV compressor as that in Flash—VP6—it also, understandably, offers a wide feature set not available in Flash. In this section we will be importing the `Tortoise` video into Flix and compressing it. Once the FLV is created, it can be used by the FLV Playback component in Flash. You can download a trial version of the application at `www.on2.com/downloads/flix-demo-software/`.

With Flix Pro open, let's discuss what we see (Figure 3-2).

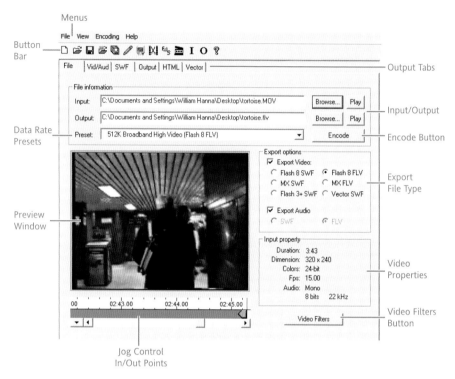

Figure 3-2. The Main interface for Flix Pro

The menus contain all of the features in the interface, and the button bar gives you one-click access to a number of encoding and playback tasks.

Be careful with the button bar because the icons perform tasks that aren't commonly associated with the icons. Figure 3-3 shows the button bar along the top of the Flix interface.

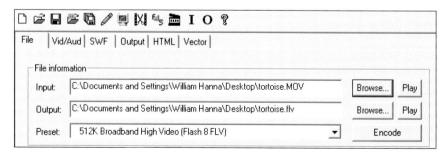

Figure 3-3. Pay close attention to the buttons because they don't always perform the task you think they should.

The buttons, from left to right, are

- Clear Settings: Click this and you clear all of the settings and fields in the file.
- Open Settings: Click this and you can navigate to an `.flx` file that contains the settings for the encoded video.
- Save Settings: Click this and you will create an `.flx` file.
- Select Input Video File: Click this to launch the Open dialog box that can be used to locate the video to be encoded.
- Batch: Clicking this opens the Batch Processing window.
- Overlay: Click this and you can add a watermark to the video.
- Player Maker: Click this and the Create Player window opens. This allows you to create standalone projectors for either a Mac or a PC.
- Edit/Crop/Filters: Click this and you open the Editor window, which does exactly what the button says.
- FLV to SWF Converter: Click this and the FLV will be embedded into a SWF file using the FLV to SWF Converter window that opens.
- Encode: Clicking this has the same effect as clicking the Encode button on the interface.
- Play Input: Click this and the video plays in the Player window.
- Play Output: Click this and the encoded file plays in the Player window.
- Help: Selecting this launches the Help menu.

Now that you have had a short walk through the main screen, let's encode a video using Flix Pro.

1. Open Flix Pro and click the Browse button in the input area of the interface.

Navigate to the Chapter 3 Exercise folder and double-click the Tortoise.mov file. The path to the file will appear in the input area, and the same path will be used in the output area. This means the FLV you create will be placed in the same folder as the source video.

2. Select the Flash 8 FLV option in the Export options and click the Vid/Aud tab (see Figure 3-4).

The Video/Audio Encoding Settings dialog box will open. Though it may at first glance appear to be a bit overwhelming, this dialog box is set up in much the same way as the Flash 8 Video Encoder and asks you essentially the same questions. Let's go through each section of this window.

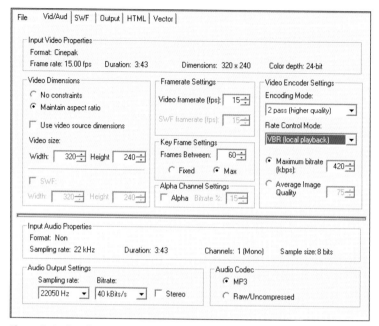

Figure 3-4. The Flix Pro Vid/Aud tab

The Input Video Properties section shows you the properties of the Tortoise video. Notice the values shown are those used in calculating the data rate.

3. Select Maintain aspect ratio in the Video Dimensions area.

This selection ensures that, should you resize the video, the 4:3 aspect ratio of the video is maintained and that no distortion occurs. For example, if you change the width of the video to 300 pixels, the height value will automatically change to 225 pixels to maintain the aspect ratio.

4. Set the Video framerate (fps) value to 15 in the Framerate Settings area.

This value matches that of the video. If the video is being placed into a Flash movie that has a different frame rate such as 12 fps or 24 fps, then change the frame rate of the FLV to match that of the FLA.

5. In the Video Encoder Settings select 2 pass (higher quality) from the Encoding Mode drop-down menu and VBR (local playback) from the Rate Control Mode drop-down menu. Then set Maximum bitrate (kbps) to 420.

The 2-pass option produces higher-quality video while requiring additional processing time. This makes sense because Flix takes two looks at the video during the encoding process. During the first look, or pass, Flix will try to figure out the best way to compress the video based on your maximum bit rate. During the second pass through the video, Flix looks at the motion in the video and allocates more bandwidth to high-motion sections and lower bandwidth to areas where nothing is really happening.

The second value—VBR, or variable bit rate—is not named correctly. You would assume, from looking at it, that you would only choose VBR if the video is playing back from your hard drive. In fact, VBR is the option to use if the video is being streamed from your web server. You choose CBR, or constant bit rate, only if the video is being streamed through a Flash Video Streaming Service, Flash Communication Server, or Flash Media Server.

The final setting, a maximum bit rate of 420, is the result of the calculation done earlier and leaves room for the audio stream.

> *If you are concerned about the final file size of the FLV, change the audio from Stereo to Mono in the* Input Audio *area by deselecting the* Stereo *check box. This has the effect of cutting the size of the audio track by about 50 percent.*

6. Click the File tab to view the file settings.

If you would rather stay out of the Vid/Aud area or find it to be rather intimidating or confusing, you can always let the software do the work for you. If you click the Preset drop-down menu on the File tab, you will be presented with a serious number of choices (see Figure 3-5).

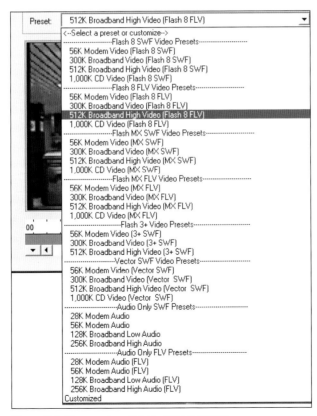

Figure 3-5. The preset encoding values in Flix Pro

Though the choices are quite extensive, for our purposes, only the Flash 8 FLV Video Presets are necessary. They anticipate a number of bandwidth situations ranging from dial-up to playback from a CD. For example, if you select 300K Broadband Video Flash (8 FLV), you are selecting one of the most common choices available. This is the one appropriate for home use. If you then select the Vid/Aud tab you will also see that the Maximum bitrate setting has been reduced to 280 kbps, which is right in the ballpark if you include the audio bit rate of 40 kbps.

7. Click the Encoding button to open the encoding window.

You will be shown the progress of the encoding process, and you can determine what happens when the encoding is completed by selecting one or all of the options in the When encoding completes area (see Figure 3-6).

Figure 3-6.
The Flix Pro encoding window

8. After you preview the video in the Flix Player (see Figure 3-7), close the Player window and quit Flix Pro by selecting File ➤ Exit.

Figure 3-7.
The FLV is playing in the Flix Player.

Now that you have created the FLV, you can open Flash and link the FLV to the FLV Playback component added to the Flash stage.

> *If you want to see the difference between 2-pass encoding and the 1-pass encoding in the Flash 8 Video Encoder, select the FLV you have just created and note the file size. In our case the video dropped in size from 41.3 MB to 12.6 MB. The same file encoded in Chapter 1 is 13.4 MB. When it comes to the Web, even a savings of 0.8 MB helps.*

Using Sorenson Squeeze 4

If any one company can claim to have sparked the streaming media boom with video, it would be Sorenson Media, Inc. When it released its Sorenson video codec a few years ago, bloated streaming video files became a thing of the past. It was no wonder then, to see Sorenson Spark appear as the video encoder in Flash.

Like the ON2 VP6 codec introduced in Flash Professional 8, Sorenson Spark is good, but, as the authors wrote in this volume's predecessor, *Flash MX Video* (friends of ED, 2002), "there is something even better. It is called Sorenson Squeeze."

Sorenson Squeeze 4.3 is a standalone product and is available in both PC and Macintosh versions. You can download a trial copy at `www.sorensonmedia.com/misc/free_trial.php`.

When you first open Squeeze, you will discover that everything you need to do is contained in the main screen, as shown in Figure 3-8.

Figure 3-8. The Squeeze interface is quite intuitive.

The compression presets are just as extensive as those in Flix, and when a video is imported, you can use the preview window to play the video, set the in and the out points if you wish to shorten the video, or use a specific clip in the video. When a video is ready to be "squeezed," the file is shown as well as the audio and the video codecs being applied to the video. When you are ready to create the FLV, simply click the SQUEEZE IT! button and the progress of the compression and conversion process will be shown in the Output Files window.

A really neat feature of Squeeze is the ability to capture video directly from a video camera. The only downside to this is if you wish to add a soundtrack to the video. You would have to do that in an audio or a video editor such as Adobe Premiere Pro.

The batch processing feature of Squeeze is found in the Watch Folder item of the INPUT area of the interface. Once a folder is identified as a watch folder, all you have to do is drop a video into the folder and Squeeze will automatically create the FLV file.

Now that you have been introduced to the interface, let's "squeeze" a video.

1. Click the Import File button and navigate to the Tortoise.mov file in the Chapter 3 example folder. The file will appear in both the preview and output windows.

> *Feeling lazy? Drag a video directly from a folder onto the preview window and it will appear in Squeeze.*

2. You now need to choose an encoding format. Click the + sign beside the Macromedia Flash Video (FLV) area in the presets area to open the preset choices available to you. Click once on the 384K selection (see Figure 3-9) and click the Apply button. The selection will appear in the output window (see Figure 3-10).

> *Do not double-click a preset. Doing so opens the preset's values in the Audio/Video Settings dialog box. Any change you make here becomes the new preset value. We'll show you how to change these values in the next step.*
>
> *Still feeling lazy? Drag a preset value to the output window and it will appear in the window.*

3. In the output area, click the + sign beside the preset, and the Spark Pro and MP3 encoders that are contained in the preset will appear. Double-click either one to open the Audio/Video Compression Settings dialog box.

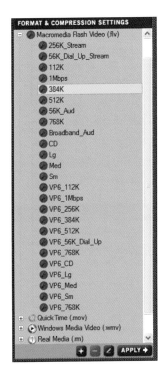

Figure 3-9.
The FLV presets in Squeeze

Figure 3-10. The preset is applied to the video in the output window.

This dialog box allows you to customize the settings without changing the preset. As you can see (Figure 3-11), the dialog box is divided into two portions. The left side is for the audio settings and the right side contains the video settings. The key value to notice in this dialog box is Total Data Rate in the upper-right corner. This represents the sum of the audio data rate and the video data rate.

Figure 3-11 shows the advanced options dialog box. If you click the Simple button in the lower-left corner, all of the video encoding options below the frame rate will be hidden (Figure 3-12).

In order to do a fair comparison between Flix and Squeeze, the Total Data Rate is going to have to be increased to about 460 kbps.

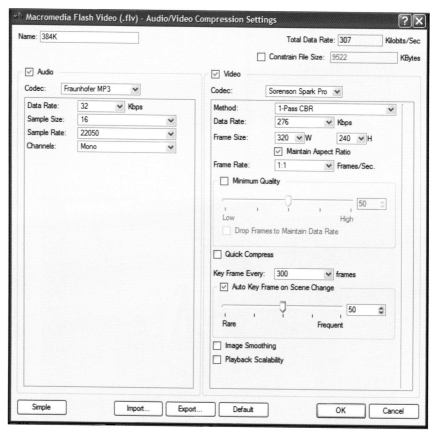

Figure 3-11. The advanced display of the Squeeze Audio/Video Compression Settings dialog box is ideal for the power user or control freak.

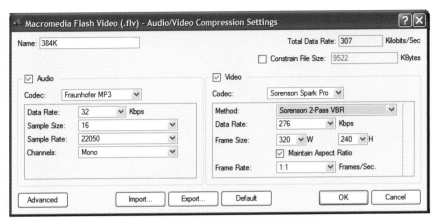

Figure 3-12. The "simple" Audio/Video Compression Settings dialog box

4. Where Squeeze differs from Spark—the Flash Professional 8 codec—is that like Flix, it too offers a 2-pass variable bit rate encoding option. In the Method pop-down, select Sorenson 2-Pass VBR.

5. Select the value in the Date Rate input box and change it to 420 Kbps. You can also choose from a number of other values in the drop-down menu.

6. Select the Data Rate value in the audio section and change it to 40 Kbps by selecting the value from the drop-down menu. Notice how the Total Data Rate value changes.

7. Select the filename in the Name text input box and change it to SqueezeTest. Click the OK button to close the dialog box and return to the Squeeze interface.

8. Click the SQUEEZE IT! button to start the encoding process. The progress bars will appear in the output window and the SQUEEZE IT! button will change its name to STOP IT!, as shown in Figure 3-13.

9. When you finish the process, select File ➤ Save Project—Ctrl+S on a PC or Cmd+S on a Mac. You won't be saving the FLV; you will instead be saving an .sqz file. This format is used by Squeeze to remember the settings used for this compression. This a really handy feature if you need to change a setting or can't remember the values used to squeeze the video. Double-clicking the .sqz file will open Squeeze and present you with the video and compression settings in the output window.

If you are at all curious, the final file size of the FLV we created in Squeeze is 12.6 MB, which is the same as the value for the FLV created in Flix.

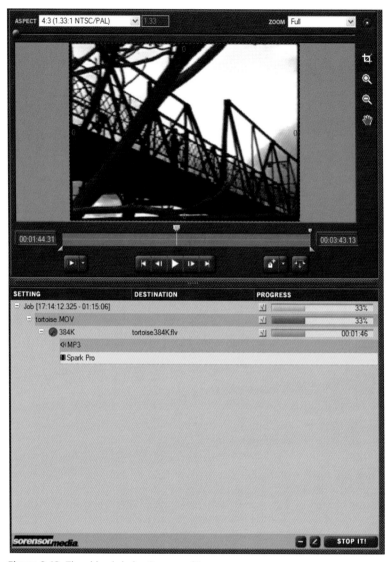

Figure 3-13. The video is being "squeezed."

Summary

So there you have it. Flix and Sorenson went head-to-head and the result is a draw. Their file sizes matched each other. Mind you, we could have brought the file sizes down even further by reducing the visual or sound quality if we had chosen to.

If the comparison resulted in a draw, then which to choose? We aren't going to endorse one product over the other because they both do an admirable job of creating an FLV that can be used in Flash Professional 8.

Based on the chatter and buzz around the inclusion of the ON2 VP6 codec in Flash Professional 8, the consensus is you get better image quality on playback if the FLV is created using Flix. Though the arguments are both complex and technical, the bottom line is that the recommendation to go with Flix is more "subjective" than "objective" because no two video producers can ever agree on a common definition of quality.

Instead, approach these applications as though they were tools. If you need to create an FLV containing an alpha channel, then Flix is the tool to use. If the video doesn't contain an alpha channel, then either tool will produce an excellent FLV file for use in Flash Professional 8. When you really think about, the user doesn't have a clue whether Flix or Squeeze was used to create the FLV. As long as the quality of the final product meets your standards, either tool does the job.

Maybe, instead of getting technical, you should take the advice we offered at the start of this chapter and simply "keep an eye on the pipe." It is the user who matters most and it is important, regardless of the tool, to keep an eye on the hardware, bandwidth, and where the video will be viewed. To achieve this, you will have to simply experiment and learn which compromises best fit which situation: high-quality audio and video versus small, quickly loading video files.

One of the authors refers to this as "The First Rule of FLV Creation." The rule states: *For every action there is an equally ugly and opposite implication.* Too many developers forget this rule in their rush to be a "cool kid" and get into the "Flash video game." The results are big, ponderous videos that take forever to download or play. Now that you know how to create a video, turn the page and let's start seeing how much fun you can have with Flash video.

4 CREATING FLASH VIDEO USING THE FLV COMPONENTS

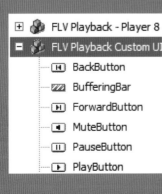

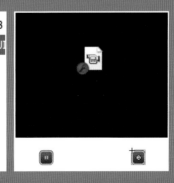

The previous three chapters have covered the creation of the raw material—the video and the FLV—and what you need to do before you "flame up" Flash. In this chapter, and the remainder of the book, we deal with many of the creative things you can do with video in Flash.

This chapter is the start of that process.

In Chapter 1, we created a simple FLV that used the FLV Playback component. This chapter expands on that one and shows you how to use many of the video tools in the application. This includes some interesting uses of the FLV Playback component: creating a set of custom controls using the FLV Playback Custom UI components and streaming and controlling an FLV using a video object from the library. Each of these approaches allows you to get your video working on the Web and gives you the flexibility to decide whether to use the components or create your own controls.

The FLV Playback component and buffering

In Chapter 1 we quickly covered how to attach a video to this component and get it playing. Rather than revisit what has already been done, let's dig a little deeper into the use of this component and examine it from the perspective of optimizing the component for a streaming video. What you learn here can be applied elsewhere.

No matter how you approach the subject, Flash video streams into a browser. This happens either through the use of the default progressive download, where the video streams from your web server, or through the use of a streaming server such as the Flash Media Server or the Flash Communication Server (FlashComm).

A couple of terms have sprung up around the subject of streaming, and this is as good a place as any to introduce them. A movie that creates a stream in a network connection is said to be *publishing* while the movie that receives the stream is said to be a *subscriber*. As you move through this chapter, be aware that at any time a stream can contain only one video and only one audio file. This means that if your boss hands you a dozen videos you can't simply toss them up to a server and expect each one to use the same stream. In this case, either the video that is currently playing has to be removed from the stream before the next video is added, or a new stream must be created and the video attached to that new stream.

Streaming in Flash is a little bit different from traditional approaches.

Think of a video stream as little packets of information being handed to the Flash Player when it needs them. Depending on the streaming choice, your video will either wait a second or two for enough packets to get going—progressive download—or the first packet essentially kicks off the movie—Flash Media Server. If it is done well, users won't have to sit around drumming their fingers on the desk waiting for the video to load and play. The key to successful playback is the data rate—the speed at which the packets are flowing into the Flash Player—which you learned about in the previous chapter. The second factor is storing enough of these packets before the video starts playing. This process is called *buffering*.

Though we could go "techie" on this, the best way to think of buffering is to imagine a dam on a river. The purpose of this dam is to help the farmers downstream from the dam keep their crops irrigated because the river has a bad habit of either flooding or drying up depending on the rainfall pattern in their little patch of the countryside.

When the dam is built, the river flows to the dam and the water starts to back up and form a lake. There is an opening in the dam to allow the water to pour out in a controlled manner that keeps the river flowing at a constant rate. This allows the farmers downstream to have a constant, controlled source of water for their crops.

So what do dams and farmers have to do with video buffering?

Think of the farmers' experience with the rainfall pattern and relate it to video playback. We have all had the bad experience of choppy video or video that starts and stops. That is due to running out of video packets. When that happens, the computer stops the process and we start drumming our fingers on the desk waiting for enough packets to load so we can continue with the video. Buffering stores those packets and releases them when there are enough in the computer to smoothly play the video.

When one packet leaves the dam, another is added to the lake to replace the packet just used. In this example, the raindrops are the data packets, the river into the lake is the data stream, the lake behind the dam is the buffer, the opening in the dam allows the packets to stream into the Flash Player, the river to the farmers' fields is the stream to the Flash Player, and finally, the field being irrigated is the video playing in the Flash Player.

The FLV Playback component makes this possible. Open Flash, drag a copy of the FLV Playback component to the stage, and link the component to the `Tortoise.flv` file created in the previous chapter. If you click the Parameters tab, you will see an item named bufferTime (see Figure 4-1). The value you enter here, measured in seconds and tenths of seconds, determines the size of the lake behind the dam. The default is one tenth of a second. This means that, if the video is playing back at 24 fps, three frames of the video, representing about one tenth of second of playback, will always be in the buffer. When a frame is released from the buffer during playback, the next one in line behind the buffer replaces it in the buffer.

There are no hard-and-fast rules regarding bufferTime. What works for you may not work for you competitor across town. Just be aware that there is little or no advantage to changing the default value if your video is playing back from your web server and using a progressive download. In this situation, the Flash Player will take on the buffering duties and essentially ignore any value you have set in this parameter. If you are using a Flash Communication Server or a Flash Media Server, values between one-tenth to one-half second are common buffer values.

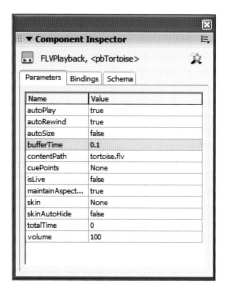

Figure 4-1.
bufferTime is a parameter used by the
FLV Playback component.

Creating a custom video controller

There are going to be occasions where you aren't going to want to give the user a full set of controls or, let's admit it, you are just fed up with the skins offered by the FLV Playback component. This could, for example, be a situation where all the user needs to do is click a start button to watch the video and click a pause button to stop it. Including volume controls, jog controls, and so on in this case would be overkill. This is where the FLV Playback Custom UI components become invaluable.

This collection of 10 components (see Figure 4-2) lets you customize the video controls and "wire them up" through ActionScript. You can do this because each component is essentially a movie clip or button, meaning they can be controlled through ActionScript. In this exercise, you will use a couple of the components shown in Figure 4-2 to create a controller for a video.

Figure 4-2.
The FLV Custom UI components

1. Open a new Flash document and drag a copy of the FLV Playback component to the stage. Click once on the Parameters tab and use these values:

   ▪ autoPlay: False

   ▪ contentPath: Tortoise.FLV. Be sure to check the Match source FLV dimensions check box.

   ▪ Skin: None

2. Select the component on the stage and, in the Property Inspector, give it the instance name of pbTortoise. Now add two more layers to the timeline and name them Controls and Actions. While you are at it, change the name of the layer containing the component to Video (see Figure 4-3).

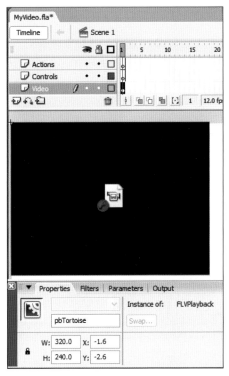

Figure 4-3. We've prepared the timeline and given the component an instance name.

3. Select the Controls layer and drag a copy of the play and pause buttons from the Custom UI panel to the stage. Place them under the Playback component. Select each button on the stage and give the play button the instance name of mcPlay (see Figure 4-4) and the pause button the instance name of mcPause.

When you drag these components to the stage, they are added to the library and a copy of the component is added to the FLVPlayback Skins folder in the library. This means the controls can be customized. If you don't like the color of the gradient used in the play button or you want to change the play button's icon color to yellow, you can open the button's movie clip in the Skins folder and make the change. Best of all, this change won't affect the original component in the UI Components panel.

You would be amazed at how many users still can't figure out which is a play button and which is a pause button. If you are at all nervous about this, add a text layer and, using the Text tool, enter the names of the controls.

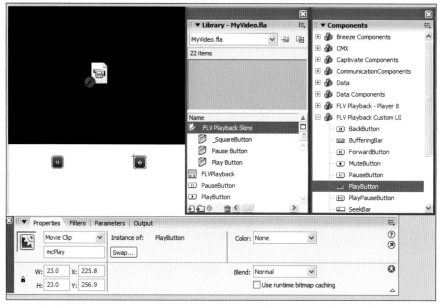

Figure 4-4. UI components appear in the library and their skins are added to the Skins folder.

With the assets assembled and on the stage, all you need to do is to add the ActionScript that controls the video.

4. Select the first frame in the Actions layer and press the F9 key (Windows) or Option+F9 (Mac) to open the Actions panel. Click once in the script pane and add the following code:

```
pbTortoise.playButton = mcPlay;
pbTortoise.pauseButton = mcPause;
```

5. Save the video and test it (see Figure 4-5). Notice how the pause button is grayed out because the video is paused—autoStart = False. Click the play button and the video will start to play. When you do, the pause button will "light up" and the play button will be grayed out. Click the pause button and the video will stop.

Figure 4-5.
The video is under the control of the two buttons.

Now that you understand how to add the UI components to a movie and control the video playback, here is how the rest of them are connected. The syntax is

```
InstancenameofFLVPlaybackcomponent.UIcomponentName =
    instancenameofUIcomponent
```

In the following examples, the instance name for the FLV Playback component is mcTortoise:

```
mcTortoise.playButton = myPlayButton;
mcTortoise.pauseButton = myPauseButton;
mcTortoise.playPauseButton = myPlayPauseButton;
mcTortoise.stopButton = myStopButton;
mcTortoise.backButton = myBackButton;
mcTortoise.forwardButton = myForwardButton;
mcTortoise.muteButton = myMuteButton;
mcTortoise.volumeBar = myVolumeBar;
mcTortoise.bufferingBar = myBufferingBar;
mcTortoise.seekBar = mySeekBar;
```

Creating a custom video player

So far we have spent a lot of time singing the praises of the FLV Playback component and the UI Playback components. They are great tools and marvelous for getting the job done. Unfortunately, many Flash developers tend to shy away from a reliance on components, claiming they "add weight to the SWF." For example, the Tortoise video, using only the FLV Playback component and no controls, weighs in at 34 KB. For serious Flash developers, to whom obtaining the smallest SWF with the highest quality is the "Holy Grail," 34 KB is seen as being somewhat ponderous... an elephant sitting on the stream.

There is a way of bringing the SWF down in size to around 1 KB with no loss of quality or sacrifice of playback accuracy. The technique involves the pairing of ActionScript with a video object.

The video object can be found in the library. Once the video object is on the stage, you can use ActionScript to feed the stream into it and manage the stream. To do this, you will need to use two classes of ActionScript. The first class you will use is the `Connection` class. As the name implies, this class is how the Flash SWF communicates—or connects—to your server. Flash doesn't care whether the server is your web server or a Flash Media Server; all it does is connect the stream from the server to your browser. The second class is the `User Interface` class in ActionScript, which does nothing more than display the video and play the sound in the SWF.

When it comes to using ActionScript to play video, it is easy to explain it in technical terms and dazzle you with our coding prowess, but drill down and you will see that it is not that difficult to understand. The process consists of just three steps:

- Connect to the server.
- Create the stream for the video.
- Play the video.

In fact, using these three steps, here is the minimum ActionScript required to play the `Tortoise.FLV` file from your web server:

```
New NetConnection();
NetConnection.connect(null);

New NetStream(NetConnection);

Video.attachVideo(netStream);
NetStream.Play("Tortoise.FLV");
```

In this code, the first two lines create the connection to the server and keep it open. The next line tells Flash the connection we have made with the server is to be used for the stream. The final two lines tell Flash which video to shoot down the stream and to attach that video to the stream. Those five lines will be used quite a bit throughout this chapter and, for that matter, the rest of this book.

Now that you understand how it is done, let's actually build a player using a video object and ActionScript.

1. Open Flash and create a new document.
2. Open the library—Ctrl+L (Windows) or Cmd+L (Mac)—and click the library's pop-down menu. Select New Video (see Figure 4-6).

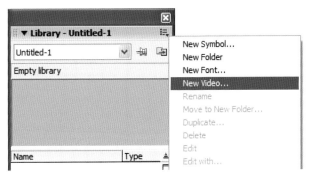

Figure 4-6. Video objects are available through the library's pop-down menu.

3. When the Video Properties dialog box opens (see Figure 4-7), select Video (ActionScript-controlled) from the Type choices and click OK. You can name the object if you wish, but for this exercise, it isn't necessary because there is only the one.

> *The* Embedded *option is rather dangerous. Select this and the entire video will be placed on the timeline with the corresponding increase in file size. There are uses for this—special effects such as rotoscoped video—but the practice of placing a video on the timeline started to disappear when video could be streamed through Flash. If you must place video on the timeline, use it for short videos lasting maybe 1 to 10 seconds.*

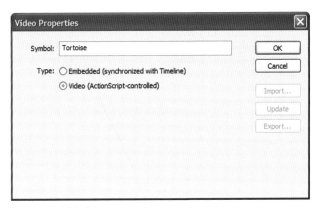

Figure 4-7. The video properties

When you click OK, the dialog box closes and, if you look at your library you will see a small video camera with the name you entered in the properties. This is the video object (see Figure 4-8).

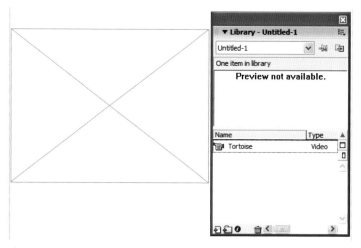

Figure 4-8. We dragged the video object from the library to the stage.

When you drag the video object from the library to the stage, you will see just how different this object is from anything else you add to the stage. It is nothing more than a box with a big "X" through it. That box is where the video will appear and will remain invisible, at runtime, until a video is fed into it. This object is quite unique in regard to ActionScript. It can only use the Video class. The Video class has methods and properties, but no events are associated with it. You can move the object, resize it, rotate it, mask it, and even stick it in a movie clip. What you can't do is use it to control a video.

The best way of understanding the video object is to look at your TV screen. The video object is the display. The knobs or buttons that turn the TV on and off or change the channel are not part of the display.

4. Select the video object on the stage and click the Properties tab of the Property Inspector. Enter the following values to resize the object to the dimensions of the video and to tuck it into the top-left corner of the stage:

- W: 320
- H: 240
- X: 0
- Y: 0
- Instance name: vidTort

Now that the properties have been set and the object given a name, you can now turn your attention to using ActionScript to "wire it up." Before you move on, it might be a good idea to save the file to the same folder used for the FLV.

Connecting the video object to a web server

As we said earlier the process involves three steps: connect, stream, play.

The first step—connect—is managed by the `NetConnection` class in ActionScript. This class manages the communication between the server and the user's computer. The `NetConnection` class has only three methods, two of which are available only if you are using a Flash Media Server or a Flash Video Streaming Service. They are

- `NetConnection.connect()`: Does exactly what it says and makes the connection request with the server where the FLV is located.
- `NetConnection.close()`: This method, only used by streaming servers, enables you to turn off the connection with the server.
- `NetConnection.call()`: This method, used only by streaming servers, is used to call remote methods from the Flash Player.

From there you simply establish the video stream using the `NetStream` class and attach the video object to the stream:

1. Open the file you have been working on and add a new layer named Actions.
2. Select the first frame in the Actions layer and press the F9 key to open the ActionScript panel. Click once in the script pane and add the following code:

```
var nc:NetConnection =new NetConnection();
nc.connect(null);
```

The first line of code defines and creates a connection object and gives it the name `nc`. We could have named the connection "bigHonkingVideoStream" but we prefer to use names that tell us exactly what the variable does. The second line uses the connect method to establish the connection. The `null` parameter is there because it establishes the connection between a local web server—IIS or Apache—or your computer's hard drive.

3. Press the Enter/Return key and add the following line of code:

```
var ns:NetStream = new NetStream(nc);
```

You have just created and instantiated—"instantiated" is a fancy name for naming a variable—a `NetStream` object using the `NetConnection` object used in the first line of the code. If you are going to be streaming a video, you need to use both a `NetConnection` and a `NetStream` if you are going to shoot a video into Flash.

With the connection made and the stream established, you can feed the stream into the video object named `vidTort` on the stage.

4. Press the Enter/Return key and add the following two lines of code:

```
vidTort.attachVideo(ns);
ns.play("Tortoise.flv");
```

71

Having established the connection to the server and created a stream, the first line entered attaches the video object on the stage to the `NetStream`. Now that the video object is attached to the stream, the last line of code essentially uses the `play()` method to load the `Tortoise.flv` to the stream and play it through the video object on the stage.

5. Save the movie and test it. First, the video plays (see Figure 4-9). More importantly is the size of the SWF. The SWF for this video, which does exactly what the FLV Playback component does, is 1 KB in size. That is a serious reduction in file size and explains why developers tend to use a code-based approach to projects rather than using the components.

Figure 4-9.
The video object and the video streaming into the object through the Flash Player

Don't panic. If you are just getting going with ActionScript and/or video, we won't suddenly start using ActionScript from this point on. There will be quite a few projects coming up in this book that are completed in a "code-free zone."

If the video doesn't play, be sure the FLV and the SWF are in the same folder.

Adding playback controls to a streaming video

Now that you have the video streaming through a video object, it would be nice if the user could control the playback of the video. In this exercise you are going to do just that. You are going to learn how to

- Pause a video before it starts playing.
- Pause a video by using a pause button.
- Play a paused video by using a play button.

1. Open the file you have just created and click once on the stage. Open the Property Inspector and click the Size button to open the Document Properties dialog box. Set the width of the stage to 320 pixels and the height to 275 pixels. Click OK. Add a new layer to the movie and name it Controls.

Reducing the size of the stage is a great habit to develop. Having a video that is 320×240 sitting on a blank stage that is 600×500 leaves a lot of unused space. In the Flash world, unused space means an extra bandwidth requirement. Considering how the whole point of this exercise is to get a video to play in the most efficient manner possible in the smallest space possible, unused stage areas defeat the purpose of the exercise.

Now that the housekeeping chores have been addressed, you can turn your attention to the controls.

Depending on personal preference, you can use either button symbols or movie clips in Flash as navigation or media controls. Both symbol types can use the `onPress`, `onRelease`, `onRollOver`, and `onRollout` event handlers commonly used in ActionScript. In our case, we are going to use a couple of buttons that were installed in a button library when you installed Flash Professional 8.

If there was a common complaint among Flash developers and designers, it was that the buttons packaged with the application were rather "lame." We aren't going to argue this observation other than to add that they were useful in situations where the client was given an idea of how controls would work. The folks at Macromedia seem to have finally gotten the message because Flash Professional 8 includes a button library that is both extensive and useful.

Yes, you can "roll your own" buttons and add them to Flash. Adobe Fireworks 8 is great tool for this, and if you really want to go to town, Adobe Photoshop CS2 is another excellent tool. Just be aware that you should have at least two button states, Up and Down, meaning that you will need two copies of each button created.

---

2. Select Window ➤ Common Libraries ➤ Buttons to open the Buttons panel.

3. Scroll down to the playback rounded folder in the Buttons panel and open it.

4. Select the Controls layer and drag a copy of each of the rounded grey pause and rounded grey play buttons to the stage.

5. Select the pause button and, in the Property Inspector, give it the instance name of btnPause (see Figure 4-10). Select the play button and give it the instance name of btnPlay. Save the movie.

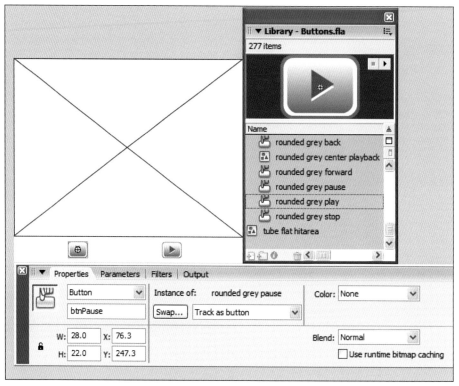

Figure 4-10. We dragged the buttons from the library to the stage where we gave them instance names in the Property Inspector.

6. Select the first frame in the Actions layer and press F9 (Option+F9 on a Mac) to open the ActionScript Editor.

7. Press Enter/Return after the last line of code and type

```
ns.pause(true);
```

This single line of code deals with our first objective. All it does is pause the stream into the video object. This means the video screen will be blank and will require the user to click a button to get it playing.

> We started off this chapter by talking about buffering video. You can also buffer video through ActionScript using the `bufferTime` property. To do this you would enter the following line of code before pausing the video:
>
> ```
> ns.setBufferTime (1);
> ```
>
> This would place one second of video in the buffer.

8. Press Enter/Return and add the following code:

```
btnPlay.onPress = function (){
   ns.pause(false);
}

btnPause.onPress = function() {
   ns.pause(true);
}
```

These two little functions play and pause the movie. The key thing you should get from this code is that video is paused or played by pausing or playing the `NetStream`.

The other important aspect of all three pieces of code is that they affect the `netStream` and don't, as you may assume, turn the connection on and off. When you think about it, this makes a whole lot of sense. The video is attached to the `NetStream`, so to pause a movie, you'd pause the flow of information into the browser. You don't kill the connection to the server.

9. Close the ActionScript Editor and save and test the movie.

When the movie starts you will see a blank screen with the two buttons thanks to the `ns.pause(true);` statement you added. Click the play button and the movie will start to play (see Figure 4-11). Click the pause button and the movie will pause. If you check the final size of the SWF, you will see the size, thanks to the buttons, has doubled from 1 KB to 2 KB.

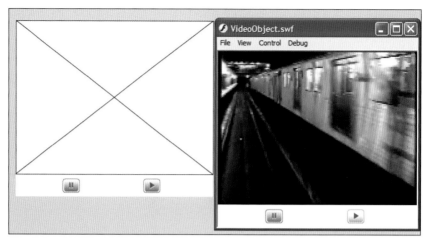

Figure 4-11. The video with buttons on the Flash stage and the video playing through the Flash Player

Summary

This marks the end of this chapter. We covered a lot of ground and, in many respects, this is one of the more important chapters in the book. It is all well and good to be able to create a video and convert it to an FLV, but if you don't know how to play it using the tools available to you in Flash Professional 8, then ... why bother?

We started off by reviewing the concept of streaming and buffering video by using the analogy of a dam upstream from a farming community. You learned the difference between publish and subscribe, how buffering a video works, and how to set the buffer time using both the VideoPlayback parameters and ActionScript.

You then learned how to build your own custom video controller using the FLV Playback UI components and how to connect them to the FLV Playback component through ActionScript.

We also showed you how to connect and play a video through a video object on the stage and stream it using ActionScript. As you saw, there was a major size reduction in the SWF because the FLV Playback component wasn't used. You also learned that streaming a video is a simple three-step process consisting of the steps connect, stream, and play.

Finally, you learned how to create a streaming video and control it with a couple of buttons contained in the button library.

Up to this point in the book, you have spent a lot of time just getting video into Flash and playing. If you were to stop here and go no further, you would have the basic skills necessary to create, encode, and deploy Flash video on your sites.

Now that you have the basics under control, turn the page and let's start seeing what you can do with your newfound skills. More importantly, let's spend the rest of the book having fun and getting very creative with video.

5 "TALKING HEAD" VIDEO AND ALPHA CHANNELS

You have seen the technique shown in Figure 5-1 used on your local television station's weather broadcast. The meteorologist will stand in front of a radar image and start pointing out the features in the image that are important. If you happened to be in the studio when all of this was going on, you would find it rather disconcerting. The meteorologist would be standing in front of a green or blue wall and pointing to it while delivering the broadcast. Meteorologists are actually looking at a monitor in which they see themselves standing in front of the radar image "behind" them. The green or blue color is being "keyed" out of the signal and replaced with the radar image.

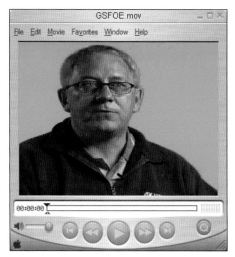

Figure 5-1. The "Talking Head" video. Note the green screen in the background.

In many respects, if you are familiar with creating masks in Photoshop or Fireworks 8, you will be quite familiar with "keying video" by default. You essentially target the color to be removed and then manipulate the edges and add a bit of feathering to smooth out the transition between the subject and the background. Premiere, Final Cut Pro, and After Effects use plug-ins for this task.

In Figure 5-2, which is taken from Premiere Pro 2.0 (if you are using an earlier version of Premiere, there may be some slight differences from the figures you see here), you can see the actual mask that is applied to the video. Anything within the black area will be masked. This type of mask differs from that in an imaging application because it moves. For example, if the subject were to lean to the right, the white area would change shape to accommodate the movement.

This is an important concept to grasp, especially in Flash Professional 8. If you place the video in a movie clip, a Drop Shadow can then be attached to the mask, and the shadow will move and change shape in conjunction with the change in shape of the video mask—you can already imagine all sorts of powerful possibilities, no? Let's explore this further.

Figure 5-2. The mask that is used to remove the green background

This chapter explores the topic of alpha channels in Flash Professional 8. It is essentially divided into three distinct sections. The first section shows you how to add an alpha channel to a green screen video using Adobe Premiere Pro 2, Adobe After Effects 7 on the PC, and Final Cut Pro on the Mac. The next section shows you how to encode it and use the video in a Flash movie, and the final section answers the question, "Yeah, that's interesting, but what can I really do with it?"

Creating an alpha channel video with Adobe Premiere Professional 2

The first thing you need to do is find out what you are working with. When creating video it is important that the project settings match those in the source file, or you will be setting yourself up for problems at a later date.

We want you to understand that this section falls into the category of "Beginner Tutorial." The process of "keying" video can be quite complex. In fact, entire chapters are devoted to this task in many of the video books on the market. Having said that, if you are familiar with the process, your first reaction will most likely be "That ain't the way I would do it." It probably isn't and, in many respects, ain't the way we would do it either. Still, our response will be, "We have to start somewhere," and this tutorial reviews the basic workflow involved.

1. Open the GSFOE.mov file from the download files for this chapter in QuickTime, and select Window ➤ Show Movie Info.

The Info dialog box provides you with the information you will need to create the project file in Premiere. You will notice that the movie is 320×240, which is a standard size for web video, and that the frame rate is 24 fps. The other bit of information you will need is the audio information. In this project the audio will remain at 16-bit 44.1 kHz. Though you could change the audio quality in a video-editing application, this project is destined for the FLV Encoder and can be changed there.

2. Open Premiere and select New Project on the splash screen. In Premiere, as well as After Effects, everything revolves around the "project." This is where you can keep track of, and assemble, the various elements that will constitute your final video.

3. When the New Project dialog box opens, click the Custom Settings tab and use the following values:

   - Editing Mode: Desktop
   - Timeline: 24.00 frames/second
   - Frame Size: 320 horizontal and 240 vertical
   - Pixel Aspect Ratio: Square Pixels (1.0)
   - Sample Rate: 44100 Hz

In the Location area, target the folder you will be using to hold the project and the files used in the project and give the project a name (see Figure 5-3). When finished, click OK.

Feel free to use the folder containing the files for this tutorial as your project folder. Regardless of what you do, don't change the folder's name or location after you create the project. Premiere stores a lot of the files associated with a project in this folder, and changing the name or the folder's location will break all of the links to the files used in the project. If you must change the location, select Edit ➤ Preferences ➤ Scratch Disks.

4. When the Premiere workspace opens, select File ➤ Import and import the CMXGS.mov file into your project. When the file appears in the Project panel, select it and click the play button, located just to the left of the small screen at the top of the Project panel, to preview the video.

5. Drag the video from the Project panel to the Video 1 layer in the timeline. You will notice that the video is now composed of an audio and a video layer and that the Monitor window opens (see Figure 5-4).

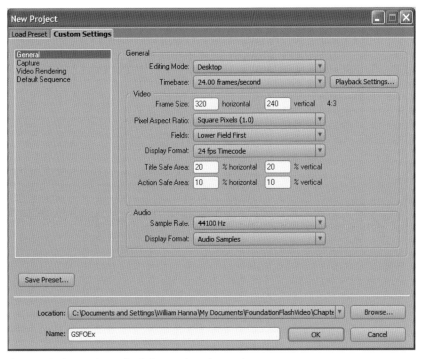

Figure 5-3. Create the project's format, location, and name.

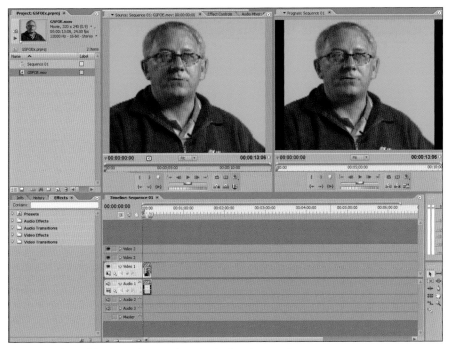

Figure 5-4. Everything is ready to work on in the Premiere workspace.

FOUNDATION FLASH 8 VIDEO

With the video on the stage, take a close look at the green background in the Monitor window. You will notice it really isn't a solid green. There are gradations of the color here and there in the background. The time you take to study the background is time well spent, because it will determine which keying effect will be used. Though there is a Green Screen Key filter, it won't be able to "get" the various shades of the green. The filter we use for this situation is the Color Key filter.

> *The Color Key filter is available in the version of Premiere Pro that ships with the Production Studio. If you do not have the Color Key filter in your copy of Premiere, use the Chroma Key filter instead.*

6. To start the process of "keying out" the green background, select Window ➤ Effects to open the Effects panel (alternatively, if it is visible, select the Effects tab.) As you can see, a lot of effects come bundled with Premiere.

7. Select Video Effects ➤ Keying ➤ Color Key in the Effects panel. With the plug-in selected, drag it from the Effects panel and drop it on top of the thumbnail in the Video 1 channel.

8. To open the Color Key plug-in settings, select Window ➤ Effect Controls. As you make changes to the settings they will be reflected in the image in the Monitor window. The window that opens contains four settings that you can adjust (see Figure 5-5):

   ▪ Key Color: You can choose a color to remove by selecting a color from the Color Picker or by using the Eyedropper to sample the color to be removed.

   ▪ Color Tolerance: If you are familiar with the Magic Wand tool in Fireworks 8 or Photoshop CS2, the tolerance specifies how wide a range of the selected color to remove.

   ▪ Edge Thin: This control expands or contacts the mask.

   ▪ Edge Feather: Does exactly what it says. The transition between the edge of the mask and the subject can be rather abrupt. This control adds a small amount of feathering to the edges of the mask to "smooth" things out.

9. Click and drag the Eyedropper in the Key Color setting onto the green area of the clip in the Monitor window. You will notice that as you drag the Eyedropper some of the green area turns black. This indicates the color to be masked. Release the mouse to sample the color.

10. Drag the Color Tolerance slider to the right. As you drag, the black area expands. As you drag, pay particular attention to the hair and the shoulders of the talking head. Try to remove as much green as possible. We found a value of 91 to be just about right.

11. Drag the feather slider to a value of about 1.6 to 1.8. When you remove the green you will also notice that the edges of the talking head become pixilated. This slider adds a bit of feather to smooth out the edge.

82

Figure 5-5. Selecting the color to remove and using the Tolerance slider allows you to control the masked area.

You don't have to use the sliders. If you wish, you can click and drag the values, the blue numbers, in the percentage area to change them. This is a neat trick but we suggest using the sliders until you are more comfortable with the application. You can also double-click the values and enter them directly.

Now that you have "keyed out" the green screen, you need to create the QuickTime file that will be used by the Flash Video 8 Encoder. Here's how:

1. Click in the Monitor window and select File ➤ Export ➤ Movie. When the Export dialog box opens, navigate to the folder where you will be saving the video and name the video TalkingHead. Click the Settings button (see Figure 5-6) to open the Export Movie Settings dialog box. The Export Movie Settings dialog box is the key to successful completion of this exercise. Here is where you choose the file type for the video and select the appropriate codec that will render the alpha channel.

Figure 5-6. Name the movie and don't click Save. Click the Settings button instead.

2. Click the General category and select QuickTime from the list in the File Type pop-down. Also be sure to select the Export Video and Export Audio check boxes. Selecting the Add to Project When Finished check box ensures you can return to these settings should changes be required after the video file is created. Select None in the Embedding options. Embedding a project in the file does nothing more than add to the metadata by letting QuickTime know the video is part of a Premiere project.

3. Click the Video category. Select Animation as the codec and select Millions+ of colors from the choices in the Color Depth pop-down (see Figure 5-7).

These two choices are the key to creating a video with an alpha channel. By selecting Millions+ of colors from the Color Depth pop-down, you have included the alpha channel created by the Green Screen Key filter in the video. Selecting Millions of colors will create a video with a lot of color but will result in the loss of the alpha channel.

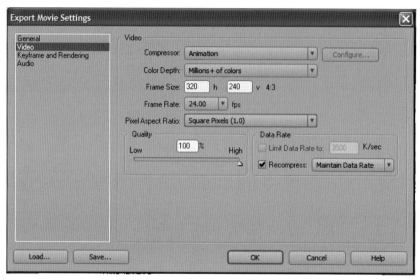

Figure 5-7. The key to retaining the alpha channel is to select Millions+ of colors from the Color Depth pop-down.

4. Click OK to close the Export Movie Settings dialog box. When you return to the Export Movie dialog box, click Save. This will open a small dialog box showing you the progress of the compression. It will close when the compression is finished.

5. Select File ➤ Save and quit Premiere.

If you open the video file in the QuickTime player now, you are in for a bit of a surprise—the green screen seems to have been replaced by a black screen. Don't worry, the alpha channel is there. This technique is most commonly used when "compositing" video. For example, you would overlay the talking head video over a video of a busy street and, if you were to play that video, you would see the head talking and cars zooming by in the background. In the case of this video, the alpha channel is there; you just aren't using it. Yet...

Creating an alpha channel video with After Effects 7 Professional

After Effects is one serious video-editing application, and the things it can do with video are simply amazing. With the advent of Flash video, this application is going to become more and more important to our workflow. Giving you a full overview of what it can do for you is well out of the scope of this book. In fact, if you get excited about how it can be used to "key" video and you use it strictly for that purpose, you are seriously limiting yourself. It would be akin to using a Formula 1 race car to drive up to the corner store for milk or a lottery ticket.

Still, a lot of Flash developers are starting to use this application and a lot of you, getting into working with video, are soon to be introduced to it. There are quite a few keying tools in After Effects; one of the most popular, for our purposes, is the Keylight filter. Talk to any video guru who uses After Effects and inevitably they will swing a "keying" conversation around to Keylight.

In many respects, Keylight is an industrial-strength keying filter with a number of tools designed to make your life easy. This filter was first developed by the Computer Film Company to help with difficult keying situations in feature-length films. In fact, this software is so good for digital compositing it won a Technical Academy Award in 1996. This plug-in lets you choose a key based on color and then allows you to carefully refine your selection using a variety of options that adjust the mask.

A custom version of the Keylight filter was introduced with version 6 of After Effects and is bundled with After Effects 7 Professional. Just be aware that we are not going to go deep into this filter. In fact, we will only be scratching the surface of what it can do. Even so, you will be amazed at its power and ease of use.

Follow these steps to create an alpha channel video using the Keylight filter:

1. Open After Effects and select Composition ➤ New Composition or press Ctrl+N (Windows) or Cmd+N (Mac). When the Composition Settings dialog box opens, enter these values (see Figure 5-8):

   ■ Composition Name: FlashVidAlpha. This is just a name for the composition.

   ■ Preset: Custom. We are going to change a few things that aren't a part of the preset values.

   ■ Width: 320.

   ■ Height: 240 (You may need to deselect the Lock Aspect Ratio option.)

   ■ Frame Rate: 24. This matches the frame rate of the clip we will be using.

   ■ Duration: 0:00:13:08. This is the duration of the clip being used.

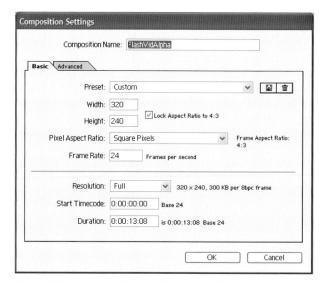

Figure 5-8. The composition settings used in this project

2. Click OK and the After Effects workspace will open. Select File ➤ Import ➤ File and navigate to the GSFOE.mov file in the Lesson 5 Exercise folder. Select it and click Open. When you do this, the clip is placed in the project window. Drag the video clip onto the timeline (see Figure 5-9).

Figure 5-9. The talking head is on the timeline and we can go to work.

3. Click once on the composition window—it contains the preview of the video—and select Effects ➤ Keying ➤ Keylight. This will open the Effects window and the controls for the Keylight filter. Though there are a lot of items contained in this dialog box, we are only going to concern ourselves with the Screen Colour control.

Click the Eyedropper and move it over the green background behind the talking head. Click once and not only does all of the green disappear but also the color just sampled appears in the Screen Colour color chip (see Figure 5-10).

> *What's with the spelling of the word "color" and "colour"? Keylight is produced by a British company and the spelling of the word colour—using the "Queen's English"—is correct.*

Figure 5-10. The green background is gone thanks to Keylight.

As it stands, you can proceed to creating the .mov file with the mask. However, there are those of you who fall into the realm of "control freak," so before proceeding let's satisfy the cravings of the control freaks and make things even better.

The control freak will look at the image and think, "Gee, I wonder if the mask is a good as we can get it?" Looking at the preview you can easily answer, "Well, looks fine to me." Let's find out if the control freaks have a point.

4. In the View pop-down, select Status. The preview will change to show us the mask, and it looks like the control freaks may have a point. The background should be a solid black, not the gray seen in the preview (see Figure 5-11).

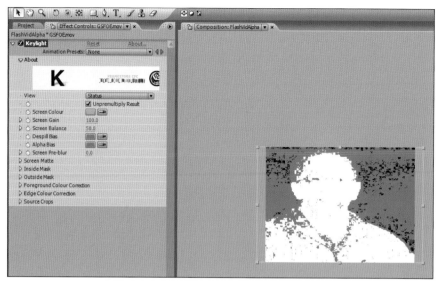

Figure 5-11. Score one for the control freaks. We didn't get all of the green.

5. To fix this, click once on the arrow, called a "twirly," beside the Screen Gain setting. When the slider appears, drag it to the right. Keep an eye on the background. When it is completely black—a value of about 118—release the mouse (see Figure 5-12).

> *There is an After Effects gotcha here that you need to be aware of. If you leave the view at* Status, *the video you see in Figure 5-11 is exactly what will be output. Be sure to change the view to* Final Result *before you create the QuickTime file.*

Now the control freaks will most likely ask, "Isn't a mask supposed to black outside and white inside?" They have another point.

6. Click the Screen Matte "twirly" to open the Screen Matte properties. Click once on the Clip White value and drag the mouse to the left until a value of about 29 is showing. What "clipping" does is essentially change any pixel in the mask with a value higher than 0 to a value of 29.

> *Twirly? If you have only lived in the Macromedia universe before now, there is some new terminology you will have to learn. The pop-down triangles used to open properties in a panel or palette in Adobe products have been given the name of "twirly" by the users. When asked to open one of these menus, the process of clicking the "twirly" is actually called "Twirl down…" Thus, if you are speaking to an Adobe user, you now know what the heck they are talking about when you are asked to "Twirl down the* Screen Matte *properties."*

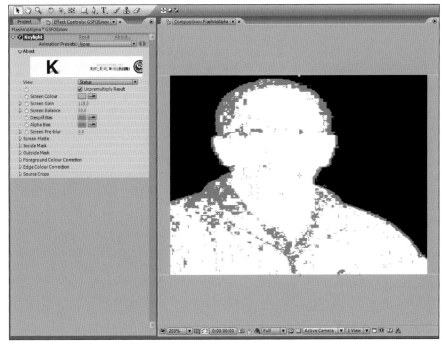

Figure 5-12. That's much better.

7. Select the Combined Matte view and you will see that things have vastly improved. Still, a little attention should be paid to the edge of the mask.

8. Twirl down the Edge Colour Correction properties and set Edge Softness to a value of about 2 (see Figure 5-13) and return to the Final Result view.

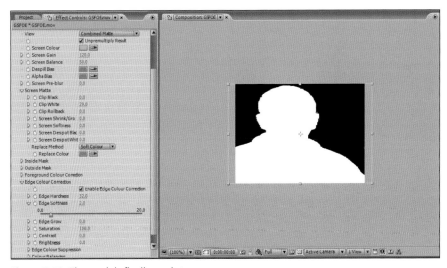

Figure 5-13. The mask is finally ready to go.

Now that the mask is vastly improved over our first effort, let's get this video created before the control freaks start looking for more improvements!

Creating the video is quite similar to what you did in the previous exercise. You are still going to need to create a QuickTime video using the Animation codec that uses Millions+ of colors to save the alpha channel. In After Effects you don't merrily "Save" the file. All that does is create an .aep file that contains all of the project settings. You have to render the composition, and to do this you have to add the project to the render queue. Here's how:

1. Click once in the composition window and select Composition ➤ Add to Render Queue. This will open the Render Queue panel. If you are new to After Effects, this can be one scary and terribly confusing place (see Figure 5-14). In actual fact, it is not all that difficult to master. All you need to do is to click the blue links.

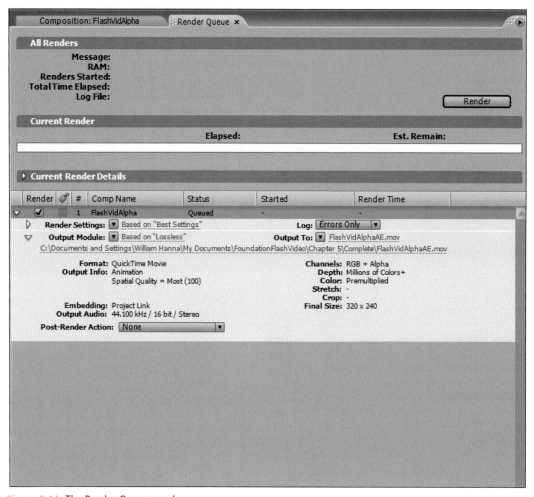

Figure 5-14. The Render Queue panel

2. Click the Best Settings link to open the Render Settings panel. This allows you to manually override the composition settings. We have no intention of changing any of the settings. The purpose of opening this dialog box is simply to answer the question, "What does this link do?" Review the settings, don't change a thing, and click OK to close this dialog box.

3. Click the Lossless link to open the Output Module Settings dialog box (see Figure 5-15). This is where the real heavy lifting is going to be done.

This dialog box lets you choose the final output and compression settings for the video. Click the Format drop-down and select QuickTime Movie. Now that we know what type of file we are outputting to, we can turn our attention to the compression settings. Open these by clicking the Format Options button in the Video Output area.

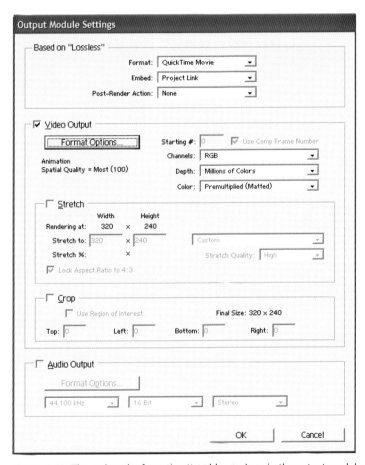

Figure 5-15. The real work of creating the video is done in the output module.

When you click the Format Options button, the Compression Settings dialog box will open. Select Animation from the pop-down list at the top of the dialog box and select Millions of Colors+ from the Color Depth pop-down. Leave the Quality slider at Best and don't change the frame rate. Click OK to close the Compression Settings dialog box and to return to the Output Module Settings dialog box. This will change to reflect the compression choices you just made.

Finally, click the Audio Output check box (see Figure 5-16). If you don't select it, the audio won't be added to the video. Click OK to close the dialog box.

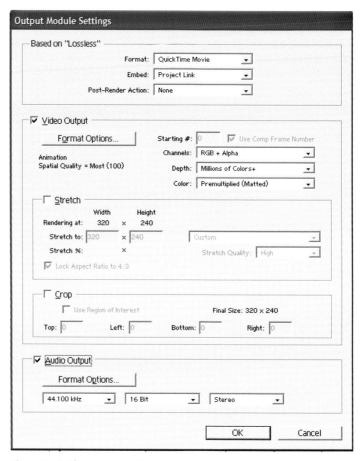

Figure 5-16. The output settings are "good to go."

4. Now all you need to do is to create the .mov file. Click the Not yet specified link in the Output To area. This will open the Output To dialog box. Navigate to the folder where you wish the video to be saved, name the file FlashVidAEAlpha.mov, and click Save. Check your final render settings and, if everything is correct, click the Render button.

When the movie "renders," you will be shown the progress of the process (see Figure 5-17) and, when it finishes, you will hear a chime. Close the Render Queue dialog box and quit After Effects.

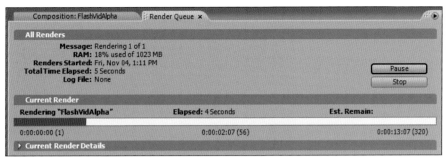

Figure 5-17. The video with the alpha channel is being created.

Creating an alpha channel video in Final Cut Pro

A few years back, Macromedia owned a video-editing product that just didn't seem to fit its product mix and corporate direction. Macromedia decided to sell it and Apple bought the application. The application became Final Cut Pro. Since then it has become a de facto video-editing standard among Macintosh users and, in many respects, among video producers. It is also a feature-rich application and, like many Apple products, has a very shallow learning curve.

If you have a Mac, here's how to create an alpha channel video using Final Cut Pro. Even if you use a PC, feel free to follow along or skip to the next section:

1. Open Final Cut Pro, create a new project—Cmd+Shift+N—and import the GSFOE.mov file into the project. Place the video on the timeline and drag the .mov file to the viewer window.

2. Click the Effects tab in the Browser panel, select the Key folder to open it, and drag a copy of the Color Key filter from the panel and drop it on the video on the timeline (see Figure 5-18).

3. Click the Filters tab in the viewer window and the Color Key settings will be available. This filter works very much like its counterpart in Premiere. You click the Eyedropper in the Color area, roll the cursor over to the video in the Sequence panel, and click the mouse to sample the color to be removed.

When the color is selected, pay close attention to the green background. You may see nothing more than a faint black smudge when you make your selection. This means you have only grabbed a few pixels. Use the Tolerance, Edge Thin, and Edge Feather sliders to adjust the selection. We found these settings worked for us (see Figure 5-19):

- Tolerance = 33
- Edge Thin = 46
- Edge Feather = 4

93

Figure 5-18. We are ready to get rid of the green.

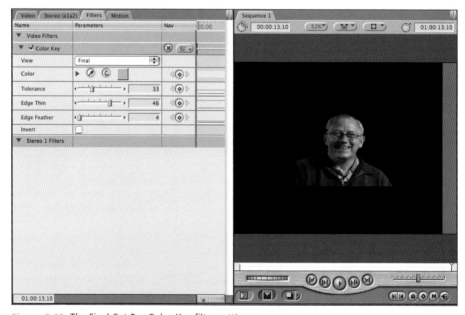

Figure 5-19. The Final Cut Pro Color Key filter settings

Just to be sure that you have everything, select Matte from the View pop-down. The screen will change to show you the mask. If there are any gray pixels in the background, adjust the sliders to remove them. When they vanish, return to the Final view (see Figure 5-20).

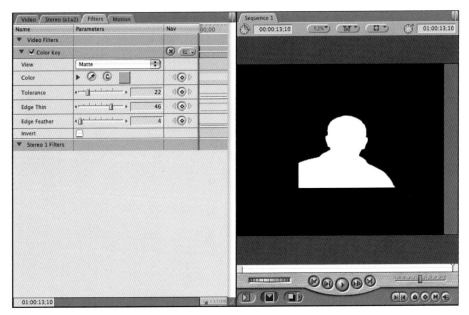

Figure 5-20. The mask is looking good.

To export the movie and the alpha channel, set the in and out points to the start and the end points of the video, respectively. Select File ➤ Export ➤ Using QuickTime Conversion, and when the Save dialog box opens, name the file and choose the location where the movie will be saved. Follow these steps to save the video and the alpha channel:

1. In the Save dialog box, click the Options button to open the Movie Settings dialog box. The Animation codec is found in the Settings area, so click the Settings button.

2. When the Standard Video Compression Settings dialog box opens, select Animation from the Compression Type pop-down menu; select 24 from the Frame Rate drop-down menu; and select Automatic in the Key Frames section in the Motion area. The alpha channel is found by opening the Depth drop-down menu in the Compressor section and selecting Millions of Colors+. While you are at it, drag the Quality slider to the Best setting (see Figure 5-21). Click OK to close the dialog box.

> *We are asking you to choose* Best *because file size isn't important. This file is destined for the Flash 8 Video Encoder where the compression will be applied and the file size reduced.*

3. When you return to the Movie Settings dialog box, deselect Prepare for Internet Streaming. Flash is going to handle the duties here, so this selection is a bit redundant.

4. Click OK to return to the Save dialog box. Click the Save button to create the .mov.

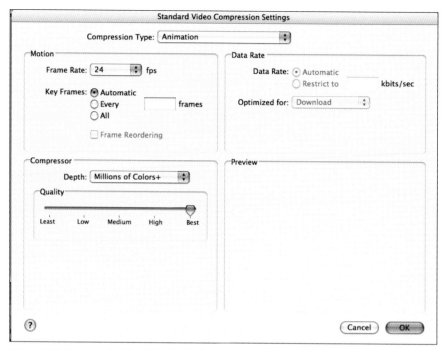

Figure 5-21. Compressing the video in Final Cut Pro

Here's something you may not have noticed when using After Effects or Final Cut Pro. If you select File ➤ Export in After Effects, you will notice that one of the choices is Macromedia Flash Video (FLV) (see Figure 5-22). Select this and you will open the Flash 8 Video Encoder. The ability to create the FLV right in After Effects is a great way of improving your workflow. In Final Cut Pro, Macromedia Flash Video (FLV) is one of the options in the Format pop-down menu found in the Save dialog box (see Figure 5-23). In Premiere you can also go direct to an FLV by selecting Export ➤ Adobe Media Encoder... and selecting Macromedia Flash Video (FLV) in the Format pop down menu. Unfortunately, you can't export any footage to which you have attached an alpha channel. This is why we suggest saving the video as a .mov file and using the Flash 8 Video Encoder to handle the duties.

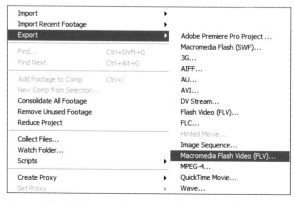

Figure 5-22. FLV files can be exported from After Effects.

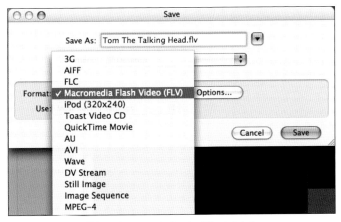

Figure 5-23. An FLV can be exported out of Final Cut Pro.

Creating an FLV file with an alpha channel

Now that you have created the video to be used in Flash, let's see how to create an FLV containing an alpha channel.

1. Open a new Flash Professional 8 document and select File ➤ Import ➤ Import Video to open the Video Import Wizard. When the Select Video dialog box opens, click the Browse button and navigate to your talking head video. When you open it, click the Next button. The window that opens is the Deployment screen. You are essentially being asked how the video will play through Flash Player 8.

2. Select Progressive download from a web server and click the Next button to open the Encoding dialog box.

This dialog box is where you will create the FLV file that contains the alpha channel. There are a few rules regarding Flash Professional 8 and FLV files with alpha channels:

- Choose one of the Flash 8 Profiles. The default is Medium Quality (see Figure 5-24), which means the data rate for the FLV is pegged at 400 kbps and the codec will be the one needed—On2 VP6.

- Alpha channels can only be added to FLV files created using the new On2 VP6 codec. This means video with an Alpha channel can only be played through the Flash 8 Player. Even though this is the default codec for the Encoder, don't click the Next button.

- You must tell Flash Professional 8 to include the alpha channel in the Advanced Settings of the Encoder dialog box.

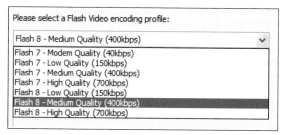

Figure 5-24. You need to select a Flash 8 encoding profile.

3. Click the Show Advanced Settings button to open the Advanced Settings dialog box. Click the Encode alpha channel radio button under the codec pop-down (see Figure 5-25).

> If you use the Flash 8 Video Encoder, you will go right to the encoding settings when you click the Settings button in the Encoder window.

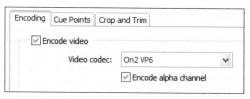

Figure 5-25. The Alpha channel is encoded in the Advanced Settings area of the Encoder.

4. Click the Next button to open the Skinning dialog box. Select None—this will be a simple talking head—and click the Next button.

   The dialog box that appears will ask you to determine where the files will be saved. Click the Finish button to open the Save As dialog box. Enter a name for the FLA file—the FLV will be given the same name—and click Save. You will be shown the progress of the FLV creation. When it finishes, the dialog box will close and you will be returned to the Flash stage, where an FLV Playback component will be visible.

5. Add a layer to the movie and move it under the video layer. Import an image into Flash and place it on this new layer.

6. Save the file and press Ctrl+Enter (Windows) or Cmd+Return (Mac) to preview your talking head video (see Figure 5-26).

Figure 5-26.
"Tom the Talking Head"

Playing with alpha channel video in Flash

Okay, the dry stuff is out of the way. Now that you know how to create the channel, compress the video, and create an FLV containing the channel—in three separate video-editing applications, we might add—you are probably wondering, "That's really great, guys, but what the heck can I do with it?"

Turns out, the answer is, "Quite a lot." To keep this chapter focused, we aren't going to cover *everything* you can do. Instead, we are going to show you how to do a few things and leave it to you to look for even more creative ways to use the techniques. We will be showing you how to

- Trim a video and use it like a banner ad
- Play "video-on-video"
- Use cue points in a video to trigger Flash events
- Have someone "walk" across your web page in a browser

Trimming video

One of the pitfalls of working with video is that sometimes the actual video is either wider or higher than the Flash stage. If you're a Flash control freak, this can be a rather disconcerting situation. Control freaks like "neat and tidy," and having a video hanging off the stage is neither neat nor tidy.

If you open `Trim.fla` in your Chapter 5 Exercise folder, you will notice that the stage dimensions are 700 pixels wide by 206 pixels high. This is due to the nature of the photo, which is a bunch of "Good Ol' Boys" hanging out in St. George's Square in Bermuda. The plan here is to use some footage whereby a young woman walks across the stage and stops to look at the guys on the bench. The problem is, the video's dimensions don't match those of the Flash stage. The video's width is 756 pixels. Here's how you fix that problem:

1. Open the Flash 8 Video Encoder and add the `betina.mov` file to the Encoder queue. When the video is added, click the Settings button and open the Advanced Settings dialog box.

2. Make sure you select the On2 VP6 codec and that you also click the Encode alpha channel check box. Now click the Crop and Trim tab of the Advanced Encoder options.

The Crop area contains four sliders, which control the cropping from the top, bottom, and two sides of the video. Knowing the width needed is 700 pixels, you can't simply enter that value. You need to remove 56 pixels from the right edge of the video.

3. Double-click in the Text input box in the right Crop area and enter the value 56 (see Figure 5-27). You could use the slider for this, but you will soon discover it is rather imprecise. In fact, it will take you longer to use the slider than to simply enter the value.

4. Click OK and when you return to the Encoder dialog box, click the Start Queue button to create the FLV file.

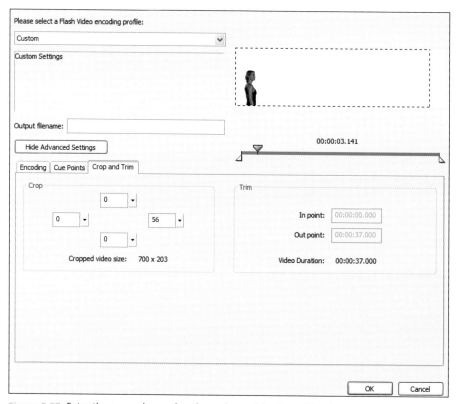

Figure 5-27. Enter the crop values rather than using a slider if precision is paramount.

Don't enter the value and then press the Enter/Return key if you want to make further changes to the file. As soon as a value is entered, it is accepted. Pressing Enter/Return is the same as clicking the OK *button, which returns you to the Encoding queue.*

Now that the FLV has been cropped, return to Flash and add a new layer. Toss an FLV Playback component into that layer and link it to the FLV just created; be sure that you check the Match Source FLV Dimensions option. Select the component on the stage and, in the Property Inspector make sure the X value is set to 0 and that the Y value is set to 3. (Remember, the stage is 3 pixels higher than the video height.) Once you have done that, save the movie and test it. Betina will walk across the stage and check out the "Good Ol' Boys" (see Figure 5-28).

Figure 5-28. Checking out the "Good Ol' Boys" in Bermuda

Video-on-video

Though we have been able to accomplish this "trick" since the advent of Flash MX and the progressive download, it is even simpler to do in Flash Professional 8. The inclusion of alpha channels kicks out the proverbial "creative jams." Need a talking head extolling the virtues of a new car model? No problem. Let him talk away while, behind him, the car is ripping through a race course. Need a talking head explaining the various new features of your product? No problem. You can "swap" videos depending on what feature is being presented.

The only caution is, don't go crazy. Videos suck up bandwidth and processing on the user's computer. Keep it simple, and the viewer's experience will be positive. Go crazy and toss in a bunch of videos, and the user will not be thanking you for the rather unpleasant experience awaiting him or her.

In this exercise, Betina walks across the stage and something in the movie trailer playing behind her catches her attention.

1. Open the VidonVid.fla file in your Chapter 5 Exercise folder. We have already included a background image and slot for the video. Add two new layers.

2. Select layer 2 and add an FLV PLayback component to the stage. Click the Parameters tab and link to component to the `Trail2-Video1.flv` in your exercise folder. Set the bufferTime to 0. Place the component over the black square in the background image.

3. Select layer 3 and drag the FLV Playback component from the library to the stage. Link this component of the `betina.flv` file in your exercise folder and set the bufferTime to 0. Place the component right at the bottom of the stage being sure to set its X and Y values to 0 in the Property Inspector.

4. Test the movie (see Figure 5-29).

Figure 5-29. Video-on-video is now easy to accomplish.

Adding cue points to video

At its most fundamental, video is a time-based medium. When you look at it in that manner, a whole world of possibilities opens up to you.

Throughout this section we have been using the Betina video from Macromedia to demonstrate a variety of techniques. You will notice that as she walks across the screen, she turns a few times to study whatever she just passed by. Each of those points in the video happens at a unique point in time. This means we can use the times where she turns to look at the screen to trigger other Flash events. This is accomplished by using cue points.

Cue points can be added to your FLV in one of three ways. The first is to embed the cue point directly into the FLV using the Flash 8 Video Encoder. The second method is to add them through the use of ActionScript. The third method is to add them as a parameter in the FLV Playback component. Any of these three methods works, but we prefer to use the ActionScript approach.

When you use the Encoder to add a cue point, it is essentially hard-wired into the FLV and can't be removed. For example, if you have a cue point located at 00:00:03.076 and subsequently discover the cue point should be set at 00:00:03:0 84, then you need to manually add a new cue point. You can't remove it or change its time.

In this section, we'll add the cue points and then use them to trigger events in Flash.

Cue points and the Flash 8 Video Encoder

Cue points can be added to the FLV when you encode the video. Here's how:

1. Open the Flash 8 Video Encoder and add the Betina.mov file from the chapter download to the queue. Click the Settings button to open the Encoder window and then click the Advanced Settings button to open the Encoder's Advanced settings.

2. Drag the jog control slider in the preview until the woman walks across the screen and makes her first turn to look behind her. This should be somewhere at the 00:00:06.050 point in the time code.

3. Click the Cue Points tab in the Encoder window.

Adding a cue point is a rather simple process. Click the + button and a cue point is added. Obviously, using the default name—New Cue Point—makes no sense. Select the name and change it to CuePointOne. At this stage of the game, if you haven't moved the jog controller, you can change the name of the cue point or even delete it completely by selecting the cue point and clicking the - button. You will next see a small dialog box asking you if you wish to delete the point.

4. Drag the jog control slider until the woman turns again—somewhere around 00:00:16.289—and add another cue point named cuePointTwo. Finally, add a third cue point, named cuePointThree, when she makes her third turn, which is close to 00:00:27.110 (see Figure 5-30).

> *At this stage of the process, before you start encoding the FLV, you can edit the cue points. Once the video is encoded, the cue points can no longer be added, changed, or otherwise edited.*

5. Click the Encoding tab and make sure you have selected the On2 VP6 codec. Name the FLV betinaqp and click the OK button to return the Encoding Queue window. Click the Start Queue button to create the FLV.

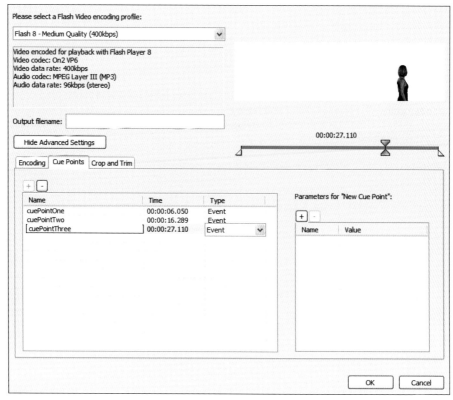

Figure 5-30. The cue points are added and named.

When you create the FLV, those cue points are embedded into the metadata and are visible when the video is linked to the FLV Playback component. You can see them in either the Parameters area of the Property Inspector (see Figure 5-31) or in the Component Inspector.

Another method of adding the cue points is to add them directly into the FLV. This is done by linking the FLV to the FLV Playback component and clicking the cuePoints strip in either the component parameters in the Property Inspector or the Component Inspector.

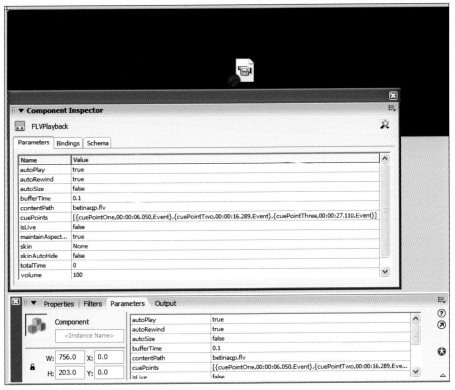

Figure 5-31. Cue points embedded into an FLV appear either in the Parameters area of the Property Inspector or in the Component Inspector.

When you do this, the Flash Video Cue Points dialog box will open (see Figure 5-32). Click the + sign, enter a name and a time for the cue point, and click OK. When the dialog box closes, the cue point will appear in the cuePoint area of the component's parameters.

> *One of the authors is constantly reminding his students to develop the habit of having a notepad on their desk to jot down ideas and so on. In the case of adding cue points, you could note the times using the values in the Encoder and then have this information at hand to add those values when they are needed.*

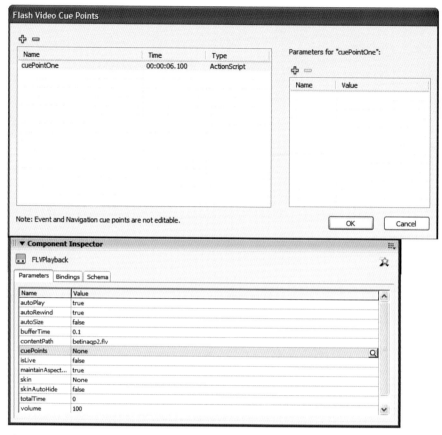

Figure 5-32. Cue points can be added by clicking on the cuePoint strip in the component's parameters.

The final method of adding cue points may just be the best, even though, in many respects, it is the most complex. In the previous examples, the cue points were essentially hard-wired into the FLV. If a value needs to be deleted or changed, you are essentially out of luck.

The method is to add them through the use of ActionScript. You must

- Add the `Video` class
- Create the cue points using the `addASCuePoint()` method
- Create listeners for those cue points
- Determine what happens when ActionScript "hears" a cue point

In this section, Betina will walk across the screen and, when she passes in front of the "Jumbotron" in the background, a video will start to play on the Jumbotron.

1. Download the Chapter 5 files and open the ASCuePoints.fla file in the Exercise folder. Everything but the ActionScript is in place for you.

2. Select the key frame in the Actions layer and open the ActionScript panel. Enter the following:

```
import mx.video.*;

var videoScreen1:MovieClip;
var videoScreen2:MovieClip;
var nc:NetConnection = new NetConnection();
nc.connect(null);
```

The first line of the code imports the video class into the movie. When you import a class—in this case the video class—you can import just the class, or if there are several class files in the package (package is a fancy programming term for "directory"), you can import the entire class package into the code. We are using the latter method, and the * is what accomplishes that task.

The next two lines of code assign variable names to the video objects in the Jumbotron. The remaining two lines create the NetConnection and allow you to test it locally on your computer.

The next step is to create the NetStream and attach the videos to the stream.

3. Press Enter/Return twice and enter the following code:

```
var ns1:NetStream = new NetStream(nc);
var ns2:NetStream = new NetStream(nc);
videoScreen1.ourVideo.attachVideo(ns1);
videoScreen2.ourVideo.attachVideo(ns2);
```

With the housekeeping out of the way, you can now turn your attention to creating the "listeners" that determine what happens when a cue point is reached.

4. Press Enter/Return twice and enter the following code:

```
var ourListener:Object = new Object();
ourListener.cuePoint = function( eventObject:Object ):Void {
  var cuePointName = eventObject.info.name;
  if( cuePointName == "trailer1" ) {
    ns1.play( cuePointName + ".flv" );
  } else if( cuePointName == "trailer2" ) {
    ns2.play( cuePointName + ".flv" );
  }
}
```

We start by creating a name for our listener—ourListener—and using it as the name for a new object. Now that the object is in place, we write a function that determines what happens when a cue point is reached.

The eventObject parameter is just that: the object passed to the event. The .info.name properties are part of the event object that is passed. The conditional statements simply say that when an event with the name of either "trailer1" or "trailer2" is reached, play the video. You will notice that we have used the actual names of the videos as the cue point names. This way when the cue point is reached, Flash grabs the name of the cue point, adds the FLV extension to the name, and goes looking, for example, for a video named trailer1.flv.

So where do the cue point names come from? That will be the purpose of the next bit of code.

5. Press Enter/Return twice and enter the following code:

```
videoComp.addASCuePoint( 8.594, "trailer1" );
videoComp.addASCuePoint( 18.354, "trailer2" );

videoComp.addEventListener( "cuePoint", ourListener );
stop();
```

The cue points are added using the addASCuePoint() method and by using the time and the name of the cue point as the method's parameters. Those times can come from a couple of places: the Flash 8 Video Encoder or through the time code shown in video-editing software.

Finally, the component, which has the instance name of videoComp, is told to listen for a cue point event and to execute the function named ourListener when the cue point is detected.

The last line of code simply holds the playback head in the first frame of the movie.

At this point, you might want to click the Check Syntax button (the check mark along the top) in the Actions panel to ensure you have no spelling mistakes in your code. If there are none, close the Actions panel, save the movie, and test it. The videos will appear in the Jumbotron as the young woman walks in front of them (see Figure 5-33).

Figure 5-33. The videos that play in the Jumbotron are triggered by the ActionScript cue points.

Alpha video and HTML

Though all of the hype around alpha video seems to be centered on Flash, you can also use an alpha video in a rather creative manner on a web page. Having someone or something walk across a web page or even interact with web page content is something sure to grab your viewer's attention. It really isn't as hard as you may think. All it requires is for you to think a bit differently.

When you embed a SWF in an HTML, you can expect to see

```
<object classid="clsid:D27CDB6E-AE6D-11cf-96B8-444553540000"
codebase="http://download.macromedia.com/pub/shockwave/
cabs/flash/swflash.cab#version=7,0,19,0" width="400" height="400">
  <param name="movie" value="file:///C|/Inetpub/wwwroot/
tomontheweb4.ca/FLVPlayer_Progressive.swf" />
  <param name="quality" value="high" />
  <embed src="file:///C|/Inetpub/wwwroot/tomontheweb4.ca
/FLVPlayer_Progressive.swf" quality="high"
pluginspage="http://www.macromedia.com/go/getflashplayer"
 type="application/x-shockwave-flash"
width="400" height="400"></embed>
</object>
```

The `Object` and `Embed` tags simply tell the browser how to handle the SWF, which SWF to use, where it is located, and the dimensions of the SWF. The important feature of the `Object` tag is the ability to add parameters or conditions to the content enclosed in the tag. Also, the use of layers in Semantic markup or CSS allows you to place content in a specific location on the web page and to then place that content above the content it covers through the use of an absolutely positioned `div`.

Rather than get into a long and involved discussion about how to create CSS web pages or use a visual web page editor such as Dreamweaver 8, let's dissect an example to see how this can be done.

1. Download the Chapter 5 exercise folder and open the VidonHTML folder.

2. Open the HTML page named Video.html in a browser. You will see Betina walk across an image in the page when you click the play button in the SWF.

Open the code view in your browser or, if you have a visual HTML editor such as Dreamweaver 8, open the HTML page in the editor and open the Code view.

The first thing you will notice, at the top of the code, is a `div` named `#videoLayer` containing the following code:

```
#videoLayer {
  position:absolute;
  width:700px;
  height:204px;
  z-index:1;
  top: 314px;
  left: 9px;
  }
```

All this says is how a `div` named `videoLayer` containing a bunch of attributes looks and behaves. The `position` attribute ensures that the layer is always in a fixed position on the page. The `width` and `height` attributes tell the browser the size of the `div`, which, incidentally, are the same measurements as the SWF. The `z-index` attribute simply tells the browser that this `div` is sitting above the page and that the top of the `div` is 314 pixels from the top of the page and its left edge is located 9 pixels from the left edge of the page. Though this may sound complex, all it does is create an empty box that sits above the page.

If you scroll down the code, you will see how the content is placed into the box and how the content below it is visible through the SWF. The code block you are looking for contains the following:

```
<div id="videoLayer"><object classid="clsid:D27
CDB6E-AE6D-11cf-96B8-444553540000" codebase="http://
download.macromedia.com/pub/shockwave/cabs/flash/
swflash.cab#version=8,0,0,0" width="700"
height="203" id="FLVPlayer">
  <param name="movie" value="FLVPlayer_Progressive.swf" />
  <param name="salign" value="lt" />
```

```
        <param name="quality" value="high" />
        <param name="scale" value="noscale" />
        <param name="wmode" value="transparent" />
        <param name="FlashVars" value="&MM_ComponentVersion=1&
    skinName=Clear_Skin_1&streamName=betina&
    autoPlay=true&autoRewind=true" />
        <embed src="FLVPlayer_Progressive.swf"
        flashvars="&MM_ComponentVersion=1
        &skinName=Clear_Skin_1&
    streamName=betina&autoPlay=true&autoRewind=true"
    quality="high" scale="noscale" width="700"
    height="203" name="FLVPlayer" salign="LT"
    type="application/x-shockwave-flash"
    pluginspage="http://www.macromedia.com/go/
    getflashplayer" wmode="transparent"/>
        </object></div>
```

This is a lot simpler than it first appears.

The code starts by placing the SWF into the `div` named `videoLayer`. When a SWF gets placed into a web page, it is placed between `Object` and `Embed` tags, which the browsers use to read SWF content.

The key to this exercise can be found in the parameters. Parameters have both a name and a value. So let's start with the parameters between the `Object` tags. The first one says to use the `FLVPlayer_Progressive.swf` to play the FLV using a progressive download. The next parameter tells the browser to place the SWF in the top-left corner of the `div`.

The next two parameters are not terribly complex. They tell the browser that the FLV will be played using the high quality setting and that the SWF can't be scaled if the page is made larger or smaller.

The key to this exercise is the next parameter: `wmode`. This parameter determines how the window in which the SWF appears is treated. By setting the `wmode` to `transparent` you are essentially making invisible the background that would normally be found in a window. If the value were not set to `transparent`, the video would appear over the image as a big black box, which defeats the purpose of the exercise. The final cluster of parameters and values tell the SWF what skin is being used for the controller, as shown in Figure 5-34; the name of the stream; to turn on auto-play; and to rewind the video when it finishes.

If you do use `transparent` in the `wmode`, be aware that any buttons or links showing through the video become inoperative. In this case, it is strongly suggested to set `wmode` to `opaque`.

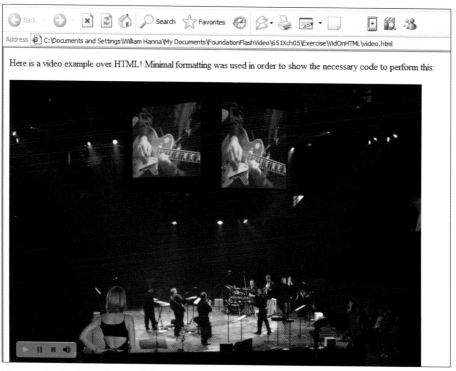

Figure 5-34. An alpha channel video can be placed over content on a web page.

Summary

The ability to use video containing an alpha channel is a major new addition to the Flash video lineup, and by now you should have a sense of the possibilities available to you by using it in your Flash movies.

Also, you now know a few ways of creating the QuickTime videos that contain the alpha channels and that the key, regardless of video editing package, is to use the Animation codec with Millions+ of colors. The + is the alpha channel. You should also be aware that you won't get the effect if you don't select Encode Alpha Channel in the Advanced Options area of the Flash 8 Video Encoder. Keep in mind as well that the only video that can contain an alpha channel is one encoded using the On2 VP6 codec and that alpha channel video can only be played through the Flash Player 8. If your target is Flash Player 7, you are essentially out of luck.

Though we showed you a number of things you can do with this type of video—video-on-video, cue points triggering other videos, backgrounds, and so on—this is just the tip of the iceberg. Why do you need a cue point to trigger a video? Why not use it to load and play another SWF? Why play video over video? Why not play video over a Flash animation in a movie clip? Why not play video over an image on a web page? Why not have it play over text or, even better, interact with another SWF on the page? All we have done is to demonstrate some fundamentals. Your job is to take those fundamentals and drive a truck through them. Your only restriction is the limit you place on your creativity.

Speaking of creativity, as we've mentioned before, the amount of fun you can have with the Flash filters and blend effects and video should be illegal. How illegal?

Turn quickly to the next chapter to find out.

6 ADDING FILTERS AND BLEND EFFECTS TO FLASH VIDEO

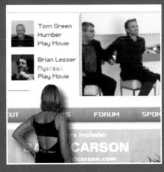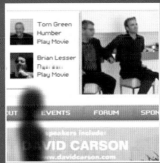

In this chapter we step away from straight video playback and explore the creative side of Flash video. When a video is on the stage, it really is no different from, say, a red box you would draw on the stage. What a video and a box have in common is that they both have properties that can be manipulated. They have position, size, color, rotation, and so on—all of which can be manipulated when a video is in a movie clip.

In Flash 8, you can go one step further. Flash Professional 8 marks the introduction of filters and blend effects. Couple those with the things you can already do with movie clips in Flash and you have a never-ending series of possibilities. Let's start with three simple video tricks designed to get you ready for some of the really cool stuff you can do with video.

Video trick #1: The "point of light" effect

This one is sort of a throwback to the early days of television. Your parents would turn on the television and the picture would grow out from the center of the screen.

1. Open the `Effects.fla` file found in your Chapter 6 Exercise folder. If you examine the library you will see we have placed an FLV Playback component into a movie clip. The FLV Playback component is linked to the `Bikes.flv` file in the Lesson folder.

> The `Bikes.flv` file is from a video done by Kyle Crockard, a student of one of the authors. The video is included as a sort of acknowledgment to Hoss Gifford, who wrote the predecessor of this book, Flash MX Video, and who, along with being one of the most creative and dynamic Flash artists on the planet, is also a partner in a BMX bike and clothing store in Glasgow, Scotland.

2. Select frame 36 of the timeline and add a keyframe.

3. Select the movie clip in frame 1 and choose Modify ➤ Transform ➤ Scale and Rotate. When the Scale and Rotate dialog box opens, set the scale amount to 3%. Click OK.

4. Click once on the timeline between the key frames and, in the Property Inspector, select Motion from the Tween pop-down menu. You could also right-click (Windows) or Control-click (Mac) between the two key frames and select Motion Tween from the resulting context menu.

5. Save the file and test the movie. The video seems to grow out of the center of the screen (see Figure 6-1).

Figure 6-1. The video is at the halfway point.

Video trick #2: The "ghost in the machine" effect

Another movie clip property that can be used to great effect is the Alpha property. Set this to a low value and the object inside the movie clip becomes transparent. This means you can use an alpha tween to actually fade a video in and out. For example, you can use a fade-in as a transition between videos or for one video. You can also use this effect to give the appearance of a "sputtering" video that seems to flicker. This is quite commonly used in games.

This one is really simple to do. Simply place the FLV Playback component in a movie clip and connect it to an FLV file. The movie clip is then placed on the stage and a key frame is added at frame 36, for example. Select the movie clip on the stage in frame 1 and select Color ➤ Alpha in the Property Inspector. Reduce the Alpha value to 5% when the Alpha dialog box appears. Click anywhere between the two key frames and add a motion tween. When you test the video, it will appear to fade in.

The "stuttering video" effect is a variation on this theme.

1. Open the video you just worked on and add several key frames.
2. Move the playback head over each key frame, select the video on the stage, and either increase or reduce its Alpha value.
3. Test the movie and it will look like the video is fading in and out (see Figure 6-2).

FOUNDATION FLASH 8 VIDEO

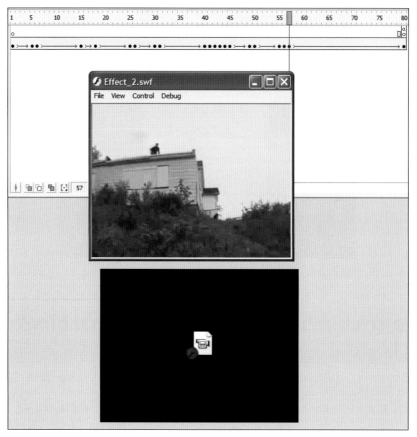

Figure 6-2. A series of tweens and changes in alpha give a flickering effect.

Video trick #3: Somebody fix the dang color!

This one gives the impression of a color TV that is about to fail. The color keeps changing and finally stabilizes.

1. Open your movie, remove the frames, and add key frames at frames 15, 25, 35, 45, and 60.

2. Select the movie clip on the stage in frame 15 and in the color area of the Property Inspector set the Color property to Tint, the color in the color chip to red, and the percentage value to 65%.

118

What this does is add a serious amount of red to the content in the movie clip. The percentage value is critical because, at 100 percent, the movie clip containing the video looks like a red rectangle, which sort of defeats the purpose of the effect. Still, feel free to experiment with various opacity values.

3. Repeat step 2 for each of the key frames at frames 25, 35, and 45. This time choose different colors and opacities. Save and test the movie. What will happen is the color you apply will affect the entire video, giving the effect of the video changing color (see Figure 6-3).

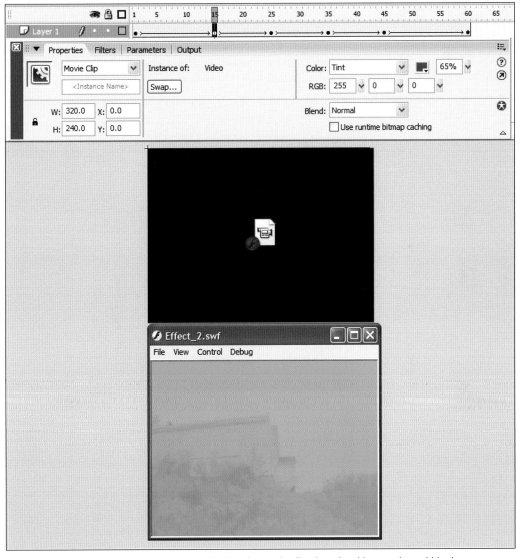

Figure 6-3. The tint color and percentage applied to the movie clip gives the video a rather odd look.

Using ActionScript to control the FLV Playback component

The purpose of those three exercises was to get the creative juices flowing. It also showed you that putting the FLV Playback component into a movie clip allows you to treat the video as nothing more than a common movie clip that can be manipulated on the stage.

There is also one other aspect of the FLV Playback component that you should also be aware of: you don't need to use the parameters in the Property Inspector or the Component Inspector to add a video to the component. This can all be done through the use of ActionScript. In fact, you can even use ActionScript to resize the component, put it above other content on the stage, add or hide a skin, and manipulate a large number of the component's properties at runtime. In this example you add a component to the stage and let ActionScript add the `Bikes.flv` file and resize the component to 180 pixels wide by 120 pixels high. Here's how:

1. Open a new Flash movie, set the stage size to 320×240, and drag a copy of the FLV Playback component from the library to the stage.

2. Select the component on the stage and give it the instance name of myFLVPlayBack in the Property Inspector (see Figure 6-4). Save the file to the Chapter 6 Exercise folder.

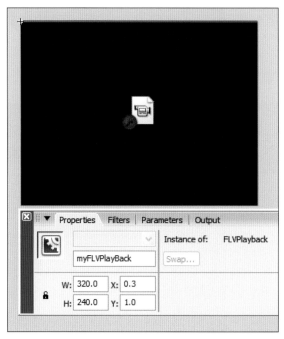

Figure 6-4. We dragged the component to the stage and gave it an instance name.

3. Add a new layer and name it Actions. Select the first frame in the Actions layer and press F9 (Windows) or Option+F9 (Mac) to open the ActionScript Editor.

4. Click once inside the Script pane and enter the following code:

```
import mx.video.*;
myFLVPlayBack.maintainAspectRatio = true;
myFLVPlayBack.width =240;
myFLVPlayBack.height = 180;
myFLVPlayBack.contentPath = "Bikes.flv";
```

Let's go through this so you clearly understand what it is you have just done.

The first line—`import mx.video.*;`—imports the entire video class package into the movie. By doing this, we ensure that all of the video class methods and properties are available when the movie plays.

The remaining four lines are properties of the FLVPlayback instance—`myFLVPlayBack`—that can be manipulated by ActionScript. For example, `maintainAspectRatio` is a Boolean value (`true` or `false`) that when set to `true` maintains the 4:3 aspect ratio of the video. If you were to change the video to another size that alters the dimensions of the video to values that are outside of that ratio, 215×96 for example, the value you would use is `false` and the video would distort to fit into that area.

The next two properties—`width` and `height`—set the dimensions of the component to 204×180.

The final property—`contentPath`—identifies the video to be played in the component. Note that the name of the video is treated as a string. The `contentPath` property can use a relative path (the FLV and the SWF are in the same directory, so you could just use the FLV filename), or an absolute path, `www.mySite.com/video/funkyVideo/ bikes.flv`, to link the FLV to the component.

This code, except for the size change, is essentially the same code that is written when you select the component on the stage and start adding the parameters in the Property Inspector. In fact, the Component Inspector uses the same syntax for the `contentPath` and `maintainAspectRatio` properties, as shown in Figure 6-5.

5. Save and test the movie. You will see that the video has changed its size from 320×240 to 240×180 and plays in the upper-left corner of the stage (see Figure 6-6).

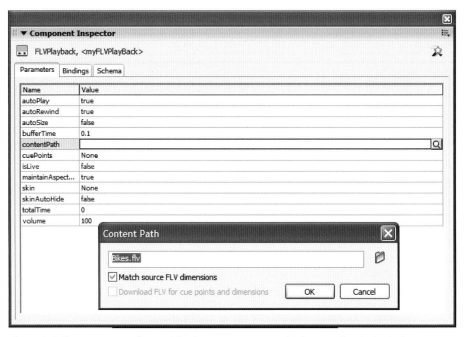

Figure 6-5. The same properties used by the component can also be set using ActionScript.

Figure 6-6. The video is managed by ActionScript and not the component's parameters in the Property Inspector.

Now that you have coded a video, let's use another property of the FLV PlayBack component to scale the video.

1. Open the ActionScript you just entered and set the `maintainAspectRatio` property to `false`.

2. Select lines 3 and 4 of the code and replace them with this line:

```
myFLVPlayBack.setScale(200, 150);
```

If you save and test the video, you will notice it is quite distorted. This is due to the `setScale` property, which sets both the `scaleX` and the `scaleY` properties simultaneously. Though you can use each one individually, by using `scaleX` and `scaleY` you avoid the automatic resizing of the component (see Figure 6-7).

Figure 6-7. Use the setScale property to automatically scale the video and distort it.

So far, most of what we have done is play the video without controls. You can also use the `skin` property to add the controls to the component. Here's how:

1. Open the code you have just written and change it to

```
import mx.video.*;
myFLVPlayBack.maintainAspectRatio = true;
myFLVPlayBack.setScale(100, 100);
myFLVPlayBack.skin = "SteelExternalAll.swf";
myFLVPlayBack.contentPath = "Bikes.flv";
```

By setting the `maintainAspectRatio` property to `true` you have ensured the video does not distort when placed into the component. The `setScale` property simply ensures the component scales to the 320×240 size or the 4:3 ratio of the video. The `skin` property tells the component which set of controls to load when the movie starts playing.

2. Save and play the movie. Kazart! The controls are missing. This is because the skin for the component is not a part of the component. Remember how, in earlier chapters, when you published a movie with a skin, a copy of the SWF containing the video and another for the controls was placed in the same directory? When you add a skin using ActionScript, you have to manually add a copy of that skin to the to the same folder as the SWF.

3. Minimize your movie and navigate to the `Skins` folder, which can be found in the Flash 8 Configuration folder in your `Programs` (Windows) or `Applications` (Mac) folder. Locate the `SteelExetrnalAll.swf` file, copy it, and then paste the copy into the directory you are using for this exercise.

4. Open the Flash movie and test it again. Still no skin. The reason is that skins are placed below the component. In this movie, the component uses all of the available real estate on the stage. To fix this, change the stage height to 275 pixels and test the movie (see Figure 6-8).

Figure 6-8. If you are adding a skin, make sure there is space on the stage to accommodate the skin.

Now that the basics are under control, let's really start to have fun with video.

Filters and Flash video

When Flash Professional 8 was still being tested, Chris Georgenes at Mudbubble did a small animation of a monkey on a swing to demonstrate how the various filters and blend effects can be applied to movie clips. When we saw it, we thought, "Hmmm, wonder if this works for video as well?" It does, and the results can be quite spectacular. The filters and blend effects are new to Flash and, if you are familiar with Photoshop or Fireworks, the odds are quite good that you have been exposed to them.

The first thing to understand about the filters in Flash Professional 8 is that they can only be applied to movie clips and text. If you select the FLV Playback component on the stage and then select the Filters tab of the Property Inspector, you will discover they are unavailable. This is because, technically, the component is not a movie clip.

The easiest way to put the component into a movie clip is to simply drag a copy of the component on the stage, select it, and right-click (Windows) or Cmd-click (Mac) on the clip and select Convert to Symbol from the context menu. When the Symbol dialog box opens, name the clip and select the movie clip behavior. When you click OK, the component will be on the stage but it will be contained in a movie clip in your library.

With the movie clip selected on the stage, you can now click the Filters tab of the Property Inspector and the + sign won't be grayed out. Select it and a pop-down menu presents you with a number of choices, ranging from a Blur to Adjust Color (see Figure 6-9).

> *We are going to demonstrate several rather interesting effects you can create with filters and blend modes. Just be aware that these effects can be quite processor-intensive for the viewer, so use them judiciously.*

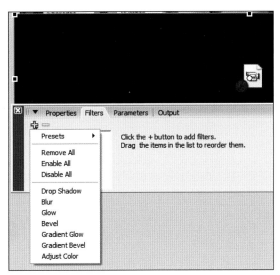

Figure 6-9. You can use the filters individually or in combination with each other.

In this first example we are going to go back to the 1940s and convert a video to a black-and-white movie.

1. Open the `Filters.fla` file found in the Chapter 6 Exercise folder.

2. Select the FLV Playback component and set the `content.Path` in the parameters to the `Bikes.flv` file in the Exercise folder.

3. With the component selected on the stage, convert it to a movie clip named Video.

4. Select the movie clip and click the Filters tab in the Property Inspector. Click the + sign and select Adjust Color from the pop-down menu.

5. When the Adjust Color menu appears, move the Saturation slider all the way to the left. The value will be -100. When you do this, the red Flash icon in the component will turn gray.

6. Test the movie (see Figure 6-10).

Though desaturating color is an interesting trick, the best place to remove the color from a video should be in a video-editing application such as Adobe Premiere or Apple's Final Cut Pro. This way, you start with a smaller video file size—grayscale images or videos are much smaller than their color counterparts—and also finish with a smaller size FLV. The other advantage of this is that the viewer's computer doesn't have to do the color change on the fly.

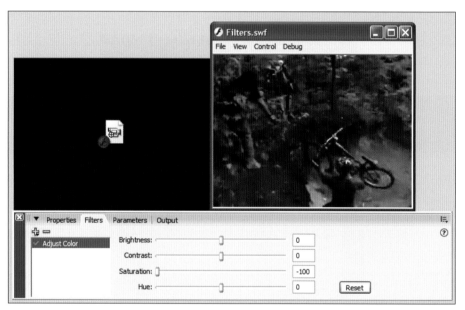

Figure 6-10. The Adjust Color filter has been used to turn a color video into a black-and-white video.

Though this is an extreme example, you can see that this filter can be used to "clean up" a video. If the video is too dark, increase the brightness. If it is too light, decrease the brightness. Adjust the contrast to increase or decrease the contrast of adjacent pixels. Saturation increases or decreases the color intensity of the pixels in the video, and the Hue slider can be used to change the color of the image.

Just be aware that you are "flying blind" when you use this filter. You can't see the effect of the selection until you test the movie. In Chapter 11, we show you how to build a controller that allows you to create and preview these effects at runtime.

Alpha channel video is where the effects really offer some potential. Filters are applied to the content in the movie clip. With an alpha channel video, that content is the image inside the mask. This means filters can be applied to the mask shape or the content.

1. Open the `Filter2.fla` file in your Chapter 6 Exercise folder. When the movie opens, you will notice that the FLV Playback component has been placed above the screenshot of the FlashinTO website. The FLV attached to the component is the Betina video used in the previous chapter. Obviously, Betina is going to take a stroll across the web page.

2. Select the video on the stage and convert it to a movie clip named Vid.

3. With the video selected on the stage, open the Filters tab on the Property Inspector and select the Drop Shadow effect from the pop-down menu. The first thing you will notice is there are quite a few choices here. The second thing to notice is that the movie clip on the stage seems to have developed a drop shadow. Don't pay attention to it.

The drop shadow selections are as follows:

- Blur X: This slider determines the horizontal distance of the shadow.
- Blur Y: This slider determines the vertical distance of the shadow.
- Strength: This slider is more of an opacity slider. A value of 100% means the shadow is full intensity and hides anything behind it.
- Quality: The three choices—Low, Medium, High—determine the quality of the shadow and the feathering on the edges of the shadow.
- Color: Click this and you can choose the color to be used for the shadow.
- Angle: This "knob" lets you determine the source of the lighting that causes the shadow.
- Distance: This slider allows you to determine the offset, in pixels, between the object and the shadow.
- Knockout: Select this and the subject will be knocked out of the shadow. It is a really neat effect because the subject is gone resulting in a shadow that moves around... sort of like a ghost.
- Inner shadow: Select this to apply the shadow inside the subject.
- Hide object: Select this and only the shadow is visible.

Now that you know what each of the selections can do, let's have some fun with Betina.

4. With the Drop Shadow menu open, use these settings:
   - Blur X: 10
   - Blur Y: 10
   - Strength: 82%
   - Quality: High
   - Angle: 45
   - Distance: 10

5. Save and play the movie. Notice that as Betina walks across the screen, she has a shadow (see Figure 6-11).

Figure 6-11. A drop shadow can be added to a video containing an alpha channel.

That is interesting, but what else can you do? How about just the shadow moving across the screen? To do this, open the filter settings for the movie clip and select Hide object. When you test the movie, only the shadow moves across the screen, as shown in Figure 6-12.

Figure 6-12. Only the shadow knows!

How about a ghost? In this case, open the filter settings and deselect Hide object. Select Knockout and Inner shadow. Test the movie and you have a ghost walking across the background, as shown in Figure 6-13.

Figure 6-13. The ghost in the machine

As you can see, the amount of fun you can have with filters should be illegal. Just keep in mind that to be effective they should not be overused.

The blend effects that ship with Flash Professional 8 are also amazing. Again, if you are familiar with Fireworks or Photoshop, they should be familiar tools. There are 14 blend effects that are available by selecting the Blend drop-down menu in the Property Inspector (see Figure 6-14).

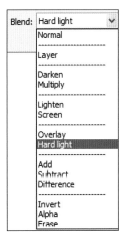

Figure 6-14. Flash Professional 8 contains 14 blend modes.

Without getting overly complex and technical—we do that at the end of this chapter when we discuss how to use ActionScript to apply a blend mode—the blend modes work with the pixels contained in the images that are over each other—in this example, the video over the image. For example, our video has the woman walking in front of an image. A blend mode would "grab" the color of the pixel in the video and the pixel in the image immediately below it. It would then manipulate the color values of the two pixels and change the color of the pixel in the video.

129

The Multiply mode is a good example of how this works. Multiply grabs the pixel values of the top and the bottom image, multiplies them together, and then divides the result by 256. The result is inevitably a darker pixel. Let's see what this means:

1. Select the movie clip on the stage and select Multiply from the Blend drop-down menu.

2. Test the movie. You'll notice that as the woman walks across the screen, the darker color results appear on the video subject. Where the color is already dark, the black top, nothing changes (see Figure 6-15).

Figure 6-15. The Multiply blend is applied to the movie clip.

Now that you have applied the Multiply filter, how about having the background look like it is projected onto the woman? Simply apply the Hard Light filter (see Figure 6-16).

Figure 6-16. The Hard Light filter applied to a video

You can also mix the filters and the blends to create some rather interesting effects. Apply a combination of the Drop Shadow and Bevel filters with the Multiply filter and you get a sort of 3-D effect. Here's the key to achieving this effect: in the Bevel settings, apply a small 2-pixel bevel, pull the opacity back to about 60–65 percent, and use the Best quality (see Figure 6-17).

Figure 6-17. Filters and blend modes can be combined.

Applying filters and blends through ActionScript

As you learned in the previous section, filters and blends can be applied without the use of code. They are all available through the Property Inspector and can be applied singly or in combination with each other. The filters and blends can also be applied through the use of ActionScript. In the first of the next two exercises, you blur a video by dragging your mouse across it. In the next exercise you add a screen blend mode that simulates the effect of a video being projected onto an underlying image... but the image shows through.

The final aspect of these two exercises is the absence of the FLV Playback component. A video object is used. The great thing about a video object is a significantly smaller SWF file.

1. Open a new Flash document and set the stage size to 320×240 to match the size of the video. Add a new layer named Actions. Rename layer 1 to Video.

2. Open the library and select New Video from the Library menu. When the New Video dialog box opens, name the video Video 1, and, in the Type area, select Video (ActionScript-controlled). Click OK to close the dialog box.

3. Select the Video layer and drag a copy of the video object to the stage. Click the object and, in the Property Inspector, resize the video object to 320 pixels wide and 240 pixels high.

4. Right-click (Windows) or Control-click (Mac) on the video object and select Convert to Symbol from the context menu. When the New Symbol dialog box opens, name the symbol Video and select Movie Clip as its property (see Figure 6-18). Click OK. Open the new movie clip in the library, select the video object on the stage, and give it the instance name of ourVideo. Click the Scene 1 link above the symbol's timeline to return to the main timeline.

These four steps are all you need to do to apply an effect to a video object. Remember, the effects and blend modes can only be applied to movie clips. By putting the video object into a movie clip, you can select it on the stage and apply a filter. In fact, you can apply any of the effects in the previous section to a video object in a movie clip. The only difference is you will need to use ActionScript to connect and stream an FLV file into the object when the video plays.

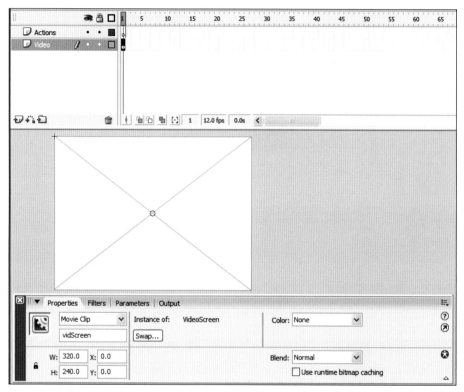

Figure 6-18. The stage is set.

5. Select the first frame in the Actions layer and open the Actions panel. Click once in the Script pane and add the following code:

```
import flash.filters.BlurFilter;

var nc:NetConnection = new NetConnection();
nc.connect(null);

var ns:NetStream = new NetStream(nc);
var vidScreen:MovieClip;
```

The first line of code imports the Blur Filter class into the movie and allows you to apply a blur effect to the content of the movie clip.

The remaining four lines open the `NetConnection`, create the `NetStream`, and ensure that the movie clip—`vidScreen`—is data typed as a movie clip.

6. Press the Enter (Windows) or Return (Mac) key twice and enter the following:

```
var blurFilter:BlurFilter = new BlurFilter(0,0,3);
var filterArray:Array = new Array();
```

The first line of the code creates a variable named `blurFilter` and a new `BlurFilter` object. The numbers—`0,0,3`—control how the blur is applied. The first number determines the amount of the horizontal blur, or the `blurX`. The second number determines the amount of the vertical blur (`blurY`), and the third number determines how many times the blur is applied to the object. If the value is 0, no blur will be applied. A value of 1 is a soft, unfocused look; a value of 2 is a strong blur; and the value used here—3—approximates a Gaussian blur. This line does not apply a horizontal or vertical blur, but when a blur is applied it makes sure it is a Gaussian blur. The maximum value for the horizontal and vertical blur values is 255.

> *When using the Blur filter using ActionScript apply blur values to the llurX and blurY parameters that are powers of 2 such as 2,4,8,16 and so on. For example this line new* `BlurFilter (4,8,3)` *is more efficient than say new* `BlurFilter (3,6,3)`. *The reason is, values that are a power of 2 are optimized to render more quickly and the result is a performance boost in the 20-30% range.*

The second line is where the various blur values will be stored as the mouse moves around the screen. Those values will be stored in a list named `filterArray`. When values change it is always a good idea to put them into a list.

7. Press Enter/Return twice and enter the following function:

```
ns.onStatus = function(eventObj:Object) {
   if( eventObj.level == "status" && eventObj.code == ➥
"NetStream.Play.Stop" ) {
   ns.play( "Trail2-Video4.flv" );
   };
};
```

All this function does is check to see whether the video has finished playing. If it has—`"netStream.Play.Stop"`—then it restarts the video (`ns.play( "Trail2-Video4.flv" );`.

> *This is a good way of looping video using ActionScript.*

8. Press Enter/Return twice and enter the following code:

```
filterArray.push(blurFilter);
vidScreen.ourVideo.attachVideo(ns);
```

The first line of code enters the initial values of the blur filter—0,0,3—into the array. Values are added to an array through the use of the `push()` method, which "pushes" them to the front of the list.

The second line attaches the video stream to the video object—`our Video`—located in the movie clip with the instance name of `vidScreen` that is on the stage.

Now that the video stream is playing through the video object, you need to write the function that blurs the video based on the movement of the mouse.

9. Press Enter/Return twice and enter the following function:

```
vidScreen.onEnterFrame = function() {
  var blurX:Number = this._xmouse / 10;
  var blurY:Number = this._ymouse / 10;
  blurFilter.blurX = blurX;
  blurFilter.blurY = blurY;
  vidScreen.filters = filterArray;
};
```

The first four lines inside the function will be used to determine the first two values in the blur. By dividing the values by 10, the blur amount is kept manageable. For example, assume the mouse is located at the 300,200 point in the video. If we didn't reduce the value, the blur applied would be `BlurFilter(300,200,3)`, which is way too strong. Values of 30 and 20 are much more reasonable. In fact, 300 is an illegal value. The maximum value, as we pointed out earlier, is 255.

The final line of the function—`vidScreen.filters = filterArray;`—reapplies the filter. You have to do this with a filter whenever the values change.

10. Press Enter/Return twice and enter the following code:

```
ns.play( "Trail2-Video4.flv" );
stop();
```

These two lines simply attach the FLV file named `Trail2-Video04.flv` (found in the Chapter 6 Exercise folder) to the stream and start playing it. The last line stops the playback head from moving to frame 2. By doing this, the combination of the `onEnterFrame` and stop actions keeps the playback head moving in the frame—called a frame loop—which allows the function with the blurs to constantly play.

At this point, check your syntax and, if everything is correct, close the Actions panel and test the movie (see Figure 6-19).

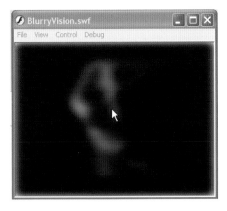

Figure 6-19. The blur on the video is a function of the position of the cursor in the SWF as it plays the video.

The final exercise for this chapter applies a blend mode to a video in a movie clip through the use of ActionScript and not the Property Inspector.

The blend is applied by the Flash Player to each pixel in a movie clip. Remember, each pixel is composed of three colors—Red, Green, Blue—and each color can have hexadecimal values, ranging from 0X00 to 0xFF, or RGB values, ranging from 0 to 255. When a blend mode is applied to a movie clip, the color values in the overlying pixel are compared to the colors of the pixel in the image directly beneath it. For example, assume a video has a dark blue pixel directly above a light blue pixel in the background. If the Lighten Blend mode were applied, the dark blue pixel in the video would be replaced with the light blue pixel from the image directly beneath it.

The blend modes are properties applied to movie clips in ActionScript through the use of `myMovieClip.blendMode = 1;` or `myMovieClip.blendMode = "normal" ;`.

The number or string, which explains why the words are between quotation marks, used determines which of the 14 modes are applied. The modes and their ActionScript values are

- 1 or `"normal"`
- 2 or `"layer"`
- 3 or `"multiply"`
- 4 or `"screen"`
- 5 or `"lighten"`
- 6 or `"darken"`
- 7 or `"difference"`
- 8 or `"add"`
- 9 or `"subtract"`
- 10 or `"invert"`
- 11 or `"alpha"`

- 12 or `"erase"`
- 13 or `"overlay"`
- 14 or `"hardlight"`

> *If you are going to use the number values, just keep in mind that their order does not match that in the Property Inspector. If they did, then* `hardlight` *would have the value* 8 *to match its position in the* Blend *drop-down menu in the Property Inspector.*

The blend mode used in this exercise will be the Screen mode. In many respects, this mode returns a somewhat similar result were you to apply a low alpha value to a movie clip. Screen mode multiplies the inverse color of the movie clip color by the inverse of the background color. The result is a faded or bleached effect. Though commonly used to add highlights or to remove the black areas of a movie clip, in this case, the video will appear to be somewhat opaque.

1. Open the `HighwaySign.fla` file located in the Chapter 6 Exercise folder (see Figure 6-20).

Figure 6-20. You will start with this file, which includes a video object over the pixel board.

2. Add a layer named Actions and open the ActionScript panel.

3. Click once in the Script pane and add the following code:

```
var nc:NetConnection = new NetConnection();
nc.connect(null);

var ns:NetStream = new NetStream(nc);
var vidScreen:MovieClip;
```

```
ns.onStatus = function(eventObj:Object) {
  if( eventObj.level == "status" && eventObj.code == ➡
"NetStream.Play.Stop" ) {
  ns.play( "Trail2-Video6.flv" );          }
};
```

This code is the same as that from the previous exercise. You create the connection, add the connection to a `NetStream` object, and write a small function that will "loop" the video.

4. Press Enter/Return twice and enter the following lines:

```
vidScreen.ourVideo.attachVideo(ns);
vidScreen.blendMode = 4;
```

The video object named `ourVideo` inside the movie clip named `vidScreen` is attached to the stream. The next line applies the `blendMode` to the movie clip. The mode applied is the Screen mode. If you can't remember the numbers for the modes, the line can also be written as `vidScreen.blendMode ="screen";`.

5. Press Enter/Return twice and enter the following lines:

```
ns.play( "Trail2-Video6.flv" );
stop();
```

These two lines first identify the video to be played in the movie clip and stop the playback head.

6. Test the video (see Figure 6-21).

Figure 6-21. The Screen blend mode give the video a bit of a transparent look.

If you are really feeling adventurous, feel free to change the `blendMode` value to another mode and test the movie to see the effect of the mode.

Summary

We think you now understand what we mean when we tell people that the amount of fun you can have with the effects, filters, and blend modes in Flash Professional 8 should be illegal. From drop shadows, to alpha channel video, to video looking like it is projected onto a surface, the creative possibilities are there and they are endless.

Just keep in mind that such effects can be processor-intensive, so keep the number of effects applied to any one video to a minimum. The other key to this chapter is that the filters and blend modes must be applied to video content in a movie clip. The fascinating thing about this is that content doesn't necessarily have to be contained in the FLV Playback component. Blends and filters can be applied to content that is streamed into a video object on the stage.

Finally, in this chapter you discovered how to add the skins and content to an FLV Playback component using ActionScript. You also saw that the filters and blend modes can be applied to video in movie clips either through the Property Inspector or through the use of ActionScript. Which method is best? We leave that to you to answer because, in the final analysis, if a drop shadow is added to a talking head video, does anybody really care how the shadow got there?

If you think the filters and blends are cool, just wait and see what you can do when it comes to masking video. To find out, turn the page.

7 MASKING VIDEO

To this point in the book, video has been treated like a television picture. It sits in a video object or the FLV Playback component and you see the full screen. This isn't, as Martha Stewart would say, "a bad thing." Still, this is Flash we are using here, and there are a lot of other possibilities for the use of video beyond simply sticking it on the stage or manipulating it. Sometimes you may want it to actually appear inside an object, such as a circle, or framed within a custom viewer. In other instances, video is to be treated like a movie clip and otherwise manipulated in a series of creative ways. This is where masking comes in.

Masking video is not exactly a complex subject. There really are only two methods of masking video. The first is to use a masking layer in Flash, and the second is to use an object with a hole in it that lets the video show through. That's it. Real simple. Where the complexity comes through is how the mask is applied and used, as shown in Figure 7-1. Those techniques range from the very simple to the very complex.

Which leads us to the point of this chapter. We will be covering a variety of techniques that start with the absolute basics and get more complex as you move through the exercises to the end of the chapter. Along the way, you will learn which masking techniques work best in particular situations, and you will also discover a "gotcha" regarding the FLV Playback component that is not documented.

Let's get creative!

Figure 7-1. Dynamically generated movie clips and a color effect can turn a simple video into something spectacular.

Creating a simple mask

You will inevitably reach a point where you are literally trying to stick a "square video" into a "round shape." Obviously that isn't going to work. You will need to use a masking layer in Flash.

1. Open a new Flash document and use these settings:
   - Width: 320
   - Height: 240
   - Stage Color: #333333
2. Add a layer, drag a copy of the FLV Playback component into layer 1, and set its X and Y positions in the Property Inspector to 0 to tuck it up against the top-left corner of the stage.

3. Download the Chapter 7 files and set the contentPath of the component to the BMX.flv file in the Media folder.

4. Select layer 2 and draw a circle on the layer (any circle will do!).

5. Right-click (Windows) or Control-click (Mac) on layer 2 and select Mask from the context menu. When you do this, the icon for layer 2 will change to show a mask; the layer 1 icon will also change and the layer name will indent. This means the video in layer 1 is being masked. You will also notice that both layers are locked.

6. Save and test the movie. The video will play inside the circle (see Figure 7-2).

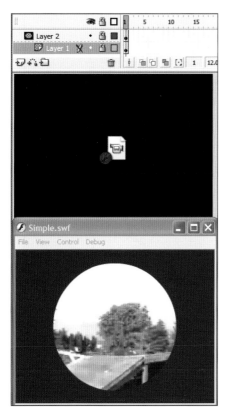

Figure 7-2. Use a masking layer in Flash to create a simple video masking effect.

Using a mask created in Illustrator CS 2

Now that you know how to use a simple shape as a mask, let's look at how a complex shape can be used. In this example, we created a simple circle in Illustrator CS2, selected it, and applied the Roughen filter to give the shape a lot of odd nooks and crannies. Then we applied a 0.5-point Chalk Scribble brush stroke to the edges of the shape. This gave us the rather "funky" shape shown in Figure 7-3. It will make a perfect mask for the BMX video.

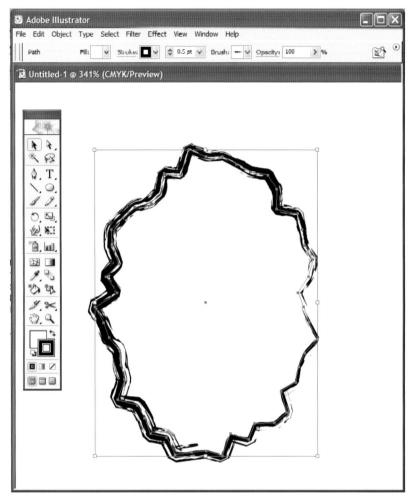

Figure 7-3. Illustrator has quite a few tools, filters, and effects that can be used to create masks.

With the mask created, we saved the image and simply dragged it from the Illustrator page to layer 2 of the Flash stage.

The relationship between Flash and Illustrator is an odd one at best, and we suspect that Adobe will make the placement of Illustrator images into Flash a bit more intuitive than is currently the case. The suggested method of placing Illustrator images into Flash is to use the File ➤ Import to Library method. This results in a rather cryptic dialog box asking about converting the image, converting the layers, and some rather mysterious options that involve rasterizing, invisible layers, and text blocks. Even then, the image comes in as a graphic and requires a bit of extra work on your part to make it into a workable mask.

Most Flash designers and artists simply ignore the import and either copy and paste the drawing from Illustrator into Flash or use the drag-and-drop method.

If you don't have Illustrator, all is not lost. This exercise, including the Illustrator image on layer 2, can be found in the file named `Simple2.fla` *in the Chapter 7 Exercise folder.*

With the mask in its proper location, we simply distorted it to fit the stage dimensions with the Auto Transform tool, then applied the Mask option to layer 2, and, when we tested the movie, the BMX video played through the inside shape of the drawing (see Figure 7-4).

Figure 7-4. The mask from Illustrator is applied.

What about the cool strokes around the Illustrator shape? Where did they go? When an object is used as a mask, only the fill is used to determine the shape of the mask. This means any stroke around the object used as a mask is essentially discarded. Let's bring the strokes back.

Now that you understand that any object used as a mask covers everything under it, you can see how to solve the lines issue. Simply place a copy of the mask object in a layer above the Mask layer. Here's how:

1. Open the `Simple 3.fla` file in your Chapter 7 Exercise folder.

2. Unlock layer 2 and select the mask on the stage. Copy the selection to the clip board and relock the layer.

3. Add a new layer, select frame 1 in the new layer, and select Edit ➤ Paste In Place. The copy of the mask will be placed directly over the original.

4. What you don't want to do at this point is to test the video. It will be hidden by the white fill of the object in layer 3. Instead, click once on the object in layer 3 and press Ctrl+B (Windows) or Cmd+B (Mac). This breaks the object apart (you can also select Modify ➤ Break Apart). Pressing that combination once separates the object into fill and stroke. Deselect the object on the stage.

5. Click the Fill area of the broken-apart object to select it—it looks cross-hatched—and then delete the selection. Just the stroke will be visible.

6. Test the movie (see Figure 7-5).

Figure 7-5. The strokes are placed on a layer above the mask.

Using an image as a mask

You have seen how vector line art can be used as a mask. Now we are going to look at how images can be used for the same purpose. Images offer all sorts of possibilities. For example, if you take a photograph of the billboards in Time Square, New York, each of those billboards can be used to hold a video. This technique is more common than you may think. For example, Vodafone makes extensive use of this technique in its Future Vision site (to access it, go to www.vodafone.com, click the Future Vision link at the top of the page, and select the high-bandwidth site option on the next page) as it places video in wristwatches, rolled-up Mylar, and other devices. It isn't only corporations that use this technique to great effect. Hit the home page of Wefail, a Flash design studio—www.wefail.com—and you will see a motion graphic, which in very simple terms, is a collection of Flash movies and video, framed in an image (see Figure 7-6).

The first thing you have to understand is that images can't be used as a mask. They can be used to mask content under them. This is an important distinction because if you were to put an image on a masking layer, the image would disappear. Flash sees an image as a bunch of pixels without a stroke around them. This means the image is seen, by Flash, as nothing more than a fill, which is why it disappears. Instead, you have to cut the shape out of the image and then save the image as a 24-bit PNG. Saving an image in this format preserves the transparency that shows through the "hole" in the image.

Figure 7-6. The Wefail home page

> If you are using Photoshop to export a PNG24 image, use the Save For Web option. If you are a Fireworks 8 user, PNG is the native format for Fireworks. Just be aware that when you import a Fireworks PNG image into Flash, a copy of the image will be added to the library along with the bitmap as a Flash movie clip.

> If you are as big a fan of drag-and-drop as we are, use Fireworks for the task. You can't drag and drop from either ImageReady or Photoshop.

Finally, using an image as a mask requires you to ask a simple question: "Does this look real?" Sometimes sliding a video under an object looks... well... like you slid a video under an object. This is because the designer didn't take the time to match the shape of the video to the "hole" and the video, perspective-wise, has the wrong angles. Also, televisions have glass screens, and inevitably a photo of a television screen will have a highlight or reflection on it. Take the time to match the geometry of the video to the shape of the mask and to incorporate any screen reflections or highlights (which can be achieved using a combination of the blend modes and effects covered in the previous chapters) and your video will look more "real."

145

1. Open the `ImageMask.fla` file in your Chapter 7 Exercise folder. You will notice we have included an image with a hole in it on a separate layer.

2. Add an FLV Playback component to the Video layer and set its contentPath to the `BMX.flv` video in your Chapter 7 Media folder. Place the component so that you can see the component's icon through the screen and then lock the layer containing the image.

3. Select the Free Transform tool, then click on the component and resize it to fit to dimensions of the hole in the image. Don't merrily start yanking corners here and there or you will distort the video. Instead, move the component so that its upper-left handle is just a bit outside the upper-left corner of the hole. Move the center point—the white dot in the middle of the component—to the upper-left corner and, holding down the Shift key, drag the bottom-right corner up toward the top-left corner. This will maintain the object's proportions.

> Don't worry if you can't get an exact fit. You rarely will. When scaling a video component or object, always leave a bit of the object covered. It looks more real that way because the video will fill the hole from edge to edge.

4. Save and test the movie. Our BMX riders should go rolling across the screen (see Figure 7-7).

Figure 7-7. Scale the component to roughly fit the "hole" in the image. Note the placement of the center point in the upper-left corner. This ensures scaling is done from or to that point.

A more complex image mask

Now that you have done something rather simple, let's deal with something a bit more complicated.

146

One of the authors has a phone sitting on his desk that contains an Information screen. He has wistfully looked at the phone on several occasions and wondered, "What would this look like if it were a video screen?" The great thing about Flash is it can be used to play these what-if games and turn a phone's information display into a video display.

Before we start, now would be a good time for you to discover a "gotcha" that is a part of the FLV Playback component: The component really hates it when you distort the component using the Free Transform tool. It especially dislikes it when you skew the component. The implication of this is you will be doing a lot of unnecessary fiddling and tweaking to get a video to fit into an oddly shaped area (see Figure 7-8).

Figure 7-8. The FLV Playback component is not exactly "distortion-friendly."

The solution is to use a video object from the library instead of the component. Let's put a video in a phone, shall we? To get started, create a new folder named `Phone` and place a copy of the `BMX.flv` file in the `Media` folder into your new folder.

1. Open the `Phone.fla` file in your Chapter 7 Exercise folder. When the file opens, you will notice we have placed the phone and the screen on separate layers and left a layer open for the video and another for the actions (see Figure 7-9).

Figure 7-9. It starts with a phone.

If you look at the screen in the phone, you will notice it is a little wider at the bottom than the top and that the sides angle in as they move upward. This is due to the perspective of the photograph. Playing a video that is rectangular in a trapezoidal area is simply not going to work. It will look a bit odd, which is why we suggest you closely match the geometry of the video to that of the area covering it.

You won't get an exact fit because the component and the video objects are not vector-based. The sides of the object, when manipulated by the Free Transform tool, can't be changed independently of each other. They all change. Moving the center point to a handle only freezes that side in place, and the other three edges will move in relation to the center point.

There are two solutions to this issue. The first is to draw a shape in Flash that matches the shape of the cutout and to use that shape to mask the video. On the surface, this sounds like a great solution, but is actually duplicating effort because that will also be the purpose of the hole in the phone. The other is to change the shape of the video object to approximate the shape of the cutout.

2. Move the Video layer above the Phone layer and turn off the visibility of the Screen layer. Open your library and select New Video from the Library pop-down menu. When the dialog box appears, name the video or leave the name suggested and click OK. You will see a small TV camera in the library.

3. Select the Video layer and drag the video object from the library onto the Video layer. Give the video object the instance name of myVideo in the Property Inspector.

4. With the video object selected, click the Free Transform tool and manipulate the shape of the object to approximate the shape of the screen area. Don't forget to move the center point—that little white dot—to make changing the sides, as shown in Figure 7-10, easier for you. When you have finished, move the Video layer below the Phone layer and turn on the visibility of the Screen layer.

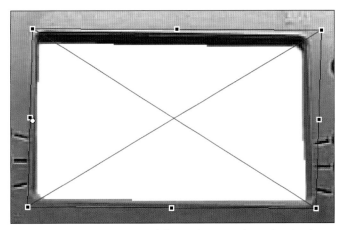

Figure 7-10. Use the geometry of the mask area to determine the shape of the video object.

5. Save the file to your Chapter 7 Exercise folder. Click once on frame 1 in the Actions layers and open the ActionScript Editor.

6. Click once in the Actions pane and enter the following code:

```
var nc:NetConnection = new NetConnection();
nc.connect(null);
var ns:NetStream = new NetStream(nc);
myVideo.attachVideo(ns);
ns.play ("BMX.flv");
```

If you test the piece right now, you won't see anything because the video is under the screen. To fix that, select the screen, and reduce its Alpha value to about 45–50 percent. Now test the movie (see Figure 7-11).

Figure 7-11. The video phone

Even though the video is somewhat distorted, it still looks fine in the viewer. However, the end result is, in many respects, an optical illusion. The user's eyes will match the video to the geometry of the hole. If you go to the Vodafone Future Vision site (www.vodafone.com), you will see this illusion used quite deliberately. For example, in the Entertainment section, Lisa has a "Visual Bracelet," which she uses to keep in touch with her friends. If you select Experience, you will watch Lisa get invited out that evening by a couple of her friends. The video plays under the bracelet, and the curve of the bracelet also gives the illusion of the video being curved to follow that geometry.

There is obviously a small problem with your video. The words on the screen still show through. You can fix this by carefully using the clone tool in either Photoshop or Fireworks to paint over the word with blank areas of the screen. Another neat trick is to simply create a new movie clip and draw a square in the clip using the Rectangle Tool in the toolbox, sample a green pixel in the screen, and fill the square with that color. Then all you need to do is to slide the Screen layer under the Phone layer and place the movie clip there. Resize it to fit the hole and apply about 50–60 percent opacity. If you want to try it, replace the Screen1 movie clip with the ScreenVid movie clip in the library.

Video masks and ActionScript

With the release of Flash Professional 8, developers are just now discovering that the manipulation of bitmap data can create some rather fascinating video effects. The three exercises that finish this chapter are based on ideas first unleashed on an unsuspecting Flash world by Guy Watson in the U.K. In typical Flash fashion, others, like Grant Skinner from Canada, have picked up on Guy's experiments and pushed the technique of bitmaps and video even further.

Now that you have had a chance to work with tangible masks—masks that you can see and manipulate—we are now going to turn our attention to the intangible—things you can't see. In the next three exercises, you will be constructing masked video movies that are composed of nothing more than a couple of objects in the library and ActionScript. The most interesting aspect of these movies will be the blank stage you will use. The only "thing" on the timeline will be several lines of code that utilize the objects in the library. ActionScript has come a long way since its earliest iterations, and in many respects a basic understanding of ActionScript is just as important as being able to move objects on the Flash stage.

In the first exercise, you will create a video on the blank stage and the mask will be used to feather the edges of the video. This is also a good time to introduce you the Drawing API (Application Programming Interface). Though this sounds rather complex, it isn't. All it does is allow you to put down your mouse or pen and let ActionScript draw the lines, shapes, and other objects on the stage. By letting Flash "draw" these shapes at runtime, you wind up with a smaller SWF because the objects aren't in the library.

The Drawing API was introduced in Flash MX and is nothing more than a subset of methods accessible to movie clips. All they do is to allow you to draw stuff—lines, circles, shapes—within the confines of a movie clip. The best way of wrapping your mind around the Drawing API is to approach its use as though you were drawing with a pencil. In the exercise that follows, you will actually draw the mask using code, so let's take a few of minutes to review or learn how to use the Drawing API.

Drawing with ActionScript

When you draw a line on a blank sheet of paper, you place the pen or pencil on the paper where the line is to be drawn and draw a line. The thing is, this whole process is unconscious. By that we mean you place the pencil on the paper and draw a line where you want it to go. When you use code to draw that same line, the phrase "where you want it to go" takes on a whole different meaning. You actually have to tell Flash these things:

- The start point of the line on the x- and y-axis
- The thickness of the line
- Its color
- The opacity of the line
- Where, on the x- and y-axis, the line ends

If you open `Drawing.fla` in the Chapter 7 Complete folder you will see how a line is drawn. When you open the file, select the code frame and open the ActionScript Editor. You will see the following code:

```
_root.createEmptyMovieClip("myLine", 5);
myLine.lineStyle(10, 0xFF0000,100);
myLine.moveTo(10,10);
myLine.lineTo(240,110);
```

If you test it, you will see a red line has been drawn from the top of the screen downward. How that happens is through the use of the Drawing API.

The first line of code creates an empty movie clip named `myLine` on the main timeline—`_root`—and places it on level 5 of the stage. The next line of code tells Flash that the line to be created—the `lineStyle()` method—is 10 points thick, is red (`0xFF0000`), and has a `100` percent opacity or `Alpha` value.

Now that Flash knows what to draw, you have to tell Flash where to draw it. The `moveTo()` method specifies that the pen should be `10` pixels across and `10` pixels down from the top of the page. The `moveTo()` method specifies that the line ends `240` pixels from the edge of the stage and `110` pixels from the top of the stage. The result is the line shown in Figure 7-12.

If you were to draw a triangle there would be three `lineTo()` methods used, and a square would use four `lineTo()` methods.

Now that you understand the basics of the Drawing API, let's see how it relates to the use of Flash video.

As you saw earlier in this chapter, a mask is really nothing more than a graphic shape that gets placed over a video. Everything outside of the shape is hidden, meaning only the part of the video, directly under the shape, is visible. That shape can just as easily be an object drawn on the stage or an object in a movie clip.

This is an important concept because there really is no distinction between whether a mask is in an object or a movie clip. This means masks can be shapes drawn into movie clips at runtime and disposed of when they are finished. These movie clips contain all of the properties of movie clips, meaning they can move, replicate themselves, fade in, fade out, change color, and so on.

So all you really need to do is to create a movie clip that contains a video object linked to an FLV, place a shape created by the Drawing API over it, and then use that movie clip as a mask using the `setMask()` method of ActionScript.

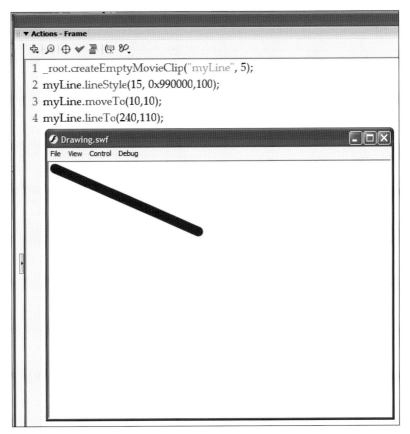

Figure 7-12. Using the Drawing API to "draw" a line

Now that you know how to draw a line, let's draw a square and actually fill it with a color. This square will form the basis for some rather fascinating video-masking effects.

1. Open Flash and create a new document.

2. Select the first frame in layer 1 and open the ActionScript Editor. When the editor opens, enter the following code into the Script pane:

```
_root.createEmptyMovieClip("videoMask",5);
videoMask.beginFill( 0x990000, 100 );
videoMask.moveTo(10, 10 );
videoMask.lineTo( 320, 10 );
videoMask.lineTo( 320, 60 );
videoMask.lincTo( 10, 60 );
videoMask.lineTo( 10, 10 );
videoMask.endFill();
```

If you test the movie you will see that you have created a burgundy rectangle on the stage. The fill is created through the `beginFill()` method and the two parameters used in the method are the fill color and its opacity. If you place the `beginFill()` method in front of a series of `lineTo()` commands, you are telling the API to get ready to fill the shape about to be drawn. How does it know to fill the shape? That is the purpose of the `endFill()` method.

Now let's try something a bit different. Remove the last line of code, or comment it out by putting `//` in front of it. It now reads `//videoMask.lineTo(10,10);`. Test the movie.

How about that? The same object is drawn even though the line of code that closes the shape, as shown in Figure 7-13, is missing. The Drawing API is not exactly stupid. When an `endFill()` method is present, a line is automatically drawn back to the starting point where the `beginFill()` method was called.

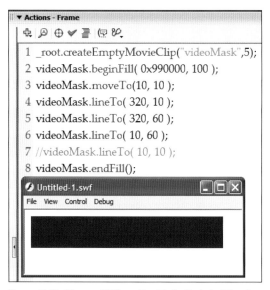

Figure 7-13. The endFill() method tells Flash to fill a shape with a solid color.

> There is a lot more to the Drawing API than lines, fills, and squares. Fully explaining what it can do moves us squarely out of this book's scope. Instead, you might want to check out Flash 8 Essentials (friends of ED, 2005).

Now let's use what you have learned to create some masks.

Creating a blurred mask

In this exercise, you will create a video that blurs the edges of a mask to create the effect of a video that is in focus in a "knockout" area while the remainder of the video, under a black bitmap, is blurred using a Threshold effect. The key to this exercise, and the two that follow, is to understand that the shapes you draw are composed of colored pixels. These pixels form a shape, and that shape, when the movie is displayed on your screen, is seen by the computer as a bitmap. Couple that concept with the `bitmapData` class and you can create some rather stunning visual and video effects with just a few lines of code.

1. Open the `BlackMaskEffect.fla` file in your Chapter 7 Exercise folder.

The first thing you will notice is that the stage is blank and only an Actions layer is present. This is all you need because everything needed for the movie will be assembled using ActionScript.

2. Open the Flash library and you will see two movie clips and a video object. One movie clip is used for the mask, and the other is the one that will "hold" the video object.

If you right-click (Windows) or Cmd-click (Mac) on each of the movie clips and select Linkage from the context menu, you will see they have each been assigned an instance name that will be used in the code and that we have selected Export for ActionScript and Export in first frame (see Figure 7-14). This ensures that they can be "called" in the code and that they load when the movie starts. Click Cancel to close the Linkage Properties window.

Figure 7-14. The movie clips in the library are prepared for use in the subsequent code you will write.

155

3. Select frame 1 of the Actions layer, open the ActionScript Editor, and enter the following code into the Script pane:

```
import flash.display.BitmapData;
import flash.geom.*;

var bitmap:BitmapData = new BitmapData( 320, 240 );
var mode:String = "<";
var fill:Number = 0;
var th:Number = 0x808080;
```

The first line imports the BitmapData class into your movie. This class allows you to create transparent or opaque bitmap images of any size and manipulate them while the movie is running. We are going to need this class because the mask will be composed of a variety of rectangles that will fade off at the edges to create the feather effects.

The next line imports the flash.geom package, which works with the BitmapData class to create points, rectangles, and transformation matrices. We will be using the rectangle and a matrix to create the fade.

The next four lines may look a bit mysterious, but all they really do is create the bitmap and set the values for the bitmap.threshold() method. The method reads the color in a bitmap up to a certain value—the threshold—and replaces them with different-colored pixels. Though the method has a number of parameters, it is not terribly complex. Let's assume we have created a rectangle that is filled with solid black pixels surrounding your name in red. The Threshold method says, "Look at all of the pixels in the bitmap, and turn to gray any pixels with a value of less than 128." When ActionScript reaches that line in the code, the black pixels turn gray and your name stays red. The three variables are the parameters, plus a rectangle from the flash.geom class.

4. Press the Enter (Windows) or Return (Mac) key twice and enter the following code:

```
var nc:NetConnection = new NetConnection();
nc.connect(null);

var ns:NetStream = new NetStream(nc);


ns.onStatus = function(eventObj:Object) {
  if( eventObj.level == "status" && eventObj.code == ➡
"NetStream.Play.Stop" )
  {
    ns.play( "Trail2-Video2.flv" );
  }
};
```

Nothing new here. You create the connection and the stream for the video and replay the video when it reaches the end.

5. Press Enter/Return twice and enter the following code:

```
var vidScreen2:MovieClip = _root.createEmptyMovieClip
( "vidScreen2", 110 );
vidScreen2.attachBitmap( bitmap, 112 );
vidScreen2.filters = [ new flash.filters.BlurFilter( 4, 4, 2 )];

_root.attachMovie( "VideoScreen", "vidScreen1", 100, {_x:0, _y:0} );
_root.attachMovie( "Mask", "videoBlack", 104, {_x:0, _y:0} );
var videoMask:MovieClip = _root.createEmptyMovieClip ➡
( "videoMask", 105 );
```

You have a blank stage and your assets are sitting in the library. These two code blocks put them on the stage. The first code block creates an `emptyMovieClip` named vidScreen2 and puts it on level `110` above the stage. The next line attaches the bitmap created earlier and moves the movie clip up two more levels above the stage. This movie clip will be used as the mask for this exercise. The feather effect will be created by blurring the fill of the bitmap. The last line of the block does just that by applying the blur across `4` pixels on the x- and y-axis and applying a medium quality blur (2) to get a nice fade on the edges.

The second code block pulls the two movie clips from the library on to the stage. The last line of the code creates an `emptyMovie` clip named `videoMask`. This clip will be used to hold the shapes about to be drawn by ActionScript through the use of the Drawing API.

6. Press Enter/Return twice and enter the following code:

```
videoMask.beginFill( 0, 100 );
videoMask.moveTo( 0, 0 );
videoMask.lineTo( 320, 0 );
videoMask.lineTo( 320, 60 );
videoMask.lineTo( 0, 60 );
videoMask.lineTo( 0, 0 );

videoMask.moveTo( 0, 180 );
videoMask.lineTo( 320, 180 );
videoMask.lineTo( 320, 240 );
videoMask.lineTo( 0, 240 );
videoMask.lineTo( 0, 180 );

videoMask.moveTo( 0, 0 );
videoMask.lineTo( 60, 0 );
videoMask.lineTo( 60, 240 );
videoMask.lineTo( 0, 240 );
videoMask.lineTo( 0, 0 );

videoMask.moveTo( 260, 0 );
videoMask.lineTo( 320, 0 );
videoMask.lineTo( 320, 240 );
videoMask.lineTo( 260, 240 );
videoMask.lineTo( 260, 0 );
videoMask.endFill();
```

Having done this earlier, you know you have just created a series of four, black-filled rectangles. So where did the values come from?

The answer is in the library. If you look at the `Mask` movie clip you can see how it will be used. The video will show through the white area. If you ignore the white area, you can easily see that the black surrounding it is composed of four black rectangles. If you open the ruler—View ➤ Rulers—and drag out guides from the rulers, the various values used to create the boxes become evident (see Figure 7-15). The `endFill()` method is used at the end of the code block because the rectangles are going to be filled with the same color—black.

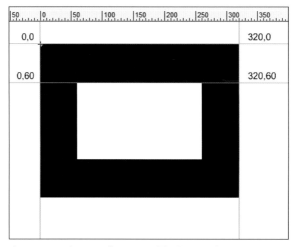

Figure 7-15. The coordinates used in the Drawing API to create the first rectangle

With the housekeeping out of the way, you can now turn your attention to assembling the movie.

7. Press Enter/Return twice and enter the following code:

```
vidScreen2.setMask( videoMask );
```

```
vidScreen1.ourVideo.attachVideo(ns);
```

The first line turns the `emptyMovieClip` named `vidScreen2` into a mask and uses the four rectangles in the `videoMask` movie clip for that purpose. The second line attaches the video that will play behind the mask to the `vidScreen1` movie clip and places it in the `NetStream`.

Now we apply the effect on top of the mask.

8. Press Enter/Return twice and enter the following code:

```
vidScreen1.onEnterFrame = function() {
    bitmap.draw( this, new Matrix( 1, 0, 0, 1, 0, 0 ) );
    bitmap.threshold(bitmap, bitmap.rectangle, new Point(), ⟾
    mode, th, fill, 0xffffff, true);
}
```

Up to this point, all you have done is create a bunch of virtual objects. The time has arrived to bring them to life and make them visible. The first line of the function draws the bitmap to be used as a mask into the `vidScreen1` movie clip.

The `newMatrix()` method is how the image will be drawn. The `Matrix` object is a transformation object that will control how pixels, when drawn, will be translated on the screen. These are determined by the arguments passed into them. The matrix determines how the image will appear on the screen by letting you tell it how to scale, skew, and displace the pixels in the bitmap by moving them over or down by a set number of pixels. As you may have guessed, this method can be a lot of fun.

The numbers are multiples for scale, skew, and displacement. The matrix is essentially a 3×2 grid. In very simple terms, the grid looks like this:

Scalex   Skewx   Skewy

Scaley   displacex   displacey

If you put the numbers in the `Matrix()` parameter on this grid, you can see how things work:

1 0 0

1 0 0

We are essentially saying keep the scale at 100 percent on both axes and don't skew or displace the pixels in the bitmap.

The second line uses the variables created at the start of this exercise to establish how the color in the bitmap is used. Though there are a lot of parameters used, they do make sense. The syntax for the `BitmapData.threshold()` method is

```
Bitmap.threshold (source Bit Map, source rectangle, ⟾
destination point, operation, threshold number, ⟾
color number, mask, Copy source);
```

Let's go through each of these and relate them to the exercise:

- `sourceBitMap`: This is the source video that we are comparing our threshold values to. In this case, we are using the bitmap we drew from vidScreen1, which is referred to as `this`.
- `sourceRect`: A rectangle created from the `flash.geom` package.

159

- ▩ destPoint: This is a point, from the flash.geom package, that corresponds to the upper-left corner of the source rectangle.

- ▩ Operation: This sets the threshold and uses the < operator we named mode earlier in this exercise. It makes sure that any pixel whose value is less than the target value is changed to the new value.

- ▩ Threshold: This is a number we set earlier and gave the variable name th.

- ▩ Color: This number is an optional value that a pixel is set to if it meets the threshold value. It isn't used in this exercise. For our purposes, we are using the variable named fill to set our color value.

- ▩ Mask: This is the mask used to isolate a color. The value 0xFFFFFF (white) is the default value and is used in this code.

- ▩ copySource: This is a Boolean value (True or False). We use the value true. This means that the pixels from the video are copied to the source rectangle if their threshold value is greater than the one used earlier.

9. Press Enter/Return twice and enter the following code:

```
ns.play( "Trail2-Video2.flv" );
stop();
```

10. Save the movie and test it (see Figure 7-16). The video appears clearly in the mask area while any portion of the video that is playing outside of the masked area looks blurred and darkened.

Figure 7-16. The final product

Playing with masking colors

In this exercise, we are going to create a mask that trims the video while still providing a backdrop for a masking effect. The idea actually came from wedding photographs. The loving couple are in full focus while the background is either faded or washed out. It is sort of like putting the subject in a window and giving the illusion of the subject being behind the washed-out area of the image. We thought, "Hey, why should the Photoshop guys have all the fun?" and then went to work (see Figure 7-17).

Figure 7-17. Flash guys should have just as much fun as the Photoshop guys!

1. Open the `StaticCutaway.fla` file in your Chapter 7 folder. Select the code in frame 1 and open the ActionScript Editor. If you take a look at the code, you will see it is not much different from that in the previous exercise apart from the fact that line 3 imports the `flash filters` package.

2. Scroll down to line 53 of the code and enter the following:

```
vidScreen2.setMask( videoMask );
videoBlack.filters = [new DropShadowFilter(8, 45, 0, .65, 8, 8)];
```

Those two lines create the cutout effect.

The first line converts the `vidScreen2` movie clip to a mask. The second line applies the drop shadow filter to the movie clip created earlier in the code. The parameters for the filter determine the alpha, angle, and blur amount on the horizontal and vertical axes and the distance of the shadow.

The square brackets denote a list because the filters that are going to be used and named need to be managed.

Now that we have the effect in place, let's have even more fun and play with the `bitmap Draw()` method to play with the color of the video under the mask by having it change, using the `ColorTransform` class, based on the position of the mouse.

3. Press Enter/Return twice and enter the following code:

```
vidScreen1.ourVideo.attachVideo(ns);

vidScreen1.onEnterFrame = function() {
    var xPercent:Number = this._xmouse/320;
    var yPercent:Number = this._ymouse/240;
```

The position of the mouse is changed to a value based on the location of the mouse on the `vidScreen1` movie clip. For example, if the mouse were at 200 x and 120 y, its `xPercent` value would be .63 and the `yPercent` value would be .5.

4. Press Enter/Return twice and enter the following code:

```
var colorTrans:ColorTransform = new ColorTransform();

colorTrans.blueMultiplier = 8 * yPercent;
colorTrans.greenMultiplier = 10 * xPercent;
colorTrans.redMultiplier = 10 * xPercent;

var trans:Transform = new Transform(vidScreen2);
bitmap.draw( this, new Matrix( 1, 0, 0, 1, 0, 0 ) );
trans.colorTransform = colorTrans;
}
```

`ColorTransform` is contained in the `flash.geom` package and lets you adjust all of the color values in a movie clip. The color change is applied to the red, green, blue, and alpha transparency channels either one at a time or all at once.

The change is done using good old math. Let's look at how it works on the blue channel in our code. As you know, each pixel in an image is a combination of red, blue, and green colors. Each color is expressed as a number from 0 to 255. Thus, a solid blue pixel would have a value of $0,0,255$. The `ColorTransform` class "plays" with those values by permitting you to change colors however you see fit.

The new blue value requires a multiplier, which means the new blue color = old blue color $\times$ `blueMultiplier`. In the case of a really dark blue pixel with a blue value of 20, the new color equals 20 $\times$ (8 $\times$ .5) and the blue value in the pixel would change to 80. The effect would be to brighten the pixel. Values in excess of 255 stay at 255.

This color change is then applied to every pixel in the movie clip `vidScreen2`.

5. Save the movie and test it.

Now it is time for you to have fun. Change the color multiplier values and those in the `Matrix` object and see what happens when you test the movie (see Figure 7-18). Remove the mouse movement and play with the multiplier values, or change the multipliers from `xPercent` to `yPercent` values (and vice versa!).

Figure 7-18. Note the position of the cursor and the color of the area of the video outside of the mask.

Masks in motion

We conclude this chapter by bringing together everything you have learned so far into one final exercise.

As you know, movie clips can be created using ActionScript, and they have properties such as position and size that can be manipulated. In this exercise, we are going have a quite a few masks—up to 30 at any given time—moving across the screen, and the color of the video will change based on the position of the mouse on the screen.

But the masks will differ from what we have done previously: as they pass over the video, the `ColorTransform` will be removed from within the mask area. To make this even more interesting, the masks will actually be a variety of shapes.

1. Open the `MovingMask.fla` file in your Chapter 7 Exercise folder.

Again we start with a blank screen. The difference is found in the library. There are a series of movie clips, each containing a different shape, that will be used as the masking object.

2. Select frame 1 of the Actions layer and open the ActionScript Editor.

The code that appears in the script is, for all intents and purposes, the same code written in the previous exercise. The only major difference is that no filters are going to be applied to the mask.

3. Scroll down to line 48 of the Script pane and enter the following function:

```
function createMovingMask() {
  var newMaskName:String = "mask" + maskCounter++;
  var selectedShape = "Shape " + ➡
  ((Math.floor( Math.random() * 50 ) % 5) + 1);
  videoMask.attachMovie( selectedShape, newMaskName, maskLevel++ );
  if( maskLevel > 2000 ) {
    maskLevel = 1000;
  }
}
```

The mask-creation process starts with an appropriately named function. The next line of code simply names each mask about to be created and appends or adds a number to the end of the mask name. The names start at 0 and the ++ adds one to the number each time a mask is created. The first mask will be named `mask0`, the second one will be named `mask1`, and so on. Now that we have named the masks, we need to identify which of the shapes in the library will be used for the mask.

The second line of code does that by randomly picking a number between 1 and 5 and adding that to the name of `selectedShape`. If the number is 1, the value of `selectedShape` will be `Shape1`, which happens to match the name of that movie clip in the library.

The third line actually pulls the movie clip out of the library, gives it a new name, and puts it on level 1000. The next mask created will be put on level 1001, and so on. The value for `maskLevel` is set at 1000 earlier in the code. That number is an arbitrary starting point but is set so high that it ensures it is above everything on the layer and that the incrementing numbers will place movie clips above each other as they are added to the stage.

With masking clips being created at a rather rapid pace, you will need to set a limit as to how high they can be stacked. The next two lines of code do just that. As soon as a `maskMovie` movie clip is placed on level 2000, the next clip to be created gets placed back on level 1000.

Now that the movie clips are stacked in much the same way planes are stacked in the air above a busy airport, let's get them moving.

4. Press the Enter/Return key twice and enter the following code:

```
var maskMovie:MovieClip = videoMask[newMaskName];
maskMovie._y = Math.floor( Math.random() * 240 );
maskMovie.delta = Math.floor(Math.random() * 10) + 1;
```

These masks are going to be created at a rather rapid pace. This is why the names of all of the masks are placed into a movie clip. You can do this because European Computer Manufacturers Association conventions (ECMA262) allow movie clips and other objects to reference their properties in array format. The mask is being referenced in this manner because our mask name is being contained in a variable. This makes them manageable. As each one hits the stage, it will appear somewhere between the 0- and the 240-pixel mark on the y-axis. The third line uses a custom delta property to determine how far along the x-axis to move the clip. By using `random` for both the x and the y position, you are assured that the clips will appear in different positions on the stage.

5. Press Enter/Return twice and enter the following function:

```
maskMovie.onEnterFrame = function() {
  this._x += this.delta;
  if( this._x > 320 ) {
   this.removeMovieClip();
   createMovingMask();
     };
      };
  }
```

This a relatively straightforward function. The `maskMovie` movie clip moves along the x-axis at a rate determined earlier. Once the clip reaches the edge of the stage—beyond the 320-pixel mark—it is removed from the movie and the computer's memory using the `removeMovieClip()` method and another one is spawned using the function in step 3.

6. Press Enter/Return twice and enter the following code:

```
for( var maskLoop:Number = 0; maskLoop < 30; maskLoop++ ) {
  createMovingMask();
  }
```

This section only deals with the number of masks that can move across the stage at any one time. The first line constantly checks to see if there are 30 movie clips on the stage. If there aren't, another one is created and added to the queue.

7. Save and test the movie (see Figure 7-19).

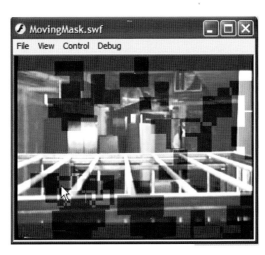

Figure 7-19. The masks are doing their job and the blue is determined by the position of the cursor within the movie. The color would be different if the cursor were in a different location within the movie clip.

Summary

In this chapter we took masking from its most basic use—a shape on the stage over a video—to some rather advanced applications of masked video driven only by ActionScript. As you have discovered, you can make your video a straight presentation or use a mask to take advantage of a wide range of creative possibilities, from playing video through the screen on a phone, to using shapes created in Illustrator, to creating the mask by using the Drawing API to draw the mask.

You've learned that masking can serve to place a video in a context. Want to demonstrate video on a cell phone? Use the cell phone as a mask. Want video to serve strictly as an artistic medium? Let ActionScript do the heavy lifting. Your only constraint is the limit you place on your creativity. You must also pay relentless attention to detail to ensure that the video follows the geometry of the mask.

To this point in the book, we have done some pretty interesting things with a single video. What happens if you find yourself in a situation where there are multiple videos to be displayed? Well, everything you have learned applies to multiple videos as well. In the next chapter, we explore what you can do with multiple videos, and we show you a couple of video wall ideas.

8 BUILDING VIDEO WALLS

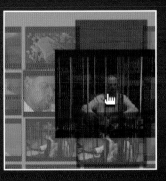

There will come a time when a client or colleague will come to you with what, at first, seems to be a rather odd video request. They don't want you to work with one video, but nine videos. The videos are not to be viewed sequentially or individually; they should be seen all at once. Obviously placing them in a neat row on the stage is well beyond boring. Maybe it is time you thought of using a video wall.

First, we are duty bound to tell you that video walls are cool. We also have to tell you that they are bandwidth pigs. If you are thinking of running nine 320X240 videos in a grid, think again. You will need a bandwidth pipe the width of the English Channel. Though we have slightly exaggerated here, you get the message: full-size video in a wall results in a really bad user experience. Having said that, of course, if you are running the videos from a hard drive... knock yourself out!

Still, it is a very eye-catching technique and, best of all, relatively easy to accomplish. We start this chapter not by creating a video wall but by revisiting After Effects 7 and showing you a couple of techniques you can use to create an interesting title sequence that will lead into the wall. We will also be revisiting the alpha channel technique from Chapter 5 and digging into making the best alpha channel video possible. From there we roll into the video wall and show you how to create a simple video wall using the Flash Media Server. We will wrap up the chapter by demonstrating how to create a wall that falls into the category of "WOW!"

There is a lot to cover here, so let's roll up our sleeves and get to work.

> *The Flash Media Server 2 is freely available from the Adobe website. It is a developer edition designed to be used on your computer. You can pick up a free, PC-only copy of the Media Server at* `http://www.macromedia.com/software/flashmediaserver`.

Flash text effects and Adobe After Effects 7

If there is one fundamental rule of media design that the authors live by, it is this: "Let the software do the work." In this case, it is an animated text sequence that could be used as the titling for a video or even as a sort of preloader while the video loads in the background. Yes, it can be done in about an hour or so in Flash. When you can do the same thing in less than 10 minutes in After Effects, using a preset animation, you come to the conclusion that maybe After Effects and Flash are a killer combination. In this exercise, you will create two animations in After Effects. The first will treat the text as though it had been dropped from the top of the stage, and then the text bounces into place. The second animation will have the title form out of a series of random letters pouring from the top of the stage, stop, and then resume pouring down the stage.

> *The following examples work just as well in After Effects 6.5. If you don't have After Effects, use the SWF files contained in the Chapter 7 Exercise folder when the example swings over to Flash for final assembly.*

1. Open After Effects and create a new composition (or *comp*) by selecting Composition ➤ New Composition.

2. When the Composition Settings dialog box opens, use these settings:

   - Composition Name: Bounce
   - Width: 500
   - Height: 400 (Note: You may need to deselect the Lock Aspect Ratio option.)
   - Pixel Aspect Ratio: Square Pixels
   - Frame Rate: 24 (You will see why in a moment.)

Leave the remaining settings at their default values. Click OK to close the dialog box. The comp will appear in the project window.

Be sure to note the frame rate. This value should match that of the Flash movie. We raise this issue now because the default frame rate for a new Flash movie is 12 frames per second and this project is going to be placed into a new Flash movie.

3. Select the Text tool, click once on the blank comp window, and enter Foundation Flash Video. Select the text and choose a font and point size that work for you. We chose Futura Md BT because it is quite readable and looks modern. We also chose 40 pixels as the size in order to have the text run across the stage. We chose white for the text color because it will eventually appear over a black Flash stage (see Figure 8-1).

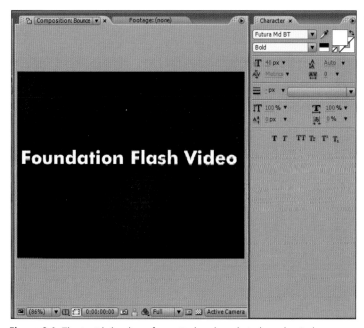

Figure 8-1. The text is in place, formatted and ready to be animated.

Next we'll apply a preset effect to the text. Quite a few of them are installed with the application. Obviously, applying each one to the text to see what it does is rather silly. Instead, click on the text and then select Help ➤ Animation Preset Gallery. This opens the list of presets in the Help menu. To see what we are going to do next, click the Organic text animation presets link. When the window opens, you will see an example of each preset in the category and what it does (see Figure 8-2). The one we will be using is Drop Bounce.

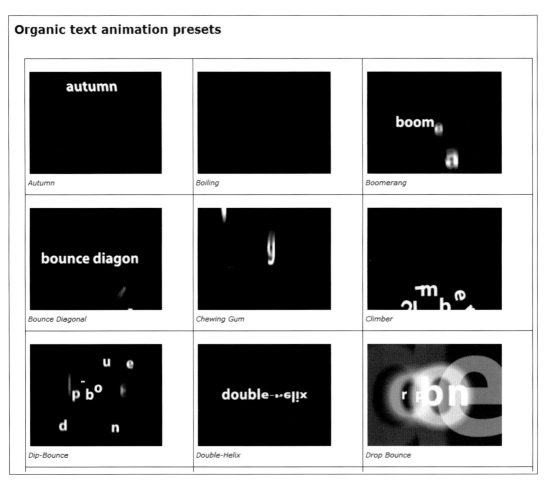

Figure 8-2. The preset we will use is in the bottom-right corner.

4. If it isn't already open, select Window ➤ Effects and Presets to open the Effects & Presets panel. Choose Animation Presets ➤ Text ➤ Organic, select the Drop Bounce preset, and drag and drop it on top of the text in the comp window, as shown in Figure 8-3.

When you drop a preset onto a text block, the first thing you see is an X over the text. Then the block expands in size to accommodate the animation when you release the mouse. (If you are using version 6.5 of After Effects, your X and comp window may look slightly different.) The text will also disappear because it has been moved above the comp window.

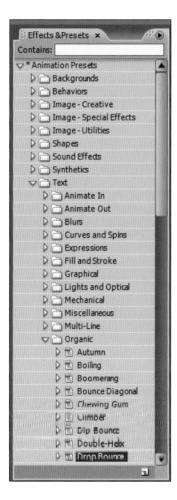

Figure 8-3.
You'll find the Drop Bounce preset in the Organic folder.

So what does it look like? Click the play button in the Time Controls panel to view a RAM preview. Alternatively, you a can scrub the playback ahead across the timeline or press the Spacebar on your keyboard.

With the effect in place, it is time to shorten it before it gets sent off to Flash. The reason it is being shortened is there is a rather small amount of text being animated. If you paid attention to the preview, it seemed to happen in a relatively short period and then just sat there. Obviously, there is a lot of wasted space and time here that should be addressed.

5. In the timeline, twirl down the Text and the Animator settings. Animator is the effect applied to the text.

> Twirl down, in the After Effects universe, means to click the arrow beside the item. In this instruction you would click the arrow beside the Text and the Animator settings in the timeline.

When you twirl down the Animator setting, you will see the key frames that compose the Drop Bounce effect. As you can see, the whole animation occurs over a space of about 3 seconds. Nothing happens for the remaining 27 seconds. This means that you are potentially looking at a very long Flash timeline where nothing happens. Not a good situation.

To fix this, drag the playback head to about the 4-second mark in the comp window. Now drag the work area bar to the same location as the playback head. This reduces the duration in the work area to 4 seconds. You need to reduce the entire comp from 30 seconds to 4 seconds.

6. Select Composition ➤ Trim Comp to Work Area. When you release the mouse, the work area is reduced to 4 seconds.

7. Select File ➤ Export ➤ Macromedia Flash (SWF). If necessary, navigate to the exercise folder, name the file Bounce (if necessary), and click OK to open the SWF Settings dialog box.

Though it may not look like much, this is one seriously cool dialog box (see Figure 8-4). Remember, text is a vector and Flash loves vectors. If you look at the top third of the box—the Images area—you are asked about JPEG compression and how to handle unsupported features. After Effects is asking you about the objects in the comp. If they can't be converted to vectors, then After Effects will apply JPEG compression to them. If you select Ignore in the Unsupported Features pop-down—go ahead and select it if it isn't there— After Effects will ignore any object it can't convert to a vector. By selecting Ignore, you have guaranteed that the output, which will eventually be used in Flash, will be pure vectors. When you click OK you will be shown the progress of the conversion. When it finishes, save the file and quit After Effects.

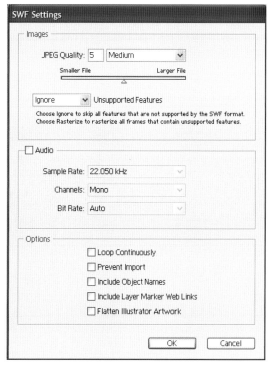

Figure 8-4. The SWF Settings dialog box

The Export process actually creates two files: the SWF and an HTML file. You don't need the HTML file. It is nothing more than a report showing you the SWF and listing the options you didn't choose. Feel free to throw it in the trash.

From After Effects to Flash

The dialog box in Figure 8-4 is the key to successfully moving an After Effects animation into Flash. The vectors created in After Effects are exactly what Flash is looking for. In fact if you have never imported a vector animation created in After Effects into Flash, you are in for a very pleasant surprise.

1. Open Flash and create a new Flash document that is 500 pixels wide and 400 pixels high. Set the background color to black and change the frame rate to 24 fps. This matches the settings of the comp in After Effects.

2. Create a new movie clip and name it Bounce.

3. Select File ➤ Import to Stage and locate the SWF created earlier.

When you click OK, each frame of the SWF created in After Effects, as shown in Figure 8-5, is imported to the timeline. If you press the Enter (Windows) or Return (Mac) key, you will see your text animation play. If you open the library, you will notice that each letter in the animation is a separate symbol as well. If you want to keep things neat and tidy, create a folder named Words in the library and place the letters there.

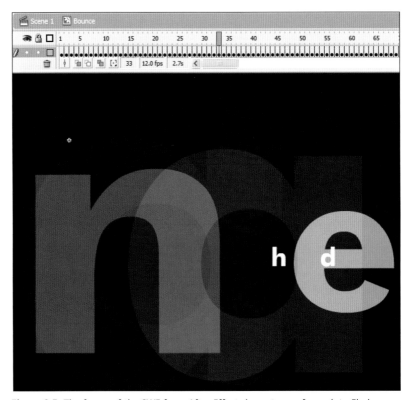

Figure 8-5. The frame of the SWF from After Effects imports as a frame into Flash.

4. Scrub the timeline by dragging the playback head; pay close attention to the movement on the screen. You should notice a series of frames at the start and the end of the animation where nothing happens. They can be removed.

5. Shift-click to select the frames that you don't need at the beginning and end of the movie. Then right-click (Windows) or Cmd-click (Mac) to open the Context menu. Select Remove Frames (see Figure 8-6) and the selected frames will be deleted. This will probably reduce the animation to about 50 frames or so (if your number varies, do not be concerned).

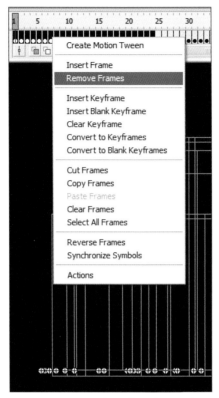

Figure 8-6. Frames where there is no action can be deleted.

6. Add a layer named Actions. Insert a key frame over the last frame of the animation and add the following code in the Actions panel:

```
stop();
```

This ensures the animation doesn't endlessly loop. This step is optional because that might be exactly what you want.

7. Return to the main timeline and drag the Bounce clip from the library to the stage. Drag the registration point of the clip—it looks like a plus sign—to the upper-left corner of the stage. Save and test the movie (see Figure 8-7).

Figure 8-7. Text effects from After Effects make life easy for the Flash artist.

It's raining letters

In this exercise you will create, in After Effects, a small animation that looks as though it is raining letters. Random letters will pour from the top of the screen to form the phrase "Foundation Flash Video," pause for about one half second, and then pour off the screen.

> *If you don't have After Effects, all is not lost. Look for the* Raining.swf *file in the* From_AfterEffects *folder in the Lesson 7 Exercise folder.*

1. Open After Effects and create a new comp, called Rain, using the same settings as in the previous exercise.

2. Select the Text tool. Click once on the stage and enter the words Foundation Flash Video. Set the text in a point size and font of your choosing and color the text green. Move the text block to the middle of the comp window. This will be the finish point for the letters raining down.

3. Open the Effects Presets panel and select Text ➤ Animate In ➤ Raining Characters In. Drag the animation on top of the text block in the comp window.

When you release the mouse, the text block is placed above the comp window and the original location is indicated by the circle with the plus sign. If you scrub the timeline, you will see the letters falling into place as you move the playback head.

4. Twirl down the comp in the timeline and then twirl down the Text and Animator 1 settings.

If you scrub the timeline, you will see the animation actually happens between the two key frames in the Animator 1 strip.

5. Twirl down the Range Selector 1 and the key frames will change from dots to diamonds. This tells you the key frames can be moved. Move the first key frame a bit to the left to start the effect a bit sooner.

6. Drag the playback head to the right until it is over the last keyframe. This will mark the point where the text rains off of the stage.

7. Open the Effects & Presets panel and select Text ➤ Animate Out ➤ Raining Characters Out. Drag the animation on top of the text block in the comp window.

If you twirl up the Animator 1 strip, you will see an Animator 2 strip has been added to the timeline and that two more key frames have been added.

8. Twirl down the Animator 2 and then the Range Selector 1 settings. Move the first key frame to a point just to the right of the last key frame in the Raining In animation (approximately 1 second).

Now you need to remove the frames where nothing happens. Move the playback head until it is over the last key frame in the Animator 2. Now drag the work area bar to the same location as the playback head.

9. Select Composition ➤ Trim Comp to Work Area, and the frames that aren't selected are removed from the timeline as shown in Figure 8-8.

10. Select File ➤ Export ➤ Macromedia Flash (SWF). Name the file and click OK to open the SWF Settings dialog box. Make sure that Ignored is selected for the Unsupported Features option, click OK, and when the export is completed feel free to quit After Effects.

Now all you have to do is to open Flash, create a new 500×400 document with a black background, and import the SWF to the stage of a movie clip named Rain. Remove any frames you don't need and add the movie clip to the main timeline. When you test the movie, you have a rather interesting effect (see Figure 8-9).

> As we did in the previous exercise, you can import the animation to a new movie clip. In addition, you can add an Actions layer and enter a stop() method to prevent the animation from continuously looping.

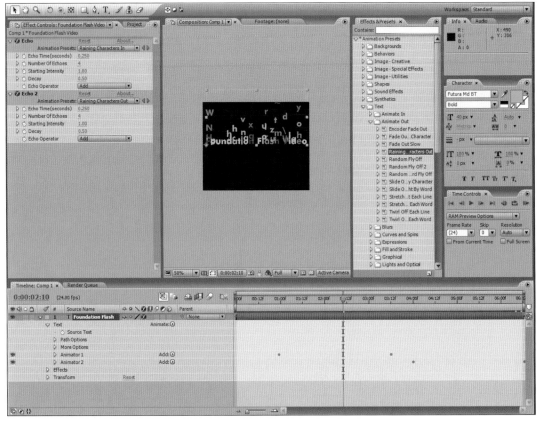

Figure 8-8. The text is raining and ready to be used in Flash.

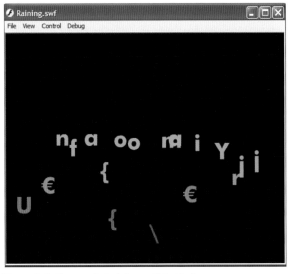

Figure 8-9. The text is "raining out" in Flash.

Advanced alpha mask creation in After Effects

In Chapter 5 we spent a lot of time talking about how to create an FLV that uses an alpha channel. The next exercise will talk about a Video Wall named "Babel" using an alpha channel video. This time, though, we are going to show you a second, slightly more advanced technique for creating the alpha channel video in After Effects. We will use a combination of filters to work on the channel, then we will skip creating the QuickTime movie and, instead, generate the FLV right out of After Effects. Though this technique works equally well in After Effects 7, we will use After Effects 6.5 Professional.

1. Open After Effects, import (File ➤ Import ➤ File) the GSFOE.mov file in your Chapter 8 Exercise folder to the project window, and create a new comp. Don't worry about the comp settings other than changing the size to 320 by 240.

2. Drag the video from the project window either to the timeline or directly into the comp window.

3. Select Window ➤ Effects & Presets to open the Effects & Presets panel. Twirl down the Keying folder and drag the Color Key filter onto the comp. When the filter window opens, click once on the Eyedropper and click once on the green area of the comp's background. Now click and drag the Color Tolerance value to the right until the green disappears and what looks like a green "fringe" appears around the subject (see Figure 8-10).

   That green fringe is actually a reflection of the key on the subject. The color has "spilled" onto the subject and should be removed.

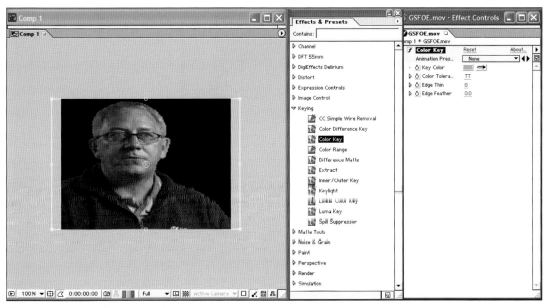

Figure 8-10. Color keying is applied.

179

4. In the Keying folder, drag a copy of the Spill Suppressor filter onto the comp. The filter will be added to the filter window. Zoom in on the left edge of the subject's neck. You will see some green pixels. Click on the Eyedropper and then click on a medium green pixel. The edge will shrink. Click on the value for Suppression and drag it to the right. As the value increases, more green disappears. Keep a close eye on the comp. As you remove the "spill," you run a real risk of giving the subject a bad haircut. We found a value of 122 works for us (if your numbers are a bit different, do not be concerned about it). Change the comp view back to 100 percent. You will notice that the spill is gone but that the edges still look a little pixilated (see Figure 8-11).

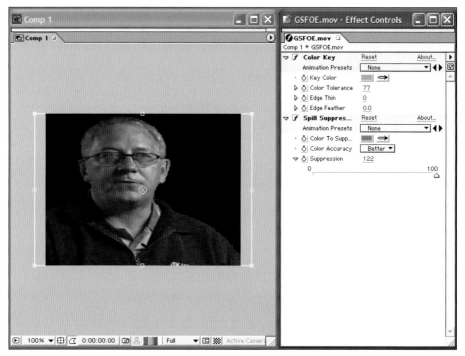

Figure 8-11. The green edge is gone.

5. Twirl down the Matte Tools folder in the Effects & Presets folder and drag a copy of the Matte Choker filter onto the comp. This filter essentially shrinks or expands the mask. Drag the Geometric Softness 1 slider all the way to the left. You will see the background start to appear around the edges of the subject. If you move it all the way to the right, the subject shrinks a bit as the mask closes around it. Paying attention to the subject's head and shoulders, drag the Geometric Softness 1 slider to the right. We have found a value of about 5.2 is best.

If you are having trouble seeing the effect of the Matte Choke filter against the black background, slide a new solid under the subject. You do this by selecting Layer ➤ New ➤ Solid and, when the New Solid dialog box opens, changing the color to white. When you close the dialog box, the solid will cover the comp. In the timeline, drag it under the comp. You can see the effect of this in Figure 8-12.

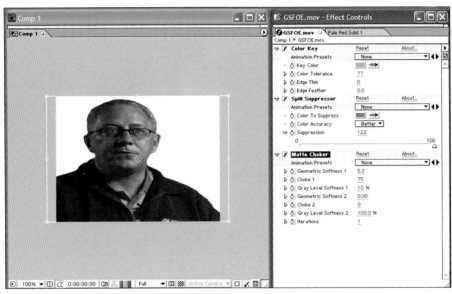

Figure 8-12. The mask is "choked" using the Matte Choker filter.

With the mask created, it is time to create the FLV. If you have added a white solid to the background, select it in the timeline and delete it.

6. Select File ➤ Export ➤ Macromedia Flash Video (FLV) (see Figure 8-13). If necessary, navigate to the Exercise folder and name the file GSFOE. This opens the Flash 8 Video Encoder. From there, you can create the FLV with an alpha channel by using the Show Advanced Settings option and then checking the Encode alpha channel option.

When you install Flash 8 Professional, the plug-in for the Flash 8 Video Encoder is installed into QuickTime and After Effects, including After Effects 7. This means you can create the FLV in the Encoder directly out of After Effects rather than rendering the video in After Effects and then opening the Encoder. This is a great time saver.

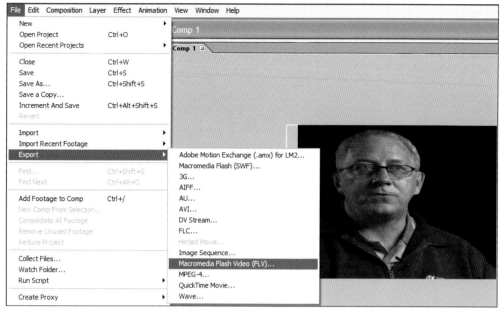

Figure 8-13. FLV files can be created using the After Effects Export menu.

A simple video wall

The first thing you need to understand about a video wall is that you shouldn't use any video that contains an audio track. Imagine nine videos with the same audio track all playing simultaneously. It would not be a pleasant experience for the user. To see for yourself, open the appropriately named Babel.swf file found in the Complete folder of the Chapter 8 folder. Not pleasant, was it?

Even though it was not a pleasant experience, the interesting aspect of the project was the size of the SWF file. You ran nine copies of a video through a SWF that was 1 K in size. The key here is to run the video through a video object embedded in a movie clip and then use nine iterations of the clip on the stage.

> *There are a couple of ways to remove the audio from an FLV. The first is to not add the audio track when the video is created. The second is to not encode the audio in the Flash 8 Video Encoder.*

One of the themes running through this book is to keep an eye on the pipe. You can actually see this when you run the Babel.swf file. There was a bit of a lag. This is because each video stream needs to compete with the other to get going. and when they do, they compete with each other for processor resources. If you are experiencing lag on your hard drive, imagine how brutal it must be if it is running through the internet. Each stream is also using audio and video. Removing the audio track reduces the file size. If you look in your Chapter 8 Complete folder, you will see two FLV files. One is named GSFOE_Small.flv and the other is named Babel.flv. The GSFOE_small.flv file is 200 K smaller than the other one simply because there is no audio track in the file.

Another major factor is the physical size of the video. The original is 320×240. It was reduced to 160×120 to fit into the video object in the movie clip. In the Complete folder is the 320×240 version of the file. It is named Original.flv, and if you compare its file size to that of Babel.flv you will see there is close to a 30 percent reduction in file size. If you compare the Original.flv to the GSFOE_Small.flv you'll see that the reduction in physical size and the removal of the audio track means a difference of 500 kb in file size.

Now that you have been sufficiently warned, let's create a simple video wall. In fact, we are going to create a version that uses the Flash Media Server 2.

> *If you don't have access to the Media Server 2, don't worry. We'll indicate the code changes necessary as a comment in the code for a normal progressive download. If you are thinking of using one of the many Flash Video Streaming Services (FVSSs) to stream your video, this section will help you to understand their requirements. This section is not intended to be a full how-to regarding the Media Server 2. There are a number of excellent books out there that deal with this subject in quite a bit of depth.*

What is the Flash Media Server 2?

If you are familiar with web servers, you'll see that this one is quite a bit different. Its sole purpose in life is to feed audio and video into a SWF embedded in a web page. The protocol used by a regular web server is HTTP. The Media Server uses what is called *Real-Time Messaging Protocol (RTMP)*. This protocol is bidirectional; information is passed to the SWF from the server and from the SWF to the server. The other thing to keep in mind is that the Media Server does not interact with HTTP. It interacts only with SWF files.

The other aspect of working with the Media Server 2 is that there are actually two paths created for the file. The first goes directly to the Media Server and the other, if you are working locally, is to IIS or Apache, which are web servers. This means file placement is critical if you want your projects to work (see Figure 8-14). Certain files are placed on the Media Server and others are placed on the web server.

Notice how the FLA and the SWF files you create will reside on a web server. But the files that actually make it work—main.asc and a Streams folder containing the FLV files are located in the Media Server folder.

The file that makes it all happen is the *ActionScript Communication (.asc)* file. It can be created in Flash, Macromedia Dreamweaver 8, or even a word processor. The code is server-side ActionScript and is based on the same ECMA standard as ActionScript. These files can run in size from one line to hundreds of lines of code. You will be using the single-line approach. Notice, though, the .asc file is located in the `Applications` directory of the Media Server.

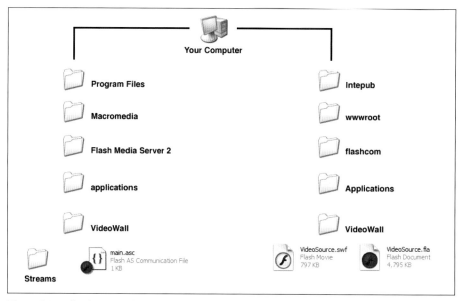

Figure 8-14. File placement is critical.

> Though there is a Streams folder, many users of the Media Server will create a folder named _definst_. This folder is placed inside the Streams folder and is used to hold the FLV and other media files used by the Media Server. Also the terminology around the server is a bit different if you are used to working on a web server. When it comes to the Media Server, the path to anything is Server/Application/ Instance; in the case of the above illustration the path would be Server/ VideoWall/. If you were to use a _definst_ folder, the path would be Server/VideoWall/_definst_. The Streams folder is always ignored.

Let's go to work.

1. Open the Flash Media Server 2 folder located in your Program folder. Now open the Applications folder and create a new folder named VideoWall. Inside this folder create another folder named Streams and inside it create another named _definst_. Place a copy of the Bikes.flv file located in the Chapter 8 Exercise folder inside the _definst_ folder.

2. Open Flash. When the Launch screen appears, select ActionScript Communication File in the Create New category (see Figure 8-15). The ActionScript Script pane opens. Enter the following code:

```
load ("components.asc");
```

Save the file as main.asc and save it to the VideoWall folder you just created. That line of code is all you need to connect any components in the SWF file to the FLV in the _definst_ folder.

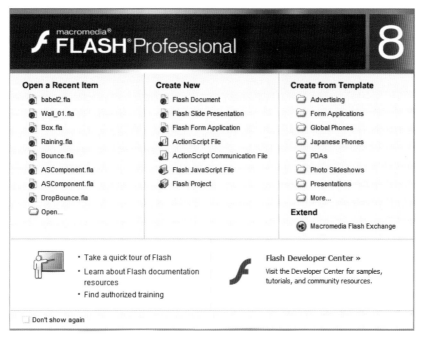

Figure 8-15. The .asc file is created by selecting ActionScript Communication File.

3. Open a new Flash document and create a movie clip named Video.

4. Open the library and add a video object from the Library pop-down menu. Name the object Video 1, select Video (ActionScript-controlled) from the Type section, and click OK.

5. Drag the video object to the stage and, using the Property Inspector, set its location to 0,0 and specify its size as 160 pixels wide by 120 pixels high. Now give it the instance name myVideo.

6. Add a new layer named Actions to the movie clip's timeline, click once on the first frame, and open the ActionScript Editor. When the Script pane opens, enter the following code:

```
var nc:NetConnection = new NetConnection();
nc.connect("rtmp://localhost/VideoWall/_definst_"),
var ns:NetStream = new NetStream(nc);
myVid.attachVideo(ns);
ns.play("Bikes.flv");
```

185

Just a bit of a warning here. We will not be going into great depth in analyzing the code. The focus of this book is Flash video and not ActionScript programming. We will just be highlighting key points while assuming you, the reader, have a knowledge of the nuls and bolts of ActionScript. Also, in any programming situation, there are sometimes multiple ways of accomplishing the same task. If you know of alternate techniques, please feel free to use them. Finally, ActionScript (like many programming languages) can sometimes be very persnickety. One misspelling could cause the exercise not to work. So please be careful when entering code into your exercises.

That is all you need to connect the video to the Media Server on your computer. The `connect()` method lets you connect to the video wall application. If you have access to a Media Server through an ISP or a FVSS provider, you will be given an RTMP address that is a series of numbers. You would add that address instead of `localhost`.

For those you who don't have a Media Server installed, the code you would use follows:

```
var nc:NetConnection = new NetConnection();
nc.connect(null);
var ns:NetStream = new NetStream(nc);
myVid.attachVideo(ns);
ns.play("Bikes.flv");
```

That last piece of code for those you without a Media Server assumes that the `Bikes.flv` *file is in the same folder as the SWF.*

7. Click the Scene 1 link to return to the main timeline and drag a copy of the movie clip to the stage. Set its location to 0,0.

8. Now we can start creating the wall. Click and hold on the movie clip. Press the Alt (Windows) or Option (Mac) key and drag a copy of the movie clip to the right. Use the Property Inspector to set its X coordinate to 160 and its Y coordinate to 0. Make another copy and set its coordinates to 320,0. You should have a neat line of movie clips across the top of the stage. Marquee all three of them and drag a copy downward. They should be sitting at 120 on the Y axis. Repeat this step one more time. When you finish, there should be nine copies of the movie clip on the stage.

When you drag the movie clips, look for a red line to appear when the edges are directly on top of each other. This is a handy little trick when you don't want to use the Property Inspector.

9. If you have some extra space on the stage, here's how to get rid of it. Click the Size button on the Property Inspector to open the Document Properties dialog box. Click the Contents button and click OK. The stage will shrink to fit the videos.

Go ahead—test the movie (see Figure 8-16).

Figure 8-16. A basic video wall

A video wall with "Wow"!

When we first saw the JC Jeans site, we confess to being wowed. Here was a Flash site (see Figure 8-17) that contained 24 interactive videos. The thing that struck us about the site— www.jc-online.com/jc/thestore/—was how quickly it loaded and how smooth everything was. Though JC isn't telling how they did it, it has stuck with us and when this book opportunity arose, we were finally given the chance to create something like it. It turns out this is not terribly difficult to do, though it does require an intermediate level of ActionScript knowledge to pull it off.

The key to this exercise is to use the technology for what it does best. For example, you want this to load fast and you want the user to click a video. They don't need to see the entire video. They just need a small three- to four-second "teaser" that loops. When they roll over the video in the wall, the loop grows and moves in front of the other videos that are playing. When they click on the video they have selected, it plays, full size, above the wall. When the user is finished, they can click the video and it disappears.

Obviously, there is going to be a bit of a wait while everything gets into place when the movie starts. This is the purpose of the Drop Bounce movie clip that will play before the video wall appears.

Figure 8-17. The JC Jeans video wall

This exercise is also a bit different from those you have done to this point. We have actually assembled the FLA, because you have already done, somewhere in this book, everything you need to know about pulling it together. At this point, we'll write the code for the engine that drives the movie. To understand the engine, you must understand the pieces that were assembled. The entire project can be found in the Chapter 8 Exercise folder, in the folder named `VideoWall2`.

When you open the folder, you will notice two folders, named `Thumbs` and `Videos`. The `Thumbs` folder contains the loops used in the wall. They are each about three seconds long, and their physical size has been reduced to 160 pixels wide by 120 pixels high. This ensures that they load and play fast. The `Videos` folder contains the full size (320X240) videos, which will load into an FLV Playback component.

1. Double-click the Video Wall 2.fla file to open it in Flash.

As you can see, there isn't much to this movie. We start with the Bounce movie clip created earlier in this chapter and have it fade out between frames 1 and 24. In many respects, it acts like a transition between the start of the movie and the video wall.

On frame 24 you find an FLV Playback component that has been centered on the stage. This will be used to play the large size video found in the Videos folder.

2. Open the library.

The library consists of two movie clips—Bounce and Video Wall—one video object that is used in the Video Wall movie clip, the FLV Playback component, and a folder to hold the various letters and words in the Bounce animation (see Figure 8-18).

If you double-click the Bounce movie clip to open it, you will see that some code has been added to frame 25. The code is

```
_root.play();
stop();
```

This code ensures that the entire animation plays on the main timeline and that it stops when it finishes.

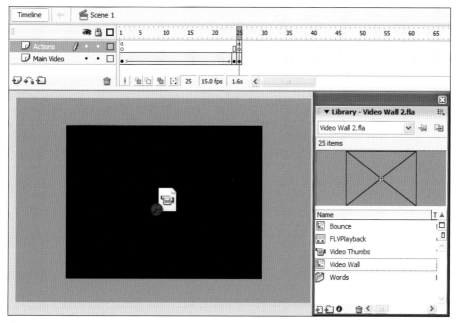

Figure 8-18. This is all you need to create a really cool video wall.

3. Return to the main timeline and open the code in frame 24. The code is

```
import mx.video.*;
import com.interactivityunlimited.video.VideoWall;

var mainVideo:FLVPlayback;
var bkgndButton:MovieClip;
var soundTrack:Sound = new Sound(this);

mainVideo.swapDepths( 100 );
mainVideo.visible = false;
mainVideo.addEventListener( "complete", this );

for( var loop:Number = 0; loop < 20; loop++ ) {
  var newMovie:String = "vid" + loop;
  var mc:MovieClip = _root.attachMovie( "Video Wall", ➥
  newMovie, loop + 1 );

  mc._x = (loop % 5) * 80 + 80;
  mc._y = Math.floor( loop / 5 ) * 60 + 60;
  mc.addListener( this );
}
```

There really is nothing new here. In fact, all this code does is create the wall on the fly and play the selected video when it is clicked. This code essentially turns the main timeline into a "major league listener."

189

The first line imports the video class that will be used to control the FLV Playback component, and the second line imports in the engine that you will write in a moment.

The code starts off by placing the FLV Playback component on level 100 of the main timeline and then turning it invisible. The listener is written to loop the video. The `for` loop actually builds the video wall using the `Video Wall` movie clip in the library and places copies of the movie clip in a series of rows across the stage until there are 20 copies of the movie clip on the stage. It also resizes those copies, which makes their "growth" on rollover so effective. It also tells each video wall clip to send event messages, such as a rollover and click, to the main timeline.

The function

```
function resumeVideoWall():Void {
  for( var loop:Number = 0; loop < 20; loop++ ) {
    var mc:VideoWall = _root["vid" + loop];

    mc.setVideoPlaying(false);
  }

  soundTrack.start();
  mainVideo.visible = false;
  bkgndButton.removeMovieClip();
}
```

ensures that the video wall will spring back to life once the main video has finished playing. The next code block starts a music track—`soundTrack`—and ensures that the component is invisible. The next line controls what happens when the user clicks the FLV Playback component. A movie clip that acts as a button is removed.

The function

```
function complete( eventObj:Object ) {
  resumeVideoWall();
}


function selectMovie( theMovie:String ) {
  var ourVideo:String = "video/" + theMovie;

  for( var loop:Number = 0; loop < 20; loop++ ) {
    var mc:VideoWall = _root["vid" + loop];

    mc.pauseVideo();
    mc.setVideoPlaying(true);
  }

  soundTrack.stop();
```

simply specifies what happens when one of the thumbnails is clicked. In addition, it puts the video wall into a state of suspended animation and stops the background audio from playing.

The final bit of code

```
bkgndButton = _root.createEmptyMovieClip( "bkgndButton", 90 );
bkgndButton.beginFill( 0, 3);
bkgndButton.moveTo( 0, 0 );
bkgndButton.lineTo( Stage.width, 0 );
bkgndButton.lineTo( Stage.width, Stage.height );
bkgndButton.lineTo( 0, Stage.height );
bkgndButton.lineTo( 0, 0 );
bkgndButton.endFill();

bkgndButton.onPress = function() {
  mainVideo.stop();
  resumeVideoWall();
}

mainVideo.visible = true;
  if( mainVideo.contentPath == ourVideo ) {
    mainVideo.seek(0);
    mainVideo.play();
  } else {
    mainVideo.contentPath = ourVideo;
  }
}

soundTrack.onSoundComplete = function() {
  this.loadSound( "selah.mp3", true );
}

soundTrack.loadSound( "selah.mp3", true );
stop();
```

actually creates the movie clip that turns the FLV Playback component on and off and fills it with a soft color so as no to distract from the videos on the wall beneath it. The function is how the component is turned off. When the user clicks it the video stops and the `resumeWall()` function, which hides the component, is called. The remaining code ensures that the sound playing in the background loops.

Now, let's turn our attention to building the engine that makes this whole thing work.

We said earlier the main timeline is turned into a major league listener. We said this because the whole key to this project is not the video object. It is the `Video Wall` movie clip. It is going to play a small video, it will start playing at 50 percent visibility, and when we roll over it, the visibility is increased to 100 percent and the video enlarges to actual size. If we click the movie clip, the video playing inside it plays, at full size, in the FLV Playback component. With 20 teasers playing at the same time, there is a lot of code, much of it the same, that will have to be written… or is there?

The neat thing about movie clips is that they are objects based on classes already built into Flash. A class is a file that contains the properties and methods that will serve as the template for creating an object. Flash has 75 built-in classes that will do such diverse things as handling text (`String`), formatting dates (`Date`), and controlling the actions of a movie clip (`MovieClip`). What makes classes so fascinating is that, if you find the methods and properties don't quite do the job you need them to do, you can extend them. This is not something to be treated at all lightly because you can get yourself into a world of grief in very short order if you don't know what you are doing. In this case, we are going to extend the `MovieClip` class to allow us to write specialized code to accomplish what we need done. Why write the same thing numerous times when you can simply write it once and be done with it?

1. Select File ➤ New and when the New Document dialog box opens (see Figure 8-19), select ActionScript File and click OK. This will open the ActionScript window.

2. Select File ➤ Save As and name the file VideoWall. Programmers follow naming conventions when working with case-sensitive languages. One of those conventions is to begin the name of a class file with a capital letter. Also, you cannot use spaces. The location is the com folder in the VideoWall folder. The actual path in that folder is com/interactivityunlimited/video. Once you are inside the video folder, click OK.

These files can reside loose in the same folder as the SWF, but it is common practice to place them in directories according to their functionality and owner's namespace. This is what is known as a "package." In this case, we are placing it a few folders deep more for example purposes than for practical purposes since we only have one class file. The reasoning behind this practice becomes more evident as more class files are added.

3. Click once in the first line and enter the following code:

```
class com.interactivityunlimited.video.VideoWall extends MovieClip {
  var nc:NetConnection;
 var ns:NetStream;
 var theVideo:Video;
 var videoSelection:Number;
 var videoPlaying:Boolean = false;

 var ourBroadcaster:Object;
```

The first line is critical. It says the file extends the functionality of the `MovieClip` class and provides the path to the file. The remainder of the code creates the variables used later in the code.

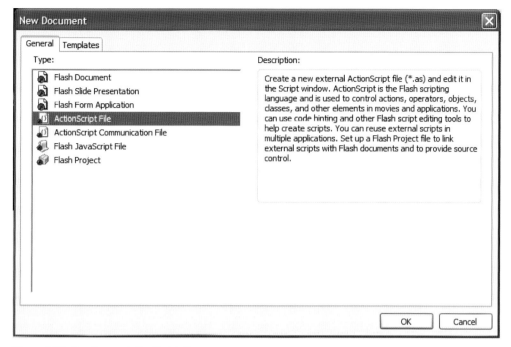

Figure 8-19. Creating an ActionScript file

4. Press Enter/Return and enter the following function:

```
function VideoWall() {
  ourBroadcaster = new Object();
  AsBroadcaster.initialize(ourBroadcaster);

  nc = new NetConnection();
  nc.connect(null);

  ns = new NetStream(nc);
  theVideo.attachVideo(ns);

  videoSelection = Math.floor(Math.random() * 6) + 1;
  ns.play( "thumbs/Trail2-Video" + videoSelection + ".flv" );
}
```

This function is also known as the constructor. Notice that it has the same name as the class file and no return type. It is designed to be automatically called as soon as the object is created from the class file. In this case, the `attachMovie()` method used in the FLA is doing that. (If you want to check, it is line 12 of the code in `Video Wall 2.fla`.) This function essentially hooks each video object in the 20 movie clips to an Internet connection and then attaches that connection and a video to a stream. The object is also set up to send event messages to any object that is willing to listen for them.

The next section randomly picks a number between 1 and 6 and starts playing the video containing that number, which is found in the `Trails` folder.

Now that we have videos actually playing in the wall, the next step is to reduce their transparency and size and have them become fully visible and grow when the mouse rolls over them.

5. Press Enter/Return key and enter the following:

```
public function onEnterFrame() {
  if( !videoPlaying ) {
    var deltaX:Number = Math.round(_root._xmouse - this._x);
    var deltaY:Number = Math.round(_root._ymouse - this._y);
    var diff:Number = Math.round(Math.sqrt((deltaX * deltaX)
    + (deltaY * deltaY)));

    if( diff > 80 ) {
        diff = 80;
      };

    this._alpha = (100 - (diff/1.5));
    this._xscale = (100 - (diff/1.5));
    this._yscale = (100 - (diff/1.5));
  }
}
```

This function (technically called an event handler) is triggered by an `onEnterFrame` event. This is no problem because the playback head is continually firing this event even if the playback head is stopped, as it is on frame 25 of the `Video Wall 2.fla` file. When the playback head enters the frame, the first thing the script does is check to see if the main video is actually playing before it goes to work. If the main video is playing, the function is exited.

The whole routine here is predicated on the movement of the mouse. If the mouse is close to a movie clip, the clip expands; if it isn't, the clip contracts. The three variables track the x and y locations of the mouse on the main timeline and then use those numbers to create another number named `diff`. In short, it uses the difference between the location of the mouse and the movie clip to set both the scale value and transparency of each movie clip on the wall.

The next two lines check to see if the value of `diff` is greater than 80. If it is, the code sets the value to 80.

With that number in place, `diff` is used to determine the `Alpha` value and the `xscale` and `yscale` values of the movie clips on the wall and under the mouse. Let's assume `diff` is equal to 80. In this case, the `Alpha` value of the clips would be 47 and the clips would be scaled to 47 percent as well. If the mouse is over the clip, `diff` would be 0, meaning that the `Alpha` value would be 100 and so would the `Scale` value. The really neat thing about this is the `Alpha` and the `Scale` values of all of the clips are affected by the proximity of the mouse to the movie clip. This technique was first discussed by Colin Moock (www.moock.org) and subsequently expanded on by Brendan Dawes (www.brendandawes.com) in his Proximity Engine.

Having dealt with a rather "slick" technique involving the movie clips, it is time to turn our attention to what happens when one of them is clicked or rolled over.

6. Press Enter/Return and enter the following functions:

```
public function pauseVideo() {
  ns.pause( true );
}

public function onRollOver() {
  if( !videoPlaying ) {
    ns.play( "thumbs/Trail2-Video" + videoSelection + ".flv" );
  }
}

public function onPress() {
   if( !videoPlaying ) {
     ourBroadcaster.broadcastMessage( "selectMovie", ➥
"Trail2-Video" + videoSelection + ".flv" );
   }
}
```

The first function simply pauses any video when it is called. The next one loads the video that has been rolled over into the video stream for the movie clip. The exclamation mark is an operator that returns the inverse Boolean value. In this case (in programming language, ! means NOT), if you go to the top of the code, we set the value of videoPlaying to false. The exclamation mark returns true if the main video is not playing. Thus, if we have no main video playing, we can play the clip in the video wall.

A similar thing happens if the mouse is pressed. If the main video is not playing, we will then send out an event that this particular clip has been selected. It is then up to the listening object to process the event and play the chosen clip. As noted earlier, the main timeline is listening to our object and will point our FLV Playback component to our video clip in the video folder. The public statement makes each of these functions available to any other function or command that may call it.

7. Press Enter/Return and enter the following functions:

```
public function setVideoPlaying( flag:Boolean ):Void {
   videoPlaying = flag;
}

public function isVideoPlaying():Boolean {
   return videoPlaying;
}
```

```
public function addListener( theListener:Object ):Boolean {
  return ourBroadcaster.addListener( theListener );
}

public function removeListener( theListener:Object ):Boolean {
  return ourBroadcaster.removeListener( theListener );
  }
}
```

The first function sets the `videoPlaying` value to `true` or `false`, set by the caller of the function. The second function simply says, "Here is the value for `videoPlaying`." This is extremely important because when a movie clip is clicked, all of the videos in the wall are paused and a stream is given to the video that loads into the FLV Playback component. Remember that the `videoPlaying` property is the flag that is set to indicate that a video is playing in the FLV Playback component. This way, the FLV Playback component can play unimpeded by any other video.

The remaining two functions are the listeners used by `Video Wall 2.fla`.

8. Save the file and open the Video Wall2.fla file. Test the file and watch what happens when you roll the mouse around the screen and click a video (see Figures 8-20 and 8-21).

Figure 8-20. The mouse is over an image; notice how the videos resize.

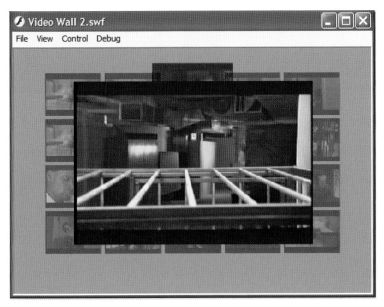

Figure 8-21. Our video is playing.

Summary

This chapter was loaded with techniques ranging from using After Effects to creating titling sequences in Flash to creating a full-blown video wall.

Though video walls are cool, be sure to take our advice and keep a close eye on the pipe. You saw this in the last exercise when 20 videos were paused to allow the FLV Playback component to play the selected video. We also hope you discovered that you simply can't "slap" one together using 320×240 videos and expect the user to congratulate you for a job well done. The odds are the opposite will occur. Still, video walls are rather cool and, in the right hands, very effective.

In the next chapter, we deal with a common situation: How do you allow the user to choose from a number of videos?

9 CHOOSING AND PLAYING MULTIPLE VIDEOS

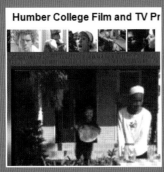 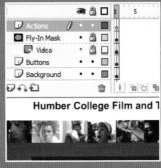 

One of the authors teaches at a college in Toronto, Canada. He teaches at the School of Media Studies, where one of the more popular programs is the Film and Television program. During their course of study, these students have a number of projects to complete, one of which is to write and produce a 30-second commercial. Considering there are some 50 students in this part of the course, putting their work on the Web for peer review and portfolio purposes can be difficult at best. In this chapter, we use the work of six of those students to demonstrate a variety of methods in which a developer can present a series of videos and let the user choose which ones to view.

The progression of exercises in this chapter will follow a line starting at dead simple and includes a rather creative technique used by such companies as the former Macromedia. You will see how movie clips can trigger videos. You will learn how to use a ComboBox component to create a pop-down menu. We will show you how short clips of the videos can be used as buttons to trigger the videos, and we will even show you how to load all of the videos into a menu and then choose which one to play right in the component.

Enough talking. Download the Chapter 9 file from the book's website and let's get to work.

1. Open the Multiple.fla file in your Chapter 9 Exercise folder.

You will see that the interface has been pretty well assembled for you. Thumbnails of each video are along the top of the page, and there is an area on the screen that serves as a backdrop for the video that will play. We have left the Video and Actions layers blank because you get to finish the project.

In case you were wondering, the background image is a shot of the interior of a restaurant on Vancouver Island that was blurred and distorted in Photoshop. The screen, with the drop shadow, was added in Fireworks 8, though they could just as easily have been added in Photoshop.

The thumbnails were screen shots taken of the videos as they played. They were placed into Fireworks 8 where they were scaled down to their current 45×35-pixel dimensions, saved as JPEG images, and imported into the Flash library. You can get them to line up on the stage in a couple of ways. The first is to do what we did, which was to drag them into position, select them, and choose Window ➤ Align—Ctrl+K (Windows) or Cmd+K (Mac)—and click the Align Centers button in the Align panel (see Figure 9-1). If you do this, be sure to deselect the To Stage option or your images will be moved to the center of the stage. Once we had our images in a line, we left them selected and set the Y position to 35 in the Property Inspector.

The other method is to "Do-It-by-the-Numbers." Each image is 45 pixels wide and the depth of the white area at the top of the stage is 70 pixels. This means the images can each be placed at 35 on the y-axis in the Property Inspector and the values for the x-axis are multiples of 45.

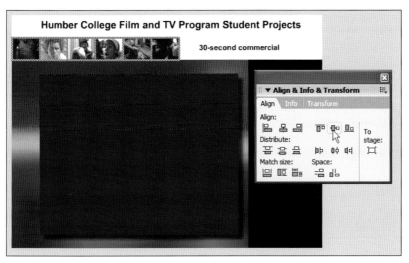

Figure 9-1. You can use the Align panel to get images or objects to line up with each other.

2. Select each thumbnail and convert it to a movie clip by right-clicking (Windows) or Control-clicking (Mac) it and select Convert to Symbol from the context menu. When the Convert to Symbol dialog box opens, name the symbol and select Movie Clip as its Type. The symbols, from left to right, should be named:

   ◾ Bread

   ◾ Hockey

   ◾ Cars

   ◾ Lemons

   ◾ Glasses

   ◾ Games

3. Select each movie clip and, in the Property Inspector, give them the following instance names:

   ◾ mcBread

   ◾ mcHockey

   ◾ mcCars

   ◾ mcLemon

   ◾ mcGlasses

   ◾ mcGames

4. Finally open the library's context menu and select New Video from the menu. When the Video Properties dialog box opens, don't worry about the name but make sure that Video (ActionScript-controlled) is selected in the Type area. Click OK to close the dialog box.

5. Select the Video layer and drag a copy of the video from the library to the stage. In the Property Inspector, set its size to 320 wide and 240 high and its X and Y coordinates to 45 and 96, respectively (see Figure 9-2). Finally, with the video object selected, give it the instance name of myVid in the Property Inspector.

That completes the assembly portion of the exercise. Now all we have to do is to wire it up with ActionScript.

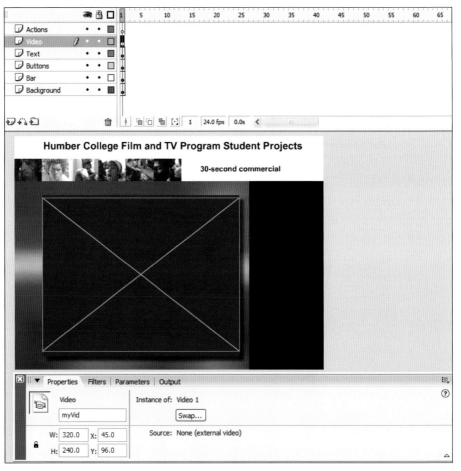

Figure 9-2. The project is ready to be "wired up" with ActionScript.

6. Select the Actions layer and press F9 (Windows) or Option+F9 (Mac) to open the ActionScript Editor. Click once in the Script pane and enter the following code:

```
var nc:NetConnection = new NetConnection();
nc.connect(null);

var ns :NetStream = new NetStream(nc);
myVid.attachVideo (ns);
ns.pause ();
```

Nothing new here. This is the code we have been using all along when we have a video object on the stage.

7. The buttons are used to control the video. Instead of repeating the same code, essentially, six times, press the Enter (Windows) or Return (Mac) key and enter the following function:

```
mcBread.onPress = function() {
   ns.play ("Bread.flv");
}
```

Now all you have to do is to copy and paste this code block into the Script pane five more times. Each time you paste a copy of the code, be sure to change the instance name to the name of the clip you are using and the name of the FLV associated with the button. They are as follows:

- mcBread = BreadQT.flv
- mcHockey = Beer.flv
- mcCars = Honda.flv
- mcLemon = Lemonade.flv
- mcGlasses = Lens.flv
- mcGames = PlayStation.flv

8. Save and play the video. As you click each movie clip, the video changes (see Figure 9-3).

That wasn't too difficult, and clicking a button accomplishes exactly what needs to be done. Unfortunately, the code is rather ugly and boxes you in. Each button has to be separately coded. This technique, therefore, is ideal for creating projects that will have short deadlines.

In the next exercise we are going to forget about the buttons. Instead, we are going to give the user the opportunity to pick a video from a list. This list will be provided through a handy little component that comes packaged with Flash Professional 8: the ComboBox component.

Figure 9-3. The video is playing.

Choosing videos from a list

In many respects, the ComboBox component functions just like a pop-down menu. If you roll over it, the menu actually pops down and you can select an item in the menu. The other neat thing about the component, which we won't be using, is that the items in the component can be made editable, meaning a user can type directly into one of the items in the ComboBox. This component is also somewhat smart. Let's assume you have placed it at the bottom of the stage and there are 10 items in the component. Obviously, the list will run off the edge of the stage and be trimmed off. Not quite. In this situation, the menu pops up, not down.

The ComboBox component can be used for forms or applications requiring a list of choices. In this example, the list of choices will be a series of videos. The user will roll over the component, the list will pop down, and when the selection is clicked on, the video starts to play. Let's get busy.

1. Open the Combo.fla file in your Chapter 7 Exercise file. When the file opens, you will notice it is the same interface you worked with previously. The major differences are the images are not movie clips, the video object is already on the stage, and there is a layer named Combo.

2. Select Window ➤ Components to open the Components panel. Locate the ComboBox component in the User Interface components and drag it onto the black area on the right side of the stage (see Figure 9-4). With the component selected, give it the instance name videoList in the Property Inspector.

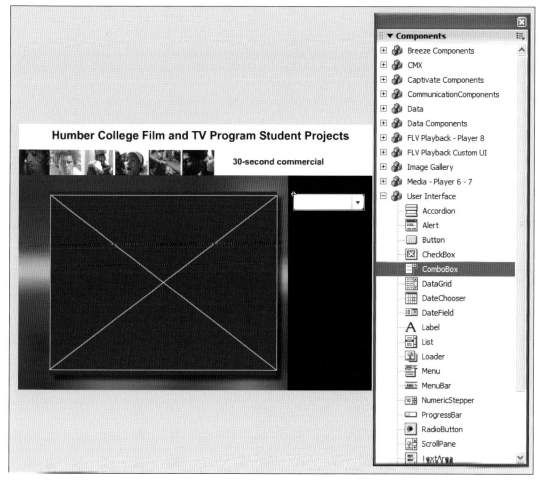

Figure 9-4. The ComboBox is on the stage.

3. Select the ComboBox and open the Component Inspector by selecting Window ➤ Component Inspector.

The Component Inspector is one of those handy tools many developers prefer over the Parameters panel of the Property Inspector. When the Component Inspector opens, you will see that it has a few more parameters than those shown in the Property Inspector.

For the purposes of this exercise, the parameters you will work with—Data, Editable, and Labels—are the same in both areas. Before we move on, let's understand why each of these parameters is so important to us.

- Data: This is the value that is generated when you select an item in the ComboBox. When you enter Data values, they are immediately available to ActionScript, and each bit of data you enter will have a counterpart in the Labels parameter (if you do not enter a Data value, the label automatically becomes the data).

- Editable: The last thing you need is to have users changing the names of the labels. The value here can be either True or False. If it is False, the labels are treated like menu items.

- Labels: This is the text that appears when the menu pops down.

4. In the Component Inspector, double-click the data area to open the Values dialog box.

The Values dialog box lets you enter the values that are associated with the menu items. To use it, click the + button. A defaultValue appears. Click once on the defaultValue to select it and enter BreadQT.flv. Click the + button to add another defaultValue. Change it to Beer.flv. Keep doing this until your Values dialog box resembles the one shown in Figure 9-5. Click OK. The dialog box will close and the data you just entered will appear in the Component Inspector as an array.

> Here's a handy ComboBox tip. If you have a number of items to add, just click the + button to add a number of slots to match the number of items in the list. Click on the first item, enter the value, and then press the Tab key to move to the next empty slot.

Figure 9-5.
The video file names are entered in the Data area of the ComboBox component.

5. Click once in the Editable area of the Component Inspector and select False from the pop-down menu. This ensures the component acts as a menu and not an input form.

6. Double-click the Values area of the Label strip to open the Values dialog box. This time, the text you enter is what appears in the menu. Enter the following labels:

- Bread
- Beer
- Cars
- Lemons
- Glasses
- Games

When you finish, click OK to close the dialog box. Now take a moment and look at the Component Inspector. Notice that each label has a data counterpart. In addition, notice how the values in the Component Inspector also appear in the Parameters area of the Property Inspector. Finally, notice how the ComboBox component has developed a label. Close the Component Inspector because it is time to write the code that will drive this.

Before you do that, save the movie and test it. When you test the movie, click on the component. Notice how the menu pops down and you can roll over the menu items (see Figure 9-6).

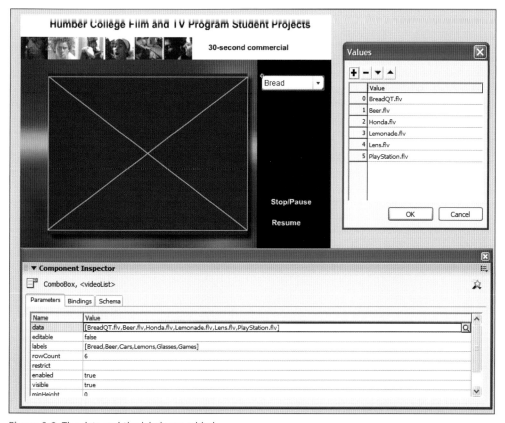

Figure 9-6. The data and the labels are added.

Now that the component is somewhat working, we now have to add the code that makes the movie functional.

1. Select the first frame in the Actions layer, open the ActionScript Editor, and enter the following into the Script pane:

```
var nc:NetConnection = new NetConnection();
nc.connect(null);

var ns :NetStream = new NetStream(nc);
myVid.attachVideo(ns);
```

2. Now that the NetConnection and NetStream have been established, we can turn our attention to making the ComboBox component act like a pop-down menu. Press the Enter/Return key twice and add the following function:

```
function playMovie():Void {
  ns.play(videoList.data[videoList.selectedIndex]);
}
```

When you entered the FLV names into the Data area of the Component Inspector you were creating a list. Lists in ActionScript are a bit different from your normal shopping list. Flash couldn't care less if you entered BreadQT.flv, Dog Food, or scumSuckingPig as the first item in the list. What it cares about is the number of the item in the list. When you entered the values for the Data in the Component Inspector, you may have noticed, as shown in Figure 9-5, that you created an array and, like all arrays, each element has an index number. The first index number is 0. For each index number there is a corresponding *value*. Now that you understand that, you can see how this function works. Instead of entering the name of the FLV to play, the second line of the code says, "In the ComboBox component named videoList, use the name of the value associated with the index number of the item just clicked on."

The beauty of this approach is its flexibility. Videos can be added and subtracted without having to make major revisions to the code.

3. Press the Enter/Return key twice and enter the following function:

```
var listenerObject:Object = new Object ();
listenerObject.change = function (eventObject:Object):Void{
  ns.close();
  playMovie();
}
```

Components like the ComboBox don't act like button or movie clip symbols and use onPress or onRelease events. They use the traditional Flash events such as onPress to generate more intricate events that other objects can readily use. The critical word in the code is change. With the ComboBox, a mouse click on a menu item is not a click but a *change*, and when one is detected the ComboBox reacts using a change event handler. In this function, when a change is detected, the stream playing the video is closed and the selected FLV is placed into the stream and starts playing.

When you have multiple videos to be placed in a stream, use the `close()` *method instead of the* `pause()` *method used in the previous example when videos are switched. This way, the video that is being replaced is totally forgotten and frees up computer resources. The* `close()` *method also deletes the local copy of the FLV that may have been downloaded by the browser.Event though the Flash Player will delete a local copy of the FLV when it finshes, a copy of the FLV may still exist in the browser cache. Think of the close method as being a way of dealing with nervous clients and security of content issues.*

4. Press the Enter/Return key twice and enter the following code:

```
videoList.addEventListener ("change",listenerObject);
playMovie();
```

The next line simply tells the component, `videoList`, what the `listenerObject` wants to listen for—`change`—and what to do: notify the `listenerObject` of any selection changes to the `videoList` component. The next line simply executes the `playMovie()` function.

5. Close the ActionScript Editor and save and test the movie. The video selected starts playing, and every time you select an item from the list, the currently playing video is replaced with the selected video. Of course, there is a problem with this approach. The user has absolutely no opportunity to stop the video from playing. Let's fix that, shall we?

6. Create a new layer directly under the Actions layer and name it Controls. With that layer selected, select the Text tool, click once near the bottom of the black area of the interface, and enter Stop/Pause.

This text is going to function as the *Pause* switch for the movie. Before proceeding, make sure the text is set to Static in the Property Inspector and that the text color is set to white. We will leave the font choice and point size to you. Now, select the text and convert it to a movie clip named Pause and, in the Property Inspector, give it the instance name of mcPause.

7. Open the ActionScript Editor and scroll down to the space under the listenerObject function. Click once and enter the following:

```
mcPause.onPress = function() {
    ns.pause (true);
}
```

If you save and test the movie, you will see this function pauses the currently playing video and you can choose a different one from the list. Of course, there is a problem with this: what if the user wants to resume playing the video?

The solution is to create another piece of text and enter the word *Resume*. Convert it to a movie clip with the instance name `mcPlay`, open the ActionScript Editor, and enter the following under the function for the Pause button:

```
mcPlay.onPress = function() {
  ns.pause (false);
}
```

This works like a charm because all you are doing is stopping and starting the `netStream` when the button is clicked (see Figure 9-7).

Figure 9-7. The code is written and the movie is doing exactly what it is supposed to do.

Changing the appearance of the ComboBox component

The ComboBox component uses the Halo theme common to many of the components that ship with Flash. You may have noticed the component has a slight "greenish" tinge to it, which tells you it uses the Halo theme. The other aspect is the style of the text in the component. You may have a corporate standard that requires a different point size and font. These can all be changed using ActionScript using the `setStyle()` method.

Let's make some changes to the ComboBox:

1. Open your Combo.fla exercise and open the ActionScript Editor.

2. Scroll down to about line 7 of the code (right after `myVid.attachVideo(ns);`), press Enter/Return, and type

   ```
   videoList.setStyle("themeColor", "haloOrange");
   ```

If you save and test the movie, you will see that the selection color is orange and that the ComboBox has taken on an orange tinge. If you change the theme to haloBlue, that color becomes predominant.

You don't have to stay with the themes. You can also change the color by substituting a hexadecimal color value for the `themeColor`. To see this, change the `"haloOrange"` to `"0xFFCC33"`. When you test the movie, the selection color changes to a light orange.

You can also change the background color for the component.

3. Press Enter/Return and add

   ```
   videoList.setStyle("backgroundColor", 0x999999);
   ```

If you save and test the movie, you will see that the orange color now contrasts quite well with a gray background (see Figure 9-8).

Figure 9-8.
You can change the selection and background colors used in the ComboBox.

Changing the size and appearance of a font is also relatively easy to accomplish. Let's change the font in the ComboBox to 14 point Times New Roman.

4. Press Enter/Return and add the following:

   ```
   videoList.setStyle("fontFamily", "Times New Roman");
   videoList.setStyle("fontSize", 14);
   ```

When you test the movie, you will see the style has changed to reflect these settings. Of course, the text is rather faint against that gray background. Let's change that:

5. Press Enter/Return and add the following line:

```
videoList.setStyle("fontWeight", "bold");
```

If you test the movie, your list will look like the one shown in Figure 9-9.

Figure 9-9.
The font is now bold.

Of course, black text against a gray background might be a bit hard to see. You can also change the text color to white by adding the following line of code:

```
videoList.setStyle("color", 0xFFFFFF);
```

At this point the code that drives the look of the ComboBox is

```
videoList.setStyle("themeColor", 0xFFCC33);
videoList.setStyle("backgroundColor", 0x999999);
videoList.setStyle("fontFamily", "Times New Roman");
videoList.setStyle("fontSize", 14);
videoList.setStyle("fontWeight", "bold");
videoList.setStyle("color", 0xFFFFFF);
```

Finally, if there is a compelling need to use a corporate or special font, you can embed it into the SWF. For example, assume your client insists that you use Times New Roman as the font in the ComboBox and you aren't sure the user has that font. All is not lost; you can embed the font used in the `fontFamily` using this line:

```
videoList.setStyle("embedFonts", "true") ;
```

The completed file is named ComboCB.fla *in the Lesson 9 /Complete folder.*

Roll your own components

Sooner or later, you are going to discover that movie clips can be restrictive. By that we mean the code in the movie clip is separate from that on the main timeline and, in many respects, locks you in to the functionality of that movie clip. There are a couple of problems with this approach. The first is there is no easy way to change the appearance or functionality of the movie clip without making the FLA available to developers. If something like the alpha value of the movie clip needs to change, whoever has the FLA has to change the code inside the movie clip's timeline. No big deal, but from a workflow perspective, it can be a cumbersome process. This highlights the second issue, which is there really is no easy way to share and distribute a movie clip and its attached code.

The balance of this chapter is designed to introduce you to using ActionScript to construct relatively simple components. These are Flash projects where the code that makes them work or extends their functionality is not inside a movie clip but resides in an external ActionScript file. This type of work is not for the faint of heart because it is complex. This explains why many Flash teams contain both designers and coders or, as we affectionately refer to them, freaks and geeks.

When you consider the makeup of project teams, you might wonder how anything gets done. Designers, the "freaks," and developers, the "geeks," populate different universes. In the geek universe, life is an orderly process that moves in a straight line. Logic is the order of the day, and all processes move in a 1-2-3-4-5 manner. The freak universe is a chaotic place where disorder is the rule and chaos is what makes life so interesting. Logic doesn't really count for much, and processes move in a 1-3-4-2-5 manner. Yet the project teams that function the most smoothly are the ones where the freaks and the geeks understand each other. Freaks need to be able to talk to their geek counterparts and understand how ActionScript works.

Our intention is not to teach you ActionScript programming or object-oriented programming, affectionately referred to as OOP. Still, it is important to understand how these projects come together and involve the active participation of freaks and geeks who are able to communicate with each other. The authors are a classic example of this concept. Jordan is the geek and Tom is the freak. Tom approaches coding in much the same way a vampire avoids sunlight, but he needs to understand what Jordan does, and, more importantly, understand just what the hell Jord is talking about when he says, "Gee, Tom, the solution is to simply extend the movie clip class. Piece of cake."

You bought this book to figure out how to work with video, not to become a geek. Still, you can't avoid some of the more advanced uses of ActionScript, especially if you are sitting around with your team brainstorming a number of what-if scenarios that incorporate a high degree of cool. The authors are just as guilty of this as the rest of you. This chapter ends with an interesting video menu project because one of us wondered, "Wouldn't it be cool if we were to create a pop-down menu that had small loops of the videos in the menu, meaning the user gets a small preview of the video, can read the video's name, and does nothing more than click on the menu strip?"

> *If you are new to ActionScript or find this whole area fascinating and wish to learn more about object-oriented programming in Flash, friendsofED has a very good book—*Object-Oriented ActionScript for Flash 8, *by Peter Elst and Todd Yard—and we suggest you pick up a copy.*

What is this "object" we speak of?

Before we start, let's get comfortable with some of the absolute basics you will encounter over the balance of this chapter and, in many respects, Chapters 10 and 11. The first is the concept of an "object." We have been tossing objects around this book like confetti at a wedding, and if you are going to start exploring ActionScript, then you need to understand that your raw material will be this nebulous thing called an object.

If you had never seen a book in your life and we handed you this one, you would wonder, "What is this thing I am holding, what are the things that make up this thing I am holding, and what does it do?" In many respects, you have just stepped into the world of objects because objects are "things." The "things that make up this thing" are pages, authors, heartless editors, and pictures, which are the properties of the object called a book. The "what does it do" question is also important because it defines the actions this thing with pages can do. When geeks talk about the actions that ActionScript can perform, they usually refer to them as methods.

Obviously, the concept of a book is rather general. This book is not even close to being like that book we call a dictionary, which isn't even close to being like the book called a novel. This means there are different types of books out there that share the same properties and methods of the object called a book but are totally different from this one.

This introduces the concept of a class because even though all books, when you move up the definition chain, derive from the same fundamental object, they are all different once you start moving downward and define their methods and properties. In ActionScript, a class defines all of the methods and properties for any object derived from it. For example, a very common class is the `MovieClip` class, which defines such properties as `alpha`, `_x`, and `_y`, and such methods as `play()`. These are all defined in the class, and each `MovieClip` object you create inherits them.

The ultimate object, by the way, is the `Object` class, and all ActionScript objects share the methods and properties of this class. In fact, the `Object` class does not pertain to any specific tasks such as location of an object on the stage, the text in a text box, or the location of an FLV file. The most common use of this class is to create simple objects that act as containers for related properties. The geeks refer to this container, or construct, as a *structure*, which is nothing more than a simple object with common properties.

Though ActionScript has quite a few classes of its own, you can create your own classes, which is something you will be doing for the balance of this chapter. An obvious question is, "Why?" The answer: to make the life of the geek and the freak easier, the code a bit more easier to understand, and to share and reuse. A video player application involves different types of concepts that range from custom control creation, video choices, and so on. Each of these can be put in a class by grouping the common characteristics and actions in one place rather than spreading them out across movie clips, components, and so on.

So what does a new class look like? Sticking with our book example, the *structure* for a class called book would contain such basic properties as bookType, bookPublisher, and imageColor. In ActionScript it would look like this:

```
var book: Object - new Object();
book.bookType " "Dictionary";
book.bookPublisher = "friendsofED";
book.imageColor = "GrAyscale";
```

> *If you want to see all of the classes available to you in ActionScript, open the ActionScript Editor. On the left side are a series of books. Click on the ActionScript 2.0 classes and you will see a listing of the classes; if you click the class you can also see all of the methods and properties associated with that class.*

Though you can create these classes in the FLA, another, more common, approach is to keep them in a file that is external to the FLA. This file is an AS or ActionScript file, and is one of the choices available to you when you select File ➤ New. Each class you create must be in its own AS file and the name of the file must correspond to the class you are creating. If you want to create a new class called Book, then the AS file containing it must be named Book.as.

Within that file, all the code relating to that class must use the following code structure:

```
class book {
// The rest of the code is tossed in here;
}
```

When you start defining the properties and methods for the Book class, you also have to determine whether they will be private or public, which we will explain in the next exercise. For now, the decision is simply whether they can be accessed by instances of the objects in the FLA.

What about simply adding new functionality to the MovieClip class, for example? One of the most powerful things you can do with classes is establish parent-child relationships between them. When you create a class that is a child of the MovieClip class, that class is said to extend (extends is so important it is a keyword in ActionScript) the MovieClip class. In fact, one of the first lines of code you will write in the next exercise does just that:

```
class com.interactivityunlimited.control.Button extends MovieClip {
// stuff goes here;
}
```

This code creates a class named `Button` (the words `com.interactivityunlimited.control` are the path to the class) that is a child of the `MovieClip` class, meaning it has all of the properties and methods of the `MovieClip` class available to it along with its own properties and methods.

Components are your friend

Now that you understand the absolute basics of classes and objects, let's move into the area of component creation because that is exactly what you will be doing in the following exercises.

If you look at the Flash workspace, one of the panels is named Components. When you really dig into components, you discover they are actually nothing more than fancy movie clips with parameters that allow you to change their appearance and behavior. They also have a "whizzy" graphical element associated with them, and we'll get into that in the exercises.

For now, it is important that you understand why the components you or your geek counterpart create can be so useful. Creating the `Button` class file as a separate AS file allows you to separate your code, including the class's properties and methods from the FLA, and also lets you create little "widgets" that can be distributed and reused without your having to understand or even change the code. Is that neat or what?

The other thing to keep in mind is that components, even though they are "movie clips on steroids," don't act like movie clips. For example, if you put a movie clip on the Flash stage, you can have it react to an *onPress* event. Components don't do "no steenkin `onPress` events." What they do is listen for a change and react accordingly. The important words in that last sentence are *listen* and *change*.

Much of the code presented will broadcast a change using a variable named, for example, `ourBroadcaster`. The component will be either listening for that broadcast or actually contain objects that will be doing the broadcasting. In either case, the component will react to the change accordingly by playing a video or performing some other function.

The final part of this discussion involves having the component's parameters show up in the Parameters area of the Property Inspector.

This occurs when the AS file is linked to the movie clip being converted to a component. This is done by right-clicking (Control-clicking if you have a Mac) on the movie clip in the library and selecting Component Definition from the context menu. A dialog box will open and you will enter the path to the AS file and the parameters for the component. These parameters will appear in the Property Inspector when you click the Parameters tab. Naturally, you are wondering, "So, uh, do the parameters just magically appear?"

The answer is you have to write them in the AS file. They look like this:

```
[Inspectable(type='String', defaultValue='Set Data')]
```

The parameters used in the Property Inspector are created by adding metadata to the AS file. Metadata is data added to a class file but is not part of the code that makes it work. It simply provides Flash with additional information about the code and lets it know which properties are to be used in the Parameters tab of the Property Inspector. The properties to be used have the `[inspectable]` metadata tag in front of them. In the case of our earlier example, the labels in the Parameters area of the Property Inspector would read *type* and *defaultValue*.

We will finish this discussion by letting you in on a little secret. If you are a geek or a freak with a bit of ActionScript knowledge, you may look at the code in the examples and mutter, "That ain't the way I would do it." It probably isn't. But the bottom line in any Flash project is that it works and that it does what it is supposed to do.

The authors discovered a very long time ago that there are probably 6,000 ways of doing everything when it comes to digital media. The best way is your way because, in the final analysis, the client wants to let the visitor choose among various videos on his page. They couldn't care less how you did it. They only care that you did it … and it works.

Creating a Button component to choose among multiple videos

In the first exercise, we showed you how to use movie clips as buttons to control video playback. If you remember, we mentioned that the code was rather "ugly" even though it was acceptable in a pinch. In this exercise you will be "beautifying" the code and actually creating your own component and building on what you learned in the last exercise and the previous chapter.

Let's get busy:

1. Open the `RYO_1.fla` file found in the `RYO_Component 1` folder in the Chapter 9 Exercise folder.

As you may have noticed, it looks a bit familiar. The major difference is the buttons along the top are simply images. You will start to deal with making them interactive later in the exercise. What you need to do now is write the code they will use when they become components. Think of this code as being the engine of a new car. Once it is created, the components will be used to screw it onto the frame.

2. Select File ➤ New and when the New Document dialog box opens, select ActionScript File and click OK.
3. When the new document opens, immediately select File ➤ Save As and name the document Button. The folder for this file follows this path in the RYO_Component 1 folder: com/interactivityunlimited/control.

4. Click once in line 1 of the file and enter the following code:

```
class com.interactivityunlimited.control. ➥
Button extends MovieClip {
[Inspectable(type='String', defaultValue='setData')]
var data:String;
var ourBroadcaster:Object;

var hitArea:MovieClip;

function Button() {
  ourBroadcaster = new Object();
  AsBroadcaster.initialize(ourBroadcaster);

  hitArea._alpha = 0;
}
```

The first line simply extends the functionality of the `MovieClip` class and provides the location of the file you are creating. The second line adds the metadata, and the next three lines set the new properties to be added to the `MovieClip` class.

The function, also known as a constructor, is called automatically as soon as the Button component is instantiated on the timeline of the FLA. The first thing it does is instantiate a new object that will act as a container for the `ourBroadcaster` properties. The `AsBroadcaster initialize()` method is applied to `ourBroadcaster` to enable it to send messages to any listening object when our button is clicked and ensures that the `hitArea`, which defines the width and height of our Button component, is transparent.

> The choice of the variable name `hitArea` is deliberate. If you place a button symbol on the stage that has nothing in the Up, Over, and Down areas but a box in the Hit Area of the symbol, you have created a hotspot that is nothing more than an invisible button on the Flash stage. By pulling the alpha for this component back to 0, you are using the component as a hot spot.

Because we are broadcasting the name of the movie, the event listener only needs to know what to play, and not which button was clicked. This is the beauty of AS 2.0 and OOP programming. The button is like its own program that communicates to another program (in this case, _root, which is the main timeline for RYO_1.fla). However, _root doesn't need to know, or care, how the Button component works.

Though we briefly explained in the previous chapter how a class is extended, let's dig a little deeper into it because extending classes or even creating a custom class is an important concept to understand. The purpose of extending a class or creating your own class is to make your life easier and make it easy to reuse and share code.

That first line of code is formally known as a classpath. A Flash classpath is a list of directories to which Flash will automatically look for the AS file. By default, Flash looks in three places:

- The file where you saved the FLA. This is the approach being used in this exercise, but if you plan to reuse the class in multiple projects, this is not a recommended location for the AS file.

- The `Classes` directory in your user configuration folder. On a PC using Windows XP, this location is `C:\Documents and Settings\ [user name]\ Application Data\MacRomedia\Flash`. If you are a Mac OS X user the path is `Hard Disk/Users/[user name]//Library/Application Support/ Macromedia/Flash 8\[language]\Configuration\Classes`. Using this area for your classes is not recommended since Flash will erase your classes when a program update—the Flash MX 2004 to Flash Professional 8 update is a good example—has occurred.

- A user-defined path that can be set up in your preferences. This is the recommended location to put all of your commonly used classes.

As you have also seen, you can add your own directories to the classpath. You can do this in a couple of ways. You can specify a path for each FLA or you can create a global classpath if the AS file is being used by other FLA files. This is done in the preferences; explaining how to do it and why it is a good thing is well out of the scope of this book.

Once the class has been declared, the next step is to determine which properties and methods will be used for the class. The variables listed after the declaration are the properties for the class. In our case they are `_data`, `ourBroadcaster`, and `hitArea`.

As we pointed out earlier, when you define a class's properties you also have to decide whether they should be `public` or `private`. Our properties will be `public`. You will notice that we didn't declare this. If you don't declare it—`public  var __data:String;`—Flash will default to `public`. A public property is one that can be accessed directly by anyone. Private properties can only be accessed by methods and properties within the same class.

Once the class members are determined, you can then define the `getter` and `setter` methods for the members. All these methods do is get data such as the name of the FLV from the Button component and then set it as the data. Here's how:

5. Press the Enter/Return key and add the following five small functions:

```
public function get Data():String {
  return data;
}

public function set Data( newData:String ):Void {
  data = newData;
}
```

```
public function onPress() {
  ourBroadcaster.broadcastMessage( "selectMovie", data );
}

public function addListener( theListener:Object ):Boolean {
  return ourBroadcaster.addListener( theListener );
}

public function removeListener( theListener:Object ):Boolean {
  return ourBroadcaster.removeListener( theListener );
}
}
```

6. Save the document and close it. This will return you to your open Flash document.

The first two functions get and set the data from the component using a `get Data()` or `set Data()` statement, respectively. That data is then identified—or `set`—as a string and the `_data` is assigned to `newData`.

Naturally, life isn't all roses or predictable. As this book is being written, a new version of ActionScript, ActionScript 3.0 or AS3, is currently in public beta. The key aspect of AS3 is its strict compliance to the ECMA standard for JavaScript. One major change resulting from this is that the `get Data()` and `set Data()` syntax used in the previous code will become the norm over the next two years.

This means there are actually two ways of using getters and setters. The method used here is called an implicit getter or implicit setter. The other way of doing it is to use `getData()`—notice the missing space between the words `get` and `Data`—which is the standard get method. Both work, though if you were to place a bet you would be a big loser by betting against the implicit getters and setters approach.

As with any emerging standard, especially this early in the process, there is now a drawback: any component done in this manner can no longer be used as a Flash element in Dreamweaver. This is because the `Inspectable` metatag cannot be used with the getter and setter as such, or it will return as undefined. It has to be placed above the variable and the variable must be public. The current Flash help documents require the use of implicit accessors if you use the `Inspectable` tag with it. Until this officially changes, we don't recommend the standard accessor method, especially if you plan to use Flash Elements in Dreamweaver.

The third function looks for a mouse click (`onPress`) and, when it detects that event, the broadcaster takes the data value and makes it available to the `selectMovie` function in `RYO_1.fla`.

Though this may seem like an awfully complex process to play a few movies, it actually makes the process more efficient. Instead of writing code for each button, you use the `addListener()` method. This allows you to add any number of buttons with listeners and leave the grunt work of requesting a new video to the `Button.as` file, which really only has to be written once. It doesn't care whether there are three or three hundred buttons.

With the `Button.as` file written, you can now concentrate on bolting the engine to the frame.

1. Choose Insert ➤ New Symbol and when the New Symbol dialog box opens, name it Hit Area and set the Type to Movie Clip. Click OK. Select the Rectangle tool and draw a rectangle that is about 50 pixels wide and 45 pixels high. Don't worry about the fill and the stroke color. The size is also unimportant because you will be resizing the movie clip later on in this exercise. Once the rectangle is drawn, set its X and Y coordinates to 0 in the Property Inspector. Click the Scene 1 link to close the Symbol Editor and return to the main timeline.

2. Create another movie clip named Button. Drag the Hit Area movie clip into the Symbol Editor and set its X and Y coordinates to 0 in the Property Inspector. Return to the main timeline.

With a hit area defined for the button, you are about to discover how easy it can be to create your own component and bolt a car engine to the frame.

3. Right-click (Windows) or Control-click (Mac) the Button movie clip in the library. Select Linkage from the context menu to open the Linkage dialog box.

This is the first step in the process. You are going to link the movie clip to an ActionScript class file that you will be writing in a moment. This file will control what happens when the button is clicked. When the Linkage dialog box opens, enter Button as the Identifier and select the Export for ActionScript and the Load in First Frame radio buttons. So far this is standard stuff.

4. Click once in the AS 2.0 class input box and enter the following text: com.interactivityunlimited.control.Button. This points to the ActionScript file you named Button, which was placed in the com/interactivityunlimited/control folder path. If you completed the previous chapter, this is similar to the path you created for the class file for the video wall. Click OK to close the Linkage dialog box.

5. Right-click (Windows) or Control-click (Mac) the Button symbol in the library and select Component Definition from the context menu.

The Component Definition dialog box will open (see Figure 9-10). First, enter the path from the previous step in the AS 2.0 Class field. That tells the component where to look for its methods, properties, and inspectable data.

Next, give your component an icon. Under Description is a small icon. Click it and a popdown menu will appear. Select Button Icon from the list and click OK to close the Component Definition dialog box. If you look at your library you will notice the icon for the Button movie clip has changed to that used for a Button component.

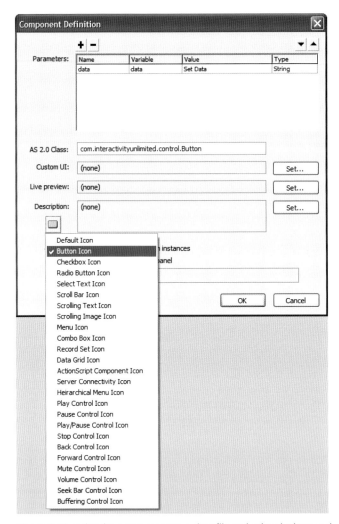

Figure 9-10. Point the component to a class file and select its icon and you, too, can convert a movie clip to a component.

6. Select the Buttons layer and drag a copy of your new Button component from the library. Place it over the first icon on the left side of the row. When you drag the component onto the stage, notice that it looks just like a button containing only a hit area. Resize the component using the Free Transform tool to fit over the image.

7. With the component selected, give it an instance name of bread in the Property Inspector. Now that it has an instance name, it should also have a parameter that points to the BreadQT.flv file. Click the Parameters tab in the Property Inspector and select the words Set Data. Replace the selected text with BreadQT.flv. Repeat the previous step and this one five more times, and use the FLV file associated with the image as the data.

As you have just seen, there is nothing mysterious about converting a movie clip to a component. The key is the Component Definition dialog box. Though there are a lot of even more complicated components that you can create with the dialog box, this isn't bad for a first effort... especially if this is the first component you have created. Now all you have to do is to "wire it up" with the necessary ActionScript. This will come from two sources: the main timeline where the components will be told where to go when they are clicked and a separate class file that will tell them what to do when they are clicked.

8. Select the first frame of the Actions layer, open the ActionScript Editor, and enter the following code into the Script pane:

```
var nc:NetConnection = new NetConnection();
nc.connect(null);

var ns :NetStream = new NetStream(nc);
myVid.attachVideo (ns);
ns.pause ();

function selectMovie( theMovie:String ):Void {
  ns.play( "video/" + theMovie );
}

bread.addListener(this);
hockey.addListener(this);
honda.addListener(this);
lemonade.addListener(this);
lens.addListener(this);
playstation.addListener(this);
```

The script starts with the usual code when a video object is involved. The rest of the code, starting with the function, is what makes things happen when your Button component is clicked.

The function simply puts the appropriate video into the `netStream` and the path to the video—`"video/" + theMovie"`—is used as the parameter for the `play()` method. The remainder of the code attaches a listener to each component using the `addListener()` method. The parameter—`this`—refers to the Button component. Close the ActionScript Editor to return to the main timeline.

9. Save the file, and open and test `RYO_1.fla` (see Figure 9-11).

Though what you have just created may seem to be an awful lot of work for a stupid button, you would be missing the point of this exercise. You haven't just created a button; you have created a button that can be used over and over for video or other Flash work. In many respects, the whole point of this exercise was to get you used to the concept of "Write once, use many." In the next exercise, we build on what you have learned here to create a really cool set of video buttons.

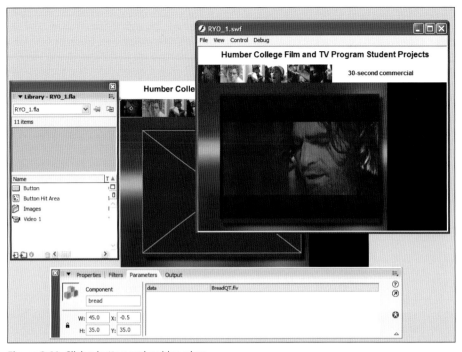

Figure 9-11. Click a button and a video plays.

Using video as a button

So far, the exercises have used graphic buttons and pop-down menus to select an FLV. In this exercise we use small clips of the video to actually "preview" the content. This is an effective technique because it gives the user the opportunity to choose a video that interests them by seeing a short loop of the video play when the mouse is over the button. In many respects, the button acts like a movie trailer.

There's really nothing to this exercise that you haven't done before. If you double-click the `VideoStrip.swf` file in the Chapter 9 Completed files folder, you can see this exercise in action. As you may have noticed, it uses the same effect as the video wall from the previous chapter, but instead of 20 videos, a strip is constructed along the bottom of the stage. When you roll over the videos in the strip, the one your mouse is over enlarges and the loop starts to play. Click the mouse and the video starts to play in the FLV Playback component.

The loops were created by opening the original QuickTime movies in a video editor, trimming out all but the first three to five seconds of the video, and reducing the physical size of the "loop" to 160 by 120. Depending on the application, the file was then exported as an FLV or saved as a QuickTime movie and converted to an FLV using the Flash 8 Video Encoder. Though you can scale and trim videos in the Encoder, we recommend using a video editor for the task. There is a higher degree of precision and a significantly reduced file size over the original QuickTime video.

Like the video wall, this exercise uses a similar AS file, so we aren't going to get you to write that code. It is already in the `VideoStrip` exercise folder in the `com` folder. Instead, we are going to let you assemble the "strip."

1. Open the VideoStrip.fla file in your Chapter 9 Exercise folder. Select the keyframe in frame 25 of the Actions layer and open the ActionScript Editor. Scroll down to line 12 of the Script pane, click once, and add the following code:

```
for( var loop:Number = 0; loop < movieList.length; loop++ ) {
  var newMovie:String = "vid" + loop;
  var mc:MovieClip = _root.attachMovie( "Video Button", ➥
  newMovie, loop + 100 );

    mc.addListener( this );
    mc._x = (loop * 80) + 80;
    mc._y = Stage.height - 60;
  mc.setOurMovie( movieList[loop] );
}
```

The `for` loop you just entered builds the strip on the stage.

The first line creates a value for the variable loop. This is a counter that will decide how many times the `for` loop will iterate. That value is 0. This number is perfect for our purposes because you are also going to use this value to position the videos on the stage. The next bit of code just establishes that the value in the `for` loop can't be more than the length of the `movieList`, the array created in line 7, and the value in the `for` loop increases by 1 because of the `++` operator.

How does Flash know the length of the `movieList`? When you were creating the data for the ComboBox component earlier in this chapter, an array was created that was numbered using an index number, which, coincidentally, started at 0. The last line of the code creates an array programmatically. Like everything else in ActionScript, an array uses a class file (in this case called `Array`). However, this class file already has the programming code built in to remember how many elements are in the array. You do not need to do any additional coding. It is held in a property called, appropriately enough, `length`. All you need to do is refer to the name of the array and add `.length` (you need the dot). This makes it easy to set the maximum value that the loop can increase. If it goes past that value, errors will occur. The last bit of coding increases the counter by 1 every time the loop runs.

Having determined how many loops will be iterated, the second line names each movie (`vid0`, `vid1`, `vid2`...), and the next line attaches them to a movie clip named `mc`, which is placed on the main timeline of the FLA at runtime. The last parameter ensures that each clip is placed on a level that is 100 pixels above the previous level. The next line attaches a listener to each of the six clips that are created.

The next two lines of the code assemble the strip and place them on the stage. Obviously, the looped video needs to grow to the height of 160 by 120. The `VideoButton.as` file sets the size of the video loops to 80 by 60 and also resizes them when the cursor rolls over one. This gives us the information necessary to build the strip.

The first line sets the `._x` position of the first video loop to 80 pixels from the edge of the stage. The next clip is placed 160 pixels from the edge, and so on. Let's do the math for the first two movie clips to see how this happens. The first value in the loop is 0; therefore (0 * 80) + 80 = 0. The second value for loop will be 1 and 80 + 80 = 160. The `._y` value might seem to be a bit odd because it uses the height of the stage to determine the position. In actual fact, that line says, "Place each movie clip 60 pixels up from the bottom of the stage."

The last line sets our button to our selected movie using the `public function` named `setOurMovie` in the AS file.

2. Press Enter/Return twice and enter the following functions:

```
function resumeVideoStrip():Void {
  soundTrack.start();
  mainVideo.visible = false;
}

function complete( eventObj:Object ) {
    resumeVideoStripl();
}
```

The first function deals with what happens when the selected video is stopped. The sound starts playing in the background and the FLV Playback component is hidden. The second function answers the question, "What happens when the video finishes?" The code calls the previous function, and then reverts the stage to black and starts playing the background sound.

Finally, you now deal with what happens when one of the videos is clicked and the FLV Playback component goes to work.

3. Press Enter/Return twice and enter the following function:

```
function selectMovie( theMovie:String ) {
  var ourVideo:String = "video/" + theMovie;

  soundTrack.stop();

  mainVideo.visible = true;
  if( mainVideo.contentPath == ourVideo ) {
    mainVideo.seek(0);
    mainVideo.play();
    } else {
      mainVideo.contentPath = ourVideo;
  }
}
```

The function starts by identifying the name of the FLV to be played. Because we are broadcasting a string for the name of the movie, we are declaring our argument to be recognized as a `String`. The next line uses that string to create a complete path to our video and assign it to our local variable `ourVideo` using a concatenation.

With the video identified, the soundtrack playing in the background is stopped and the FLV Playback component is made visible. The next line checks the `contentPath` for the component to see if it is the same movie that we had selected. If they are the same movie, the component is simply instructed to rewind our video using the *seek()* method to the beginning of the FLV and starts playing it. If it is not the same movie, we assign our FLV Playback component's `contentPath` to `ourVideo`, which will automatically start playing the new video.

> The `seek()` *method is a great way of ensuring that you start right at the beginning of the video. The method looks for the nearest keyframe in the FLV to the time, in seconds—in our case* 0*—specified in the parameter.*

4. Save and test your movie (see Figure 9-12).

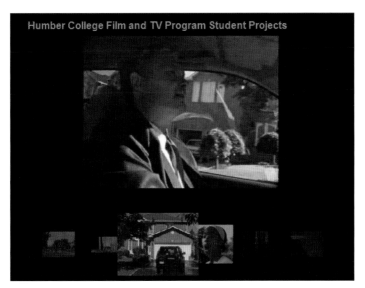

Figure 9-12. Videos loops can do double duty as buttons.

Using transitions with multiple videos

This exercise answers that age-old question: "How did they do that?"

When the Studio 8 line of products was introduced in the fall of 2005, Macromedia ran a series of customer testimonial videos. There were usually three to six of them, depending on the products, and once they loaded, if you selected a video testimonial it seemed to slide over the currently playing video. To say this was a cool effect would be an understatement, and we were constantly being asked how they achieved that effect when we spoke at seminars or did workshops. Though Macromedia isn't telling, here is one approach to the task.

There is an ActionScript class called the `Transition Manager` (you can read all about it by opening the Flash Help file and searching for "Transition Manager Class") and a series of effect-defining transition-based animations that can be applied to movie clips. Here's a little-known aspect of the FLV Playback component: it can load multiple videos and play them in the order you choose. Put those two ideas together and you have the makings of a rather interesting method of playing multiple videos.

The `Transition Manager` class regards transitions as animations and applies the animations to movie clips. The ten transition-based classes are as follows:

- `Blinds transition`: Uses rectangles to give the appearance of a blind opening or closing
- `Fade transition`: Does what it says
- `Fly transition`: Slides an object in or out using a direction you specify
- `Iris transition`: Uses a square or a circle to zoom an object in or out
- `Photo transition`: Looks as if someone uses a camera flash to have an object appear or disappear
- `PixelDissolve transition`: Shows or hides a movie clip using a bunch of randomly disappearing rectangles
- `Rotate transition`: Does what it says
- `Squeeze transition`: Scales the movie clip either horizontally or vertically
- `Wipe transition`: Uses an animated horizontal mask to reveal or hide an object
- `Zoom transition`: Gives the effect of a zoom by scaling the object

Let's go to work.

1. Open the Transitions folder in your Chapter 8 Exercise folder. Double-click the transition.fla file to open it. When the file opens, you will see we have constructed the interface and placed an FLV Playback component with the instance name of vidcomp on the stage.

2. Select the Buttons layers. Next open the Components panel—Window ➤ Components—and drag a copy of the Button component from the UI components group to the stage. Place the component in the white area between the last line of text in the headline and the background image. This will be our "Next Video" button. Select it and give it the instance name of nextVideo in the Property Inspector. With the Button still selected, click the Parameters tab of the Property Inspector and change the Label parameter from Button to >>. Open the library and drag another instance of the button to the stage to the left of the Next Video button. Give it the instance name of previousVideo and change the Label to << (see Figure 9-13).

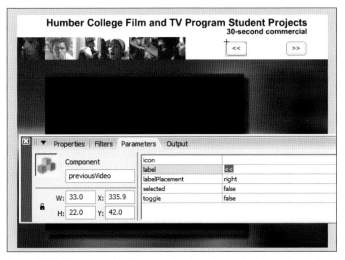

Figure 9-13. The control buttons are in place, instantiated and labeled.

The next step in the process is to pay attention to the video component. You are going to apply the Fly transition to the component. The problem is, when the movie plays, the component will move across the stage when the next iteration of the component flies in from the left. Though it may look cool, the objective here is to have the transition occur only in the area where the video is visible. The solution is to mask the video area to ensure the effect is "confined" to the video area of the stage. With the mask in place, you can now write the code that makes it all happen.

3. Add a new layer to the timeline above the video layer and name it Fly-In Mask. Select the rectangle tool and draw a rectangle in the new layer. Use the Property Inspector to set the width to 321 pixels and the height to 253 pixels. Set the X location to 43 and the Y location to 91. Right-click (Windows) or Control-click (Mac) on the layer name and select Mask from the context menu. Now we need to write some code (see Figure 9-14).

> If you do apply a mask, be sure the controls for the FLV Playback component have the word "Over" in the skin name. This means the controls will appear over the video. If you don't, anything in the component that appears below the mask—such as a skin with the word "External" will be hidden. We also make it a habit of setting the skin autoHide parameter to true. This means the controls will only be visible if the user rolls over the video.

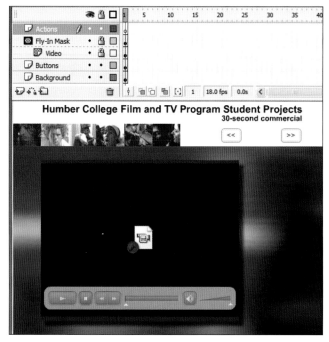

Figure 9-14. All that's left to do is to write some code.

4. Select the first key frame in the Actions layer, open the ActionScript Editor, and enter this code into the Script pane:

```
import mx.transitions.*;

var videoLoadedCount:Number = 0;
var videoPlayerIndex:Number = 1;
var videoList:Array = new Array("Beer.flv","BreadQT.flv", ➥
"Honda.flv", "Lemonade.flv", "Lens.flv", "PlayStation.flv");

for (var loaderLoop:Number = 1;
loaderLoop <= videoList.length; loaderLoop++ ) {
    vidcomp.activeVideoPlayerIndex = loaderLoop;
    vidcomp.load( "video/" + videoList[loaderLoop - 1] );
}
```

This code block imports the entire transitions class into the movie. The variables count the number of videos that have been loaded into the component, iterate the video list—videoPlayerIndex—to tell the component which video to play, and, finally, create a list of the videos—videoList—that will play in the component. The last for loop creates a list of players if it hasn't already done so and assigns the video from our list to the requested active player in the component's list of players.

5. Press Enter/Return twice and enter the following functions and listener:

```
function eready(e:Object):Void {
   ++videoLoadedCount;
      if ( videoLoadedCount == videoList.length ) {
      for (var playerLoop:Number = 1; playerLoop ➥
<= videoList.length; playerLoop++ ) {
         e.target.activeVideoPlayerIndex = playerLoop;
         e.target.play();
         }

         e.target.visibleVideoPlayerIndex = videoPlayerIndex;
   }
}


vidcomp.addEventListener("ready", eready);

function ecomplete(e:Object):Void {
      for (var playerLoop:Number = 1; playerLoop <= ➥
videoList.length; playerLoop++ ) {
         e.target.activeVideoPlayerIndex = playerLoop;
         e.target.play();
   }
}
vidcomp.addEventListener("complete", ecomplete);
```

The first function—eready—checks to see if each player actually has a video loaded into it, and the second one—ecomplete—starts the video playing and then rewinds and restarts the video when it finishes. With the videos loaded and playing in six players, we can now use the Fly transition to navigate between the videos.

6. Press Enter/Return twice and enter the following functions:

```
function transDone(e) {
   vidcomp.visibleVideoPlayerIndex = e.target.content._name;
   trace(e.target.content._name);
}

function buttonTransition(m:MovieClip) {
      if (videoPlayerIndex != m.visibleVideoPlayerIndex) {
      var other:MovieClip = m.getVideoPlayer(videoPlayerIndex);
      m.bringVideoPlayerToFront(videoPlayerIndex);
      var vp:MovieClip = other;
      TransitionManager.start(vp,{type:mx.transitions.Fly, ➥
      direction:Transition.IN,
      duration:4,
        easing:mx.transitions.easing.None.easeNone,
        startPoint:4});
```

```
vp.__transitionManager.addEventListener
("allTransitionsInDone",transDone);
 }
}
```

The purpose of the first function—`transDone`—is to identify which player is the next one to be played once the transition has been completed. As we said earlier, though this whole thing can be random, we are using the buttons to move through the players in a linear order. All of the code, to this point, has created a stack of players. And each is playing a separate FLV. We need to identify which players in the stack will have the transition applied to them. That means if the video is playing in Player 3, then the transition will occur either between 3 and 4 or between 3 and 2.

The second function deals with what happens—which transition and how it is applied—when a button is clicked. The first line identifies the target player that will be transitioned to, and the next line brings it to the top of the stack. The third line attaches a reference to `vp`, and any changes applied to this player will be applied to the requested player in the stack.

The change is the transition and the `TransitionManager,start();` make the effect occur. It only requires two parameters: the *content* to which the transition is applied—`vp`—and the transition effect class to be applied that includes the parameters for that transition class.

The parameters specify that the direction of the transition is to be `IN` and its duration is 4 seconds. There is no easing in or easing out when the transition occurs, and the `startPoint` of the transition is the center point of `vp`.

The final line listens for the end of the transition and fires the `transDone` function.

Now that you have put the transition in place, all you need to do now is code the buttons to switch between movies in the stack and to add the listeners that tell the buttons what to listen for.

7. Press Enter/Return twice and add the following code:

```
var buttonListener:Object = new Object();
buttonListener.click = function( eventobj:Object ) {
    f( eventobj.target == previousVideo ) {
    --videoPlayerIndex;
    if( videoPlayerIndex < 1 ) {
      videoPlayerIndex = videoList.length;
    }
  } else {
    ++videoPlayerIndex;
    if( videoPlayerIndex > videoList.length ) {
      videoPlayerIndex = 1;
    }
  }
```

```
    buttonTransition( _root.vidcomp );
}

previousVideo.addEventListener( "click", buttonListener );
nextVideo.addEventListener( "click", buttonListener );
```

8. Save and test the movie (see Figure 9-15). Notice how, when you click a button, the next video in the stack slides into place. If you press the back button, you will see that the previous video is still playing. It is a lot like TV and channel surfing. If you want to stop and rewind the video, simply place the cursor over the video to reveal the skin.

Figure 9-15. One video slides over the other thanks to the Fly transition.

A video menu

We finish this chapter with a rather interesting, and somewhat advanced, exercise that adds the FLV loops to a drop-down menu. Rather than end the chapter with a rather long and involved exercise, let's dissect the project instead.

In the Chapter 10 Completed folder is another folder named VideoMenu. Open that folder and double-click the Video Menu.fla to open Flash. When the file opens, open the library and the Video Menu Assets folder in the library.

As you can see, this movie is somewhat similar to the one created in the "Roll Your Own Components" exercise from earlier in this chapter. The major difference is that odd icon in the library, as shown in Figure 9-16, for VideoMenu. In actual fact, that icon indicates that it is a ComboBox component. You can check this by right-clicking (Windows) or Control-clicking (Mac) the component and selecting Component Definition. When the Component Definition dialog box opens, click the component icon and you will see that it is, indeed, a ComboBox component.

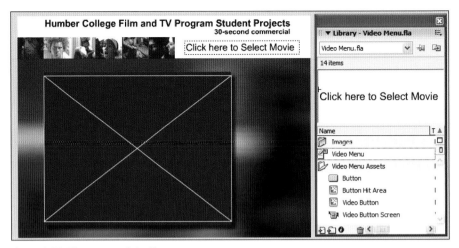

Figure 9-16. The stage and the library

This component will act very much like a pop-down menu, but it will have a major difference: when you play the movie and select the menu, the video titles pop down but, beside each name, a small loop of the video plays as well. You can see how this is constructed by opening the `Video Button` movie clip in the `Video Menu Assets` folder. The button is nothing more than a video object and a dynamic text box named `._textDisplay`. The choice of a dynamic text box is important. This way, we don't have to add the names of the videos to the list in the component. These names will be added at runtime. If you do click on the component on the stage and open the Parameters tab in the Property Inspector, you will see that the list has a name, `movieList`, but the actual `Value` list is blank (see Figure 9-17). If you open the AS in the Actions layer, you will see the list of values is constructed in line 1 of the code. This should tell that you can either enter these values programmatically or through the component parameters.

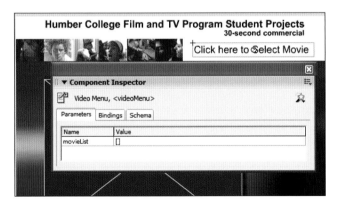

Figure 9-17. The values for movieList will be added to the component when the movie plays.

To understand how the menu is constructed, double-click the VideoMenu component on the stage to open the Symbol Editor. You will notice it is composed of text in a dynamic text box with the instance name of ._selectedMovie. Now open the Video Menu Assets folder library and you can see how the menu is put together.

The Button component consists of nothing more than a hit area. Obviously, each strip in the pop-down menu will be a copy of the VideoButton movie clip and the Button component will be how the video loops and the video names are added to the component.

Each strip in the pop-down menu will consist of two elements. The first will be one of the small looping movies, and the second will be a text area containing the name of the movie. This text area will be used as the button.

Tying all of that together is the job of the three AS files in the com folder.

If you open that folder, you will see two more folders. One is named video and the other is named control. The video folder contains two AS files, named VideoButton.as and VideoMenu.as. The Button.as file in the com folder will be used as a hot spot in the menu, which will be used to send data to the various listeners in the AS files and the main Flash file.

If you look at the code in the Actions layer, you can see how the whole process starts. The last two lines

```
videoMenu.movieList = videoList;
videoMenu.addListener( ourListener );
```

assign the list of videos for the videoMenu and listen for the user to click one of the items in the menu. This is where the relationship between the VideoButton.as and VideoMenu.as files comes into play. With the component on the stage, the code driving VideoMenu.as file is already being called by the SWF.

If you open the VideoMenu.as file, your first reaction may be, "Wow, this is complicated." Actually there is nothing here that you haven't done somewhere in this book. So let's follow the code to see how this whole thing works.

The code starts off with a number of variables that will be used to construct the menu or manage data that is used in the code.

The first function

```
public function VideoMenu() {
  movieList = new Array();
  ourBroadcaster = new Object();

  AsBroadcaster.initialize(ourBroadcaster);
  __menuButton = this.attachMovie ➡
  ( "Button", "__menuButton", 200 );
  __menuButton._width = __selectedMovie._width;
  __menuButton._height = __selectedMovie._height;
  __menuButton.message = "processMenu";
  __menuButton.addListener(this);
}
```

starts by creating an empty array in case we didn't assign any values earlier. The next two lines create a broadcaster that will send data back to our user, who will assign a listener to our component. We then create the button over the text field; this button, if clicked, executes the `processMenu()` function.

This function is the key to the whole exercise:

```
public function processMenu( theData:String ) {
  if( __menuExtended ) {
      for( var iterator:Number=0; iterator < ➥
  __movieList.length; iterator++ ) {
          this["vbutton" + iterator].removeMovieClip();
      }
      __menuFrame.removeMovieClip();

      __menuExtended = false;
```

The first statement checks to see if the menu is extended; if it is, it should clear out the data in the menu and close it. The next one actually draws the menu if the menu is not active or in its closed state.

```
  } else {

      var menuFrameStart:Number = this._height;
      __menuFrame = this.createEmptyMovieClip ➥
      ( "menuFrame", this.getNextHighestDepth() );
      __menuFrame._y = this._height;
      __menuFrame.beginFill( 0xffffff, 50 );
      __menuFrame.moveTo( 0, 0 );
      __menuFrame.lineTo( 200, 0 );
      __menuFrame.lineTo( 200, __movieList.length * 35 );
      __menuFrame.lineTo( 0, __movieList.length * 35 );
      __menuFrame.lineTo( 0, 0 );

      __menuFrame.filters = [new flash.filters. ➥
DropShadowFilter( 6, 45, 0, 65, 6, 6 )];
```

Now that the menu has been drawn, we can create each menu item and decide how the video buttons will react to a rollover and a click.

The first line

```
for( var iterator:Number=0; iterator\ ➥
  < __movieList.length; iterator++ ) {
```

determines how many items are to be displayed in the menu. The next line

```
var vbtn:MovieClip = this.attachMovie( "Video Button", ➥
  "vbutton" + iterator, this.getNextHighestDepth(), ➥
  {_x:0, _y:(35 * iterator) + menuFrameStart });
```

creates the button movie clip. The important method here is attachMovie(). It contains a call to the Video Button.as file. This file simply adds the short loops to the menu and also listens for clicks and rollovers. Once that is done, the rest of the code in the function

```
vbtn.setOurMovie( __movieList[iterator] );
  vbtn.addListener( this );
  }

  __menuExtended = true;
  }
}
```

creates the items in the component and extends the menu (see Figure 9-18).

Figure 9-18.
The menu is extended.

Now that you have a menu that is open, you need to select items on the menu. Once a selection is made (see Figure 9-19), you want the menu to close. That is the purpose of this function in VideoMenu.as:

```
public function selectMovie( theMovie:String ):Void {
processMenu();
  var movieIndex:Number = -1;
  for( var iterator:Number=0; iterator ➡
  < __movieList.length; iterator++ ) {
    if( theMovie == __movieList[iterator] ) {
      movieIndex = iterator;
      break;
    }
  }

  if( movieIndex != __selectedIndex ) {
    __selectedIndex = movieIndex;
    __selectedMovie.text = theMovie;
    ourBroadcaster.broadcastMessage( "change", theMovie );
  }
}
```

Figure 9-19. The menu allows you to pick a video from a looping preview.

Summary

As you may have noticed, there are a lot of ways to play multiple movies. They range from the simple, such as a series of buttons, to the quite complex, which is where we finished the chapter. We aren't going to claim this chapter is all you need to know, but it did give you a rather extensive overview of some of the more common techniques available to you.

We also introduced you to the transitions class, which is really handy to know if you want to add jazz to how Flash moves between videos. We also showed you how small looping videos can add some pizzazz to your work.

In the next chapter we don't deal with FLV files. We are going to show you how to add a feed from a web camera to a movie. From there, we answer the question, "What else can I do with it?" Turn the page to find out.

10 THE CAMERA OBJECT AND FLASH VIDEO

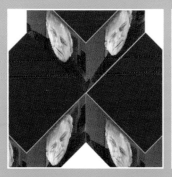

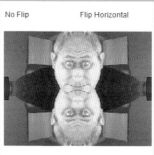

No Flip   Flip Horizontal

One of the authors is fond of telling anybody who will listen, "You know, the amount of fun you can have in this business should be illegal." When it comes to connecting a web camera to your computer and seeing what you can do in Flash, that statement takes on even more importance. It is both easy and fun to connect a webcam to a Flash movie. The only problem is once you do it, you will discover the creative possibilities are unlimited and you are facing a life sentence.

How easy is it? A webcam and two lines of ActionScript get you into the game. Really!

In this chapter we will start slowly with simply connecting a webcam to a Flash movie. After that, we kick out the jams and explore some of the more interesting things you can do with a webcam. Download the Chapter 10 Exercise file and let's have some fun with a webcam.

Flash and the camera object

The first thing to understand about using the camera object is that its primary purpose is to broadcast a video feed from your camera through the Flash Media Server 2 to a SWF in a web page. This means that if you have a Flash Media Server account with your ISP you can wave at Aunt Millie in Manchester, England, from your computer and, if she has a webcam, you can see her wave back at you. Though that is the primary purpose, you can also allow users with webcams who only use HTTP to stream video to see themselves and even put themselves into some rather interesting circumstances you devise.

The other aspect of using a webcam with the Flash Player is that any SWF that tries to access a camera will kick out a Privacy Settings dialog box that lets the user choose whether to allow or deny access to the camera. This dialog box also lets you choose the camera to be used. More about that in a minute. Finally, though you can connect a number of cameras to your computer, the camera object will only let you display them one at a time.

Connect your webcam to your computer and let's start looking at different ways of using a webcam.

1. Open a new Flash document. Open the library and create a video object. Drag the video object to the stage from the library.

2. Click once on the video object and give it the instance name of myVid. Also set its size to 320 pixels wide by 240 pixels high.

3. Add an Actions layer to the main timeline, open the ActionScript Editor, and enter the following two lines of code in the script pane:

```
var myCamera:Camera = Camera.get();
myVid.attachVideo (myCamera);
```

The first line retrieves the camera object using the `Camera.get()` method and gives the camera a name by assigning it to myCamera. (You can find out more about the Camera class by using Flash help.) The second line simply attaches the feed from the

240

camera to the video object on the stage as shown in Figure 10-1. That is all you need to get in the game. Go ahead; test the movie.

> *Though you are using a video object that is 320 by 240 to play the video feed, you can use any size you wish. Just be aware that every time the camera is detected, the Privacy Settings dialog box will appear over the SWF. This means if you have a video object on a stage that is 160 by 120, your user is going to have a real problem because the Privacy Settings dialog box will be larger than the stage. If you do use a webcam, the minimum stage size is 215 by 138 pixels, which is the minimum size required by Flash to display the dialog box.*

Figure 10-1. Hello World

You may have noticed the empty parameter in the `Camera.get()` method. That directs Flash to use the first camera it finds that is connected to your computer. If you had three cameras, they would have index values of 1, 2, and 3. If you wanted to use the second camera the method would be

```
Camera.get(2);
```

If you haven't been able to get your camera to connect to the video object, all is not lost. Sometimes multiple camera drivers are installed and Flash may have picked the wrong one. To choose the proper driver, test the movie again and follow these steps:

1. Right-click (Windows) or Control-click (Mac) on the SWF to open the context menu. Choose Settings. The Macromedia Flash Player Settings dialog box will open.

2. Along the bottom are four icons. The last two look like a microphone and a camera. Click the camera icon.

3. This is the area where you can choose your camera. Just click on the pop-down list and, when you find your camera (see Figure 10-2), select it and click the Close button.

Figure 10-2. Choose your camera through
the SWF Settings dialog box.

If you are a Mac user and connect an Apple iSight camera to your computer, the camera settings may give you a bit of grief. You may see your iSight listed as a choice. If you
choose it, the image quality will be absolutely terrible. Instead, choose the generic
FireWire camera—IIDC FireWire Video—shown in Figure 10-2.

A video box

In Chapter 8 you created a video wall. In this exercise you will create a video box.

1. Open a new Flash movie and create a new movie clip named Vid. Add a video
   object to the library and drag that object to the stage. In the Property Inspector, set
   the instance name of the video object to myVid, set the dimensions of the video
   object to 240 wide by 180 high, and set its X and Y coordinates to 0,0.

2. Add a new layer to the movie clip timeline and name it Actions. Select the first
   frame in the Actions layer, open the ActionScript Editor, and enter these two lines
   of code:

```
var myCam: Camera = Camera.get();
myVid.attachVideo (myCam);
```

3. Close the ActionScript Editor and click the Scene 1 link to return to the main timeline.

4. Drag two copies of the Vid movie clip to the stage and place them beside each
   other. Select both clips, open the Transform panel by selecting Window ➤
   Transform, and set the width to 130.0%. Before you do the scale, make sure the
   Constrain check box is deselected.

5. Select the movie clip on the left and, using the Transform panel, set its vertical
   skew to 45%. Do the same thing with the movie clip on the right but set its skew
   value to -45. Align the edges of the movie clips as shown in Figure 10-3.

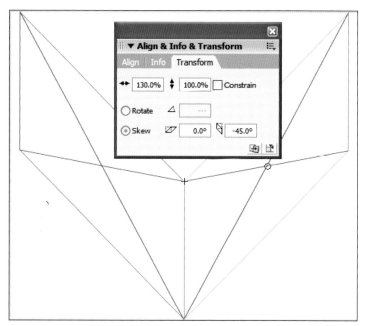

Figure 10-3. Use the Transform panel to scale and skew by the numbers.

6. Lock Layer 1 and add a new layer named Top. Draw a rectangle in this layer and fill it with a color of your choosing. Select the Free Transform tool and manipulate the rectangle to fit on top of the two movie clips. When you finish, it should look like a box. Unlock the layers.

7. Select Edit ➤ Select All and convert the selection to a movie clip named box.

8. Using the Free Transform tool, scale the box to about half the size of the height of the stage. Move the box to the lower-left half of the stage, as shown in Figure 10-4.

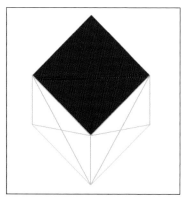

Figure 10-4. The first box is in position.

243

9. Alt+Shift-click (Windows) or Option+Shift-click (Mac) once on the box, drag a copy of the movie clip to the right, and align it with the right edge of the other movie clip. Make another copy and this time drag the copy to the top of the two boxes on the stage.

10. Save and test the movie. You are boxed in, as shown in Figure 10-5.

If you really want to have some fun with this, put a bunch of the movie clip boxes on the stage and, using the `startDrag()` *and* `stopDrag()` *methods, let the user stack the blocks.*

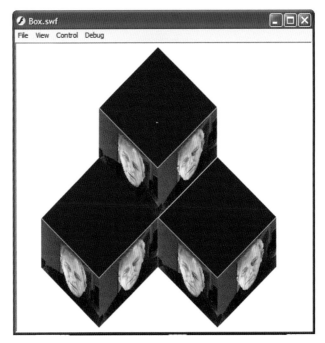

Figure 10-5. Boxed in

Flipping video

As you discovered in the previous exercise, you don't always need to have the video on a flat plane. In this section you keep the video on that plane but the end result is a sort of kaleidoscopic effect. This is accomplished by simply "flipping" the movie clips containing the video object.

One of the authors has been teaching this and the previous technique under the category of "Stupid Web Camera Tricks" to his students for a couple of years. When doing the research for this book he noticed that Hoss Gifford in the friendsofED book Flash MX Video *also presents these techniques. Regardless of who was first, Hoss, if you are reading this, this one's for you.*

1. Open the Flip.fla file in your Chapter 10 Exercise folder. Everything is wired up and ready to go with this exercise. All you need to do is to flip the videos.

2. Select the movie clip under Flip Horizontal and select Modify ➤ Transform ➤ Flip Horizontal (see Figure 10-6). You will know the movie clip has flipped because its registration point will move to the upper-right corner from the upper-left corner of the movie clip.

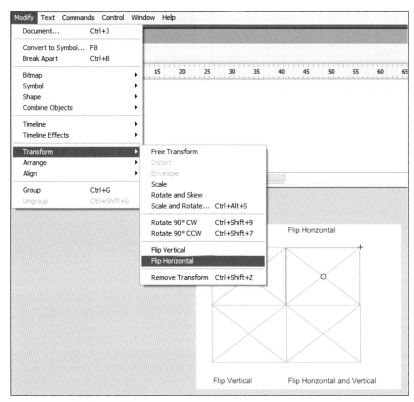

Figure 10-6. A horizontal flip

3. Select the movie clip over Flip Vertical and apply a vertical flip transform to the selection.

4. Select the last clip and flip it vertically and then flip it horizontally.

5. Save and test the movie. As you move around, you start to look a bit "odd," as shown in Figure 10-7.

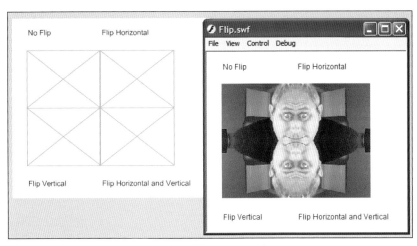

Figure 10-7. Why should carnival fun houses have all the fun?

Playing "Blade Runner" in Times Square

A couple of years ago one of the authors was in New York attending the East Coast version of FlashForward. As he was wandering around the vendor displays, he happened to see an orange booklet— *Web Video with Macromedia Flash*—put out by Macromedia. He stuck a copy of the booklet in his pocket and, when he had a couple of minutes to spare, he pulled the booklet out of his pocket and started flipping through it. What really caught his attention was the page with the interesting title of "No faking it." In particular, this passage came flying off the page and into his "creative cortex:"

Using Flash it's possible to toss videos around 3D space like a leaf blowing in the wind. Resist the urge. Nothing turns viewers off more than pointless cool effects. That's not to say there aren't great ways to make use of the advanced technology of Flash. Take a picture of Times Square and composite your video over the Sony JumboTron...

Having wandered through Times Square the previous afternoon, it suddenly hit the author, "Why not?" In fact, why not go them one better and create a sort of "Blade Runner" effect using the screens and billboards in Times Square? He rummaged through his photos from the previous day and settled on the one shown in Figure 10-8. Let's see if we can't get you on the billboards in Times Square as well.

Figure 10-8. Screens galore on Times Square

Open the `TimeSquare.jpg` image in your Chapter 10 Exercise folder and let's take a minute or two to plan out our approach to this exercise.

When you first look at the image, a couple of issues immediately arise:

- The areas for the camera object are not perfectly square. There is some perspective involved.
- There are objects such as street lamps and so on in front of the areas. In order to maintain the "realism," you can't simply remove them. You have to work around them.

This means you have to

- Make the camera and video objects fit the area through the use of Flash's Free Transform tool.
- Keep the objects in front of the videos in place by masking the video or camera object.
- Create the masks in Adobe Illustrator CS2 or a similar application such as Fireworks, because Flash is not an industrial-strength imaging application.
- Place the masks in Flash as graphic symbols.
- Place the masks and the camera objects into separate movie clips where you can apply the mask.

Now that we know what needs to be done, let's go to work.

> If you don't have Illustrator CS2, don't worry; you can find each of the masks created in this exercise in the Illustrator Masks folder in the library for the `TimeSquare.fla` file used later in this exercise.

> The final file we will be producing will result in a rather hefty SWF file. The implication of that is a rather "lengthy" download for people with speedy connections. This project, therefore, is best played back from your desktop.

1. Open Illustrator CS2 and create a new document. When the new document appears, locate the image named `TimeSquare.jpg` in the Chapter 10 Exercise folder and drag it from the folder on to the Illustrator page. When you release the mouse, the image will drop into its own layer in Illustrator.

2. Select the magnifying glass and zoom in on the green sign on the left of the image. As you can see in Figure 10-9, there are some features that will have to be accommodated. There is a light pole going across the top of the image and a traffic signal in the bottom-left corner.

Figure 10-9.The light pole and the traffic signal will have to be accommodated in the mask.

3. Select the Pen tool and click on each point of the area where a line changes direction.

4. When the shape is completed, turn off the stroke around your shape. Then select the Direct Selection tool, click and drag the points, and manipulate the handles until you have the area covered. When you finish, your shape should resemble that shown in Figure 10-10.

Figure 10-10. The Mask shape to be used in Flash

5. At this stage you can either choose to create a layer in Illustrator for each shape or just continue building them until you have the masks in place. Create the remaining masks and save the file as an Illustrator file. When finished, your image should resemble the one shown in Figure 10-11. Don't quit Illustrator; you are about to discover how easy it is to add Illustrator objects to Flash.

Life is not a series of straight lines. Things tend to shift their shape, due to perspective, as they recede into the distance. Simply adding the video to a sign and then expecting the viewer to believe it belongs there is a bit optimistic. It will look totally out of place. Also, there are obstructions in front of each video's final location. It would look odd to have the video sitting in front of them. The masks created in Illustrator are the key. They match the lines of the area where the video will be placed. All you have to do is create the camera objects and distort them to follow the lines of the mask.

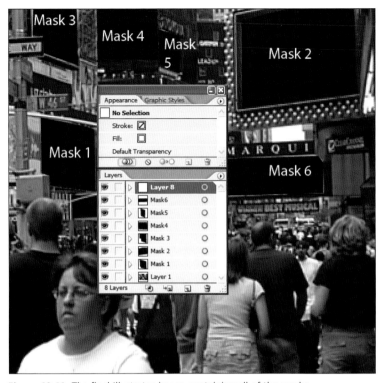

Figure 10-11. The final Illustrator image containing all of the masks

We will only be describing how to create the video that will go into Mask 1. The remaining screens follow the same technique.

6. Open the `TimeSquare.fla` file in your Chapter 10 Exercise folder. When the file opens, create a new layer named Vids.

7. Create a new movie clip named Mask 1. This is where the relationship between Illustrator and Flash gets really cool. When the Symbol Editor opens, return to your Illustrator document and click and drag a copy of `Mask 1` from the Illustrator document into the Flash Symbol Editor. When you release the mouse, the mask will drop onto the Flash stage. Use the Property Inspector to set the location of the Mask 1 object to 0,0.

8. Create a new video object in the Flash library. When you see the object in the library, create a new layer named Video and drag the new layer under the mask shape layer.

9. With the Video layer selected, drag a copy of the video object from the library to the stage. Use the Property Inspector to set its location to 0,0 and give it the instance name of myVid. Now select the Free Transform tool. You will put the video into "perspective" using the sides of the mask. Click on the video object and reduce its size to a close approximation of the mask.

10. Select the magnifying glass and zoom in on the mask and the video object. Reselect the Free Transform tool and change the shape of the video object to roughly follow the edges of the mask as shown in Figure 10-12. Keep in mind what we told you about this in Chapter 7. You only need to be close because the eye will add the distortion.

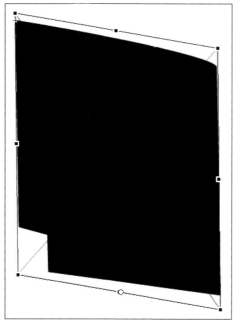

Figure 10-12. "Close" only counts in video masking and the game of horse shoe throwing.

11. Select the layer containing the mask. Right-click (Windows) or Control-click (Mac) on the layer name. Select Mask from the pop-down menu. The video object now takes on the shape of the mask.

12. Add a new layer named Actions. Open the ActionScript Editor and enter the following code in the script pane:

```
var myCam: Camera = Camera. get();
myVid.attachVideo (myCam);
```

13. Close the ActionScript Editor and click the Scene 1 link to return to the main timeline.

14. Add a new layer named Video1 and drag a copy of the Mask 1 movie clip from the library on to the stage. Then place it in its correct position over the image. Go ahead and test the file. Now you, too, can have a billboard (see Figure 10-13) in Times Square.

Figure 10-13. "Live. From Times Square in New York. It is...me!"

From here on, it is nothing more than creating the masks and putting them in place using the objects from Illustrator. One of the things we do, though, is to give each video object a unique name in order to avoid confusion.

Another little trick is to simply get the video and the mask sized up against each other in the movie clip. Then you drag the movie clip from the library into the video layer and move it into position. This way, you have the black shape to help guide you in lining up the object where it is supposed to go. Then you simply double-click on the movie clip to open the Symbol Editor and then apply the mask and add the code.

Keep in mind that those users without webcams will not see the image. The camera objects are transparent until a webcam is detected, meaning nothing will appear in the masked area of the image unless a camera is attached to the computer and Flash detects the camera.

The completed file, shown in Figure 10-14, can be found in the Chapter 10 Complete folder. It is named `TimesSquare.fla`. We have also included the Illustrator file in Illustrator CS2 format.

Figure 10-14. The completed file

Put your user into the action

Like many of the great Flash artists out there, we are huge movie fans. Whereas most people are content to watch a movie, we tend to play close attention to the title sequences because they are a great source of motion graphics ideas.

One of our favorite sequences is for the film *Altered States*. What really caught our attention was the movie's title sequence (created by Richard Greenberg of R/Greenberg Associates). As the movie starts, William Hurt rises in the tank and the camera comes in tight on his head through the window of the tank. The movie title then moves across the screen in a rather disorienting manner. The title moves across the screen, but it is very difficult to make out the letters as they overlap and create rather abstract shapes. Eventually they get smaller and the title gradually becomes both readable and legible.

One of the neat features of the title is the letter A. The right arm of the letter is missing and the letter beside it is used to fill the space. This exercise creates a similar title, only we are going to use the words *FLASH VIDEO* and put the user into the action.

One of the great maxims of this business is, "Use the right tool, at the right time, for the right job." In this case we are going to create the lettering in Illustrator and do the motion graphics in Flash. Let's go to work.

Creating the title in Illustrator

Flash 8 and Illustrator CS2 are an ideal pair when it comes to the creation of vector-based art for Flash. Illustrator objects can be dragged and dropped or copied and pasted right onto the Flash stage. If that doesn't appeal to you, you can easily import Illustrator files into the Flash library.

1. Open Illustrator, and when the New Document dialog box opens, name the file Flash Video, set the units to pixels, the height and width to 320 by 240—the size of the Flash stage we will be using—and the Color Mode to RGB. Click OK.

2. Select the text tool, click once on the page, and enter the words FLASH VIDEO using all uppercase letters. Select the text and, in the Object panel, set the size to 48 points and the font to a bold Avant Garde or Arial. We used ITC Avant Garde Gothic Demi. as shown in Figure 10-15.

Figure 10-15. The text is formatted in Illustrator.

3. The word VIDEO is a bit spread out and could use some tightening. Select the word and click once on the Character link in the Object toolbar to open the Character Settings dialog box. Set the tracking value to about –20 and press Enter/Return. Tracking reduces the space between letters in a word.

4. Add a new layer from the Layer panel's pop-down menu. Name this layer A.

With the housekeeping out of the way, we can now "break" the letter A in the word FLASH. Removing the right stroke of the letter A is actually a bit complicated and involves converting text to an outline and playing with various masks and objects. There has to be a quicker way! There is: draw the shape. Here's how:

5. Select the Selection tool and click once on the text block. Now select Type ➤ Create Outlines. This will convert each letter of the text to a PostScript shape. By doing this you can treat the text as a graphic in Flash. This means the user doesn't need the font to view the movie, nor does the developer have to embed the font into the SWF. Select View ➤ Outline. You need the Outline view because as you draw, a fill will be added, which will make it very difficult for you to see the lines you will need to use.

> This works well for a couple of words, but don't use this technique on entire paragraphs of text.

6. Click once on the A layer. Select the magnifying glass and zoom in on the letter A. Select the Pen tool and draw the shape shown in Figure 10-16 over the letter.

7. Hide the A layer by clicking the eyeball in the layer. Select the Direct Selection tool (the hollow arrow) and click once on the A in the word FLASH. Delete the letter and turn on the visibility of the A layer. Select Window ➤ Preview and you have a broken A. Move the S and the H closer to the broken A, select the word VIDEO, and press the left arrow key a couple of times to move it closer to the word FLASH.

8. Click once on the broken A, copy it to the Clipboard, and paste it into the bottom layer. Keep it selected, and using the mouse and arrow keys, move it into position (see Figure 10-16). When you have finished, delete the A layer. You are now ready to work in Flash.

Figure 10-16. Ready to go to Flash

Creating the title sequence

We do a lot of classes and seminars on the integration of the Flash with other applications. There is always an inevitable "Holy smokes!" moment when we demonstrate how to bring Illustrator objects into Flash. The official way involves saving and importing and getting the file formats correct. Here's the unofficial way.

With Illustrator still open, open Flash and create a new document that has a stage size of 320 by 240. Now select the words in Illustrator and drag them onto the Flash stage.

With the words created and in Flash, you can now turn your attention to creating the title sequence.

The visitor, peering through their webcam, will be moved right into the action. The words will move slowly across the screen a couple of times and then slowly recede to reveal the title. This tells you a few things:

- The whole sequence should only require one frame on the main timeline. This means it should be a movie clip.
- You need to create a camera object to "hold" the video stream.
- The words must move over the video image but shouldn't hide the image. The words, therefore, must be converted to symbols

Let's get started:

1. Right-click/Control-click the word FLASH and select Convert to Symbol. Name the symbol Flash and select Graphic as the behavior. Click OK. Repeat this for the word VIDEO. Select both words on the stage and delete them.

2. Open the library and create a new video object.

3. Click on the library pop-down and select New Symbol to open the New Symbol dialog box. Alternatively, press Ctrl+F8 (Windows) or Cmd+F8 (Mac). Name the new symbol FlashVideo and select Movie Clip as its property. Click OK to close the dialog box.

With the assets in place we can begin to assemble the animation. This will require getting the video on the stage and "wiring it up" to a camera. Each of the words will be put in motion across the screen and the animation will need to loop.

4. Open the FlashVideo movie clip, if it isn't already open, and add three layers to the movie clip's timeline. Name the layers as follows, from the top down:
   - Action
   - Video
   - Flash
   - Vid

5. Select the first frame of the Vid layer and drag a copy of the Embedded Video symbol from the library onto the stage. Click once on the video symbol on the stage and set the following properties in the Property Inspector:

- Width: 320
- Height: 240
- X: 0
- Y: 0
- Instance Name: myVid

6. Click once in frame one of the Vid layer and press the F9 key (or Option+F9 if you are using a Mac) to open the ActionScript Editor. Enter the following line of code:

```
myVid.attachVideo(Camera.get());
```

This code should be familiar. It is essentially the same line used elsewhere in this chapter. The difference is that instead of creating an explicit camera object to store the results of our `Camera.get()` method, you are passing a camera object, using the `Camera.get()` method, directly into the parameter of the `attachVideo()` method. Essentially the line says, "Use myVid to play any video from the first camera that is found." Close the ActionScript Editor.

We are firm believers in the New Media axiom: "Trust nothing and trust no one. Especially yourself." At this stage of the process it might not be a bad idea to save the movie, drag the movie clip onto the stage in the main timeline, connect your camera to the computer, and select Control ➤ Test Movie. If you appear in the video instance (see Figure 10-17), everything is working as it should and life is wonderful.

Figure 10-17. It works.

Pulling it together

The first hurdle—does the video stream?—has been overcome. The time has come to add a little "disorientation" to the experience.

Before we start it would make sense to map out what we intend to do. The words are going to slide across the screen in a horizontal direction and move forward and backward.

The video image is going to be under the words but will still be able to be seen through the words. At the end of the sequence the words will turn white and recede to form the title. After a short time the whole animation starts over again.

This can only be done with symbols. In Flash all symbols have properties that can be manipulated. In our case the properties being manipulated are opacity (Alpha), size, movement (Motion Tween), and color (Tint).

1. Open the `FlashVideo` movie clip and select frame 200 of the Vid layer. Right-click/Control-click on frame 200 and select Insert frame from the context menu. Lock the Vid layer.

2. Select the first frame in the Flash layer and drag an instance of the Flash graphic symbol from the library onto the stage. Select Modify ➤ Transform ➤ Scale and Rotate, and set the scale value to 450%. Click OK. Drag the word FLASH and place the edge of the H against the left edge of the video instance. Set the Y value for this instance to 77 in the Property Inspector.

3. Select the first frame of the Video layer and drag a copy of the Video graphic symbol from the library onto the stage. Give it the same scale and Y value as the word FLASH. Place the edge of the first S against the right edge of the video instance. Your stage should resemble the one in Figure 10-18.

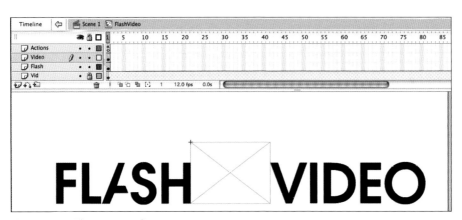

Figure 10-18. The stage... so far

Movie clips have a stage size that is always appears larger than that used in the main timeline. If you can't tell what the final stage size is going to be, how can you exercise the precision required of this project? The answer is: the video instance. The final file is going to have a stage size that precisely matches the size of the video instance. In this manner, we can accurately animate and manipulate the words because the video will be standing in for the stage. This also explains why the Vid layer was locked in the first step of this section.

Another good way of figuring out where items in a movie clip will appear on the main stage is to place the movie clip on the timeline and then double-click the movie clip on the stage. This will open the movie clip on the stage and still allow you to see other objects on the stage and how they interact with the content in the movie clip.

4. Click on the word FLASH on the stage. Click on the color pop-up on the Property Inspector and select Alpha. Move the Alpha slider to a value of 50%. Repeat this with the word VIDEO. You have just set the opacity of the words to 50%.

5. Right-click/Control-click on frame 60 of the Flash layer and select Insert keyframe from the context menu. Do this for frame 60 in the Video layer as well.

6. Select the word FLASH and, using the right arrow key, move the word until the H is partially outside the right edge of the video. Select the word VIDEO in frame 60 and, using the left arrow key, move the word until the O is partially outside the left edge of the video. Finally, Right-click/Control-click anywhere between the two key frames in the Flash layer and select Create motion tween from the pop-down menu. An arrow will appear between the two key frames. Add a motion tween to the Video layer.

The reason we chose 60 frames as the length for the first sequence is time. The movie plays at about 12 fps, the Flash default, and we wanted this sequence to last about 5 seconds. We are also using the arrow keys to move the objects to ensure there is no vertical movement in the tween.

> *If you are really picky about smooth animations in Flash, a frame rate of between 20 and 24 fps is recommended.*

7. Add key frames in the Flash and Video layers at Frame 100. Select the word VIDEO on the stage and, using the right arrow key, move the object until the V touches the inside right edge of the video. Select the word FLASH and, using the left arrow key, move it to a point where the D and the S appear intertwined (see Figure 10-19). Add a motion tween between the new key frames in both layers.

Figure 10-19. The second tween

8. Add key frames in the Flash and Video layers at frame 140. Select the word VIDEO on the stage and, using the right arrow key, move the object until the V touches the inside right edge of the video. Select the word FLASH and, using the left arrow key, move it to a point where the A is just outside the left edge of the video. Add a motion tween between the new key frame's in both layers. The next tween finishes the sequence. The words are going to shrink and change color.

9. Add a key frame at frame 200 of the Flash and Video layers. With the playback head over frame 200, select the word FLASH on the stage and add the following properties:

   ▪ Tint: 255 255 255

   ▪ Tint Amount: 96%

   Repeat this with the word VIDEO as well. Now, with the word VIDEO selected, select Modify ➤ Transform ➤ Scale and Rotate. Set the scale amount to 15%. Repeat this for the word FLASH. Add the motion tweens.

Though the animation works, the small words won't be on the screen all that long before the animation starts over. Let's add a couple of seconds at the end of the movie to give the viewer a chance to read the title.

10. Click and drag through frame 240 of all four layers. Open the context menu and select Add Frame.

The movie is complete. Now for some housekeeping.

1. We are currently working in the movie clip. We need to pull this whole thing together on the main timeline. Click the Scene 1 button to return to the main timeline.

2. Click once on the stage and click the Size button in the Property Inspector. When the Document Properties dialog box opens, set the stage size to 320 pixels wide by 240 pixels high. Set the stage color to white and click OK.

3. Drag the FlashVideo movie clip from the library and place it on the stage. Set its X and Y coordinates in the Property Inspector to 0 to ensure that it tucks up against the upper-left corner of the stage.

4. Save the movie. Connect your camera to your computer and test the movie (see Figure 10-20) by pressing Ctrl+Enter (Windows) or Cmd+Return (Mac).

Figure 10-20. The movie clip is on the stage.

259

Call out the "bucket brigade"

In the days before fire departments had fire trucks or other pumping apparatus, if there was a fire, a line of men would form from a water source to the fire and they would pass buckets of water up the line to throw on the fire. These firefighters were known as a "bucket brigade." In this example, we are going to use Flash to create the bucket brigade.

The exercise is rather simple. You are going to create a movie that uses a webcam but with a difference. Whenever you move it will look like your movement is happening in slow motion. Flash will create a series of 10 bitmaps that will be laid over the image from the webcam. These images will be somewhat opaque and will be placed over the image, beginning with the first instant that the camera starts feeding a signal into the video object on the stage.

So where does the "bucket brigade" come in? The images will essentially be passed up the "line," and when an image is finished, instead of passing the image back down the line, the image is thrown out or, to stay with the analogy, destroyed by throwing it on the fire. These images will appear and disappear so quickly that they will give the illusion of a slow-motion image that has a "trail."

Let's get started.

1. Open Flash and create a new document that has a stage dimension of 240 by 160. Add a new video object named `Main Video` to the library. Drag the video object from the library to the stage and give it the instance name of `mainVideo`. It is important that the position of the video object be exact on the stage. If it isn't, the whole effect will be lost. For this exercise, use the Property Inspector to position the X and Y at 40 and 20.

2. Rename layer 1 to Video. Add a new layer named Actions and open the ActionScript Editor. Click once in the script pane and add the following code:

```
import flash.display.BitmapData;
import flash.geom.Matrix;
import flash.geom.ColorTransform;
```

The new class here is `Matrix`. This class is part of the `flash.geom` package that contains classes for handling, as the name implies, geometry issues such as points, rectangles, and the movement of points from one place to another (we are slightly simplifying here). The `BitmapData` class allows you to create transparent bitmap images and manipulate them. You first encountered a matrix in Chapter 7 when you created a feathered mask. The `flash.geom.Matrix` class allows you to map pixels from one coordinate space to another. Though that may sound like a rather complex explanation, it is actually quite simple if you think about a screen shot. When you take a screen shot, it sits on your computer's Clipboard. The image, sitting on the Clipboard, has coordinates determining the size of the image and the color of each pixel in the image. In this case the desktop is one coordinate space. When you place the image from the Clipboard into an application such as Word, the image moves from one coordinate space—the desktop—to another—the Word page.

3. Press Enter/Return and add the following lines of code:

```
var mainVideo:Video;
var bitMapArray:Array = new Array();
var maxImages:Number = 10;
var mainBitmap:BitmapData = new BitmapData( 160, 120 );
var bitmapMovie:MovieClip = _root.createEmptyMovieClip ➥
( "bitmapMovie", _root.getNextHighestDepth() );
bitmapMovie._x = 40;
bitmapMovie._y = 20;
var vidCamera:Camera = Camera.get();

bitmapMovie.attachBitmap( mainBitmap, _root.getNextHighestDepth() );
```

Having brought in the classes needed to make this example work, we can now declare the variables used throughout the movie. The array—`bitMapArray`—will be used to store the bitmaps used in the bucket brigade and the next variable—`maxImages`—determines how many bitmaps will be stored in that array. The next two variables—`mainBitmap` and `bitmapMovie`—build the image for the screen and the movie clip into which it will be placed.

> *Keep in mind that the use of the* `BitmapData` *class is deliberate. Creating bitmaps on the fly using ActionScript lets you create rather complex vector images without having to redraw them on every frame while the movie plays. The bottom line is smooth and efficient playback.*

We created an empty `MovieClip` to serve as an overlay to the video object on the stage. We will change the transparency (alpha) of this clip so that the time delay, which we will create between the two objects, will create the effect of slow motion. It is important that the two objects be placed exactly in the same position. That is why we added the next two lines positioning the empty clip at 40, 20. If we did not do this, the empty clip would default to position 0, 0.

The last two lines get the camera object and attach our main canvas bitmap to the `bitmapMovie` movie clip on the stage. With the housekeeping finished, you can turn your attention to building the main engine that drives the bucket brigade.

4. Press the Enter/Return key twice and enter the following function:

```
function slomotion():Void {
  if( bitMapArray.length >= maxImages ) {
    bitMapArray.shift().dispose();
  }

  var bitmap:BitmapData = new BitmapData( 160, 120 );
```

First, we check to see if we have our maximum number of bitmaps in our bucket-brigade list—if(bitMapArray.length >= maxImages). If we do, then remove the oldest image from our list and get rid of it. It's no longer of any use. In this exercise the oldest image is the first snapshot taken. Remember we are grabbing ten images from the webcam and the newest image is image 10. Once the first image is finished and thrown on the fire—dispose()—each of the images moves up one position—shift()—and a new image 10 is added to the array due to the last line in the code block.

> *An instance of the* BitmapData *object can eat up the viewer's memory quickly. Every pixel in a bitmap is stored using 4 bytes of memory (1 byte per color channel ARGB). If you create a bitmap that is 500 by 500 pixels in size, it will take up close to 1 MB of RAM. If you don't need a* BitmapData *object anymore, then it is good practice to free the memory that the bitmap is using. The* BitmapData *class has a method that enables you to do just this, which is why we use the* dispose() *method.*

5. Press Enter/Return and add the following code:

```
var alpha:ColorTransform = new ColorTransform➡
( 1, 1, 1, .30, 0, 0, 0, 0 );
bitmap.draw( mainVideo );
bitMapArray[bitMapArray.length] = bitmap;
```

The first line will instruct our draw routines below to draw at 30 percent of the current alpha level. The first four numbers of our ColorTransform object are multipliers and the last four are offsets that are added after the multipliers have been applied.

To understand how powerful the colorTransform class can be, let's look at each of the values used.

The first four numbers are the multiples for the red, green, blue, and alpha values of the pixels in the image. The remaining four numbers are offset values applied to the colors.

The multipliers can have any decimal value between 0 and 1. This means, for example, if you want to change the red color in the image to half of its intensity (the term is *saturation*), the value would be .5. A color square solely composed of red pixels with the maximum red value of 255 would see the red reduce to a medium red as all of the pixels are reduced to a value of 128.

The value used in this exercise is 1. The three ones in the code essentially tell Flash not to play with color and to leave the values at their current settings. The next value, .30, is the important change. It reduces the alpha of the image in the movie clip to 30 percent opacity.

The offset value can be misinterpreted. It has nothing to do with moving pixels from here to there. The value for the offset can be any number between -255 and 255. When you add an offset value to the parameters for the colorTransform, that number is added to the multiplier result. The bottom line is that the Hue value of the color is shifted. In the case of a red pixel, it will take on a green or blue tinge depending on the value used. The calculation is *New red value = (old red value X redMultiplier value) + redOffset value.*

The next line of the code takes the screen shot and the last line places it at the end of the line of the bucket brigade.

6. Press Enter/Return and add the following code:

```
for( var bitmapLoop:Number = 0; bitmapLoop ➥
< bitMapArray.length; bitmapLoop++ ) {
  var tBitmap:BitmapData = BitmapData(bitMapArray[bitmapLoop]);
  mainBitmap.draw( tBitmap, new Matrix(), alpha );
  }
}
```

Now, we're going to cycle through our list of images and draw them to our main canvas. The `for` loop iterates through the images in our bucket brigade. The next line pulls the indexed image in the array, and draws it in the `BitmapData` object `mainBitmap` at 30 percent opacity. Each time it cycles through the loop, it grabs the next image in the array and overlays it on top of the previous image in our `mainBitmap`. Because we will only have a maximum of 10 images stored, the loop will only execute a maximum of 10 times.

This explains how the effect works. At any one time there are 10 images on the screen stacked above the feed from the video camera. The opacity of these 10 images creates what appears to be a trail. When the image at the bottom is finished, the new image is placed at the top of the stack and the old one is forgotten.

We finish the exercise by showing you how to detect a camera and utilize a couple of features of the camera class.

7. Press Enter/Return and add the following code:

```
if( vidCamera != null ) {
  vidCamera.setMode( 160, 120, vidCamera.fps );
  mainVideo.attachVideo(vidCamera);
  var ourIntervalID = setInterval( slomotion, 100 );
}
```

The first line checks to see if a camera is attached. When a camera is attached to a Flash movie, the value is not equal to null—`!-null`. From there it sets the size of the image using the `setMode()` method. Note how the parameters set the size of the capture and use the default frame rate of the camera.

> The `.fps` value in the `setMode()` method is optional. By not setting an `.fps` value in the method, you are essentially using the default value for the webcam, which is 15 fps.

The next line—`attachVideo()`—is quite familiar but the one after it, which uses `setInterval()`, is most likely unfamiliar to you. This line tells the function `slomotion` how often it should run. By using the `setInterval()` method, you control the timing of a specific function. In this case the `slomotion` function will grab an image every `100` milliseconds.

8. Close the ActionScript Editor and save and test the movie. When it plays, move from side to side to see the effect shown in Figure 10-21.

Figure 10-21.
Gimme that old "slo mo"!

A little game of "gotcha"

Our final exercise will appeal to the security freaks. We are going to create an app that makes it so that, whenever the camera detects a certain level of motion, it takes a picture.

1. Open the Gotcha.fla file in your Chapter 10 Exercise folder, select the first frame of the Actions layer, open the ActionScript Editor, and enter the following:

```
import flash.display.BitmapData;
import flash.geom.Matrix;
import flash.geom.ColorTransform;

var mainVideo:Video;
var mainBitmap:BitmapData = new BitmapData( 160, 120 );
var bitmapMovie:MovieClip = _root.createEmptyMovieClip➥
( "bitmapMovie", _root.getNextHighestDepth() );
var vidCamera:Camera = Camera.get();
```

This should look familiar because you used it in the previous exercise.

2. Press Enter/Return twice and enter the following code and function:

```
bitmapMovie._x = 200;
bitmapMovie.attachBitmap( mainBitmap, _root.getNextHighestDepth() );

function gotcha( movement:Boolean ):Void {
  if( movement ) {
    mainBitmap.draw( mainVideo );
  }
}
```

The first line tells Flash to place the emptyMovieClip 200 pixels to the right of the video movie clip and the second line attaches the bitmap object to that emptyMovieClip.

The function named `gotcha` specifies that if motion is detected Flash should capture the image from the camera and place it using the `draw()` method in the bitmap named `mainBitmap`.

Now all you have to do is to make sure a webcam is attached to the computer and set the motion sensitivity level of the camera.

3. Press Enter/Return twice and enter the following:

```
if( vidCamera != null ) {
mainVideo.attachVideo(vidCamera);
vidCamera.setMotionLevel( 40 );
vidCamera.onActivity = gotcha;
}
```

The last two lines are the key. The `setMotionLevel()` and `onActivity()` methods are intertwined.

The first method sets the sensitivity of the motion level to be detected. The values you can use range from 0 to 100. These values are a bit backward. If the value is 100, then the camera will be prevented from detecting any motion at all and the `activityLevel()` method won't be invoked.

In our case, Flash is going to wait until a `motionLevel` of 40 is detected. When that happens, an `onActivity` event will occur. In our case, when a `motionLevel` of 40 is detected the `gotcha` function is triggered and the picture (see Figure 10-22) is placed on the screen.

> Try using different motion level values and testing them to see how this method works.

Figure 10-22. There's a burglar in the house!

Summary

As you have discovered, two simple lines of code make for an outrageous amount of fun. All you need to do is to create a video object on the stage or in a movie clip and feed a webcam signal to it.

We showed you how to create a simple webcam feed, how to place a feed into blocks and stack them, and how to use a webcam feed to create a kaleidoscope effect. These are fairly simple techniques that can be used with FLV files as well. We also demonstrated a couple of intermediate-level techniques that place the user in the action. The Times Square exercise showed how Illustrator can create some rather precise masks for you and the title sequence shows how text can create a rather interesting experience.

The final two exercises were slightly more advanced and demonstrated how a webcam and the bitmap class can work together to create interesting effects, such as a slow-motion effect we call "bucket brigade," and how the webcam can be used as ...well... a camera.

In the next chapter you are going to build a really useful tool that will allow you to apply all the filters and blend modes to a video in order to answer that age-old question: "I wonder what that looks like?"

11 ACTIONSCRIPT AND FLASH VIDEO

On the surface, this chapter title might seem a bit out of place. You are most likely looking at it and wondering, "So, dudes, we have been using ActionScript throughout this book." Our reply is "Absolutely, but this chapter is just for you." Everything done so far in this book is intended to give you some hands-on experience with a variety of techniques. This chapter is designed to make your life easier.

Though you can add the blends and the filters to your video projects, you may have noticed that you really can't see what you have done until you test the movie. In this chapter we are going to build a little widget we call "Jordievision" that plays with the color in a selected FLV in real time, and lets you see the result without your going back and forth between the FLA and testing the effect.

For example, want to see how blend mode pairs up with a glow filter? Simple! Just identify the FLV and apply the blend and the filter. Want to adjust the colors and alpha in the video? Simple! Just move the sliders to make the change.

There is, of course, a hidden agenda here. This chapter gives you a grounding in how filters and blend effects can be applied using a code-based approach.

Let's get busy and make our lives easier. You can start by downloading the Chapter 11 files to your computer.

Creating the "Jordievision" assets

To start, let's open `jordievision.swf` in the Chapter 11 Complete folder and see how the movie works.

When the movie starts, all of the sliders are sitting at the bottom of the control. When you click a slider or drag it, the effect will change. This is because the sliders are waiting for you to click on them and move them up or down.

As you can also see, the video listed in the Movie area starts to play. When you move the sliders up or down in each of the areas, the image will change. You can also apply a blend mode by simply selecting the mode from the Blend pop-down. If you pull the Alpha setting in the Color area back to around 0, you will see the video is laid over a gradient. This enables you to see how the color in the video will interact with the colors below it when a blend mode is applied. Apart from the brushed metal effect, this entire interface was constructed using the tools in Flash Professional 8.

If you wish to substitute your own FLV, place a copy of the FLV in the same folder as your SWF and enter the filename in the MOVIE input box. When you press Enter/Return, that FLV file will play.

When you "play" with the SWF, you will discover you need to create the following interface elements:

- The sliders
- The gradient behind the video
- The Blend pop-down menu
- The text input box

The last two items are nothing more than a ComboBox component and a text input area. As you can see (Figure 11-1), there isn't much to this interface that you can't create or that you haven't created at some point in this book. Enough playing around; quit the SWF and let's get to work.

Figure 11-1. The Jordievision interface

1. Open the jordievision.fla file in the Chapter 11 Exercise folder. When it opens, you will see we have included the layers and placed the interface and the video object on the stage. If you open the library, you will see that the only items within the library are the PNG for the interface, a video object, a movie clip named Slide, and the movie clip containing the video object (see Figure 11-2).

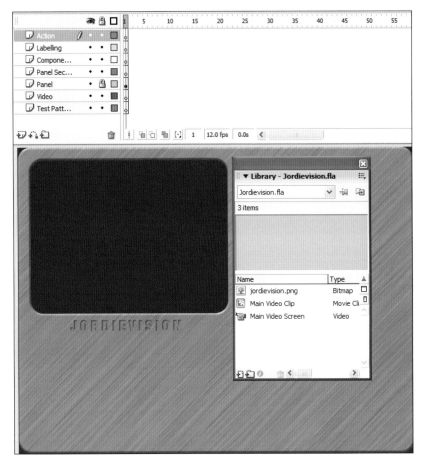

Figure 11-2. You don't need much to get started.

2. Create a new movie clip symbol named Test Pattern. When the Symbol Editor opens, select the Rectangle tool and deselect the Stroke option on the toolbar. Draw a rectangle that is 338 pixels wide and 259 pixels high.

   With the rectangle still selected, click the Fill Color chip on the Property Inspector to open the color picker. At the bottom of the color picker are a couple of radial and linear gradients. Click on the rainbow liner gradient at the end of the swatches. The rectangle will fill with that gradient. In the Property Inspector set the location of the gradient rectangle to 0,0 and click the Scene 1 link to return to the main timeline. Select the Test Pattern layer and drag the gradient from the library to the stage. When the movie clip is in its final position, set X = 10 and Y = 11 in the Property Inspector, and lock the layer.

3. Select the Video layer and drag the Main Video Clip movie clip to the stage and place it over the gradient with an X position of 20 and a Y position of 19 in the Property Inspector. Once it is in position, as shown in Figure 11-3, lock the layer.

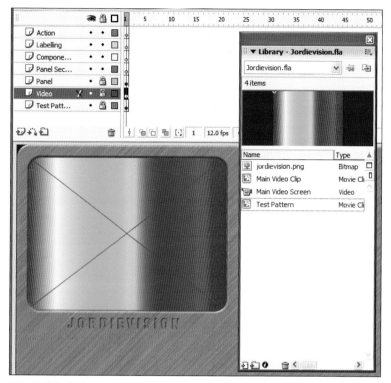

Figure 11-3. So far so good...

The next step is to create the three panel sections that will "hold" the various sliders. In many respects, they are a snap to do in Flash. They are nothing more than rounded rectangles with an opaque fill color.

4. Unlock and select the Panel Sections layer and select the Rectangle tool. In the toolbar set the Stroke to black and the Fill to a dark gray color—#333333—with an Alpha value of 40%.

   Before you start drawing squares, click the Set Corner Radius button in the Options area of the toolbar. This will open the Rectangle Settings dialog box. Set the corner radius to 10 points, as shown in Figure 11-4, and click OK. When the dialog box closes, draw a rectangle on the layer and use these settings in the Property Inspector:

   ■ Width: 200

   ■ Height: 200

   ■ X: 392

   ■ Y: 60

271

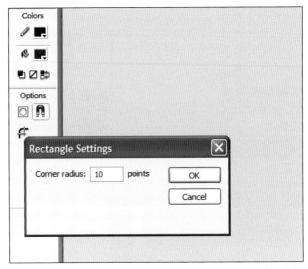

Figure 11-4. Click the Set Corner Radius button to open this dialog box.

5. Having created the Blur area of the interface, select the Text tool, click once on your new box, and enter Blur. Though we used the _sans font at 90 points for our project, feel free to use a font of your choosing. Set the Text color to white—#FFFFFF—and push the opacity back to 40%.

The next two boxes—Glow and Color—use the same text and color properties as the Blur box. Use these settings:

Glow box:

- Width: 320
- Height: 186
- X: 19
- Y: 289
- Text: Glow

Color box:

- Width: 275
- Height: 185
- X: 355
- Y: 289
- Text: Color

When you finish, your interface should resemble that shown in Figure 11-5.

Figure 11-5. The holders for the sliders are in place.

Now that the easy stuff is done, it is time to tackle the construction of the slider used throughout the movie. There will be ten copies of this slider on the stage.

This tells you a couple of things. The first is that it really should be converted to a component. This way, the slider can be treated in a rather versatile manner. The second is that you only need to create the two pieces used in the slider—a vertical scale bar and the thumb—and let ActionScript do the "heavy lifting" for you.

Let's start with the Thumb.

6. Create a new movie clip named Thumb. Select the Rectangle tool and set the Stroke to 1 point and the stroke color to a medium gray—#999999. Set the fill to the linear black-to-white gradient in the color picker. (The gradient you need appears in the bottom-left corner of the color picker.) Draw a rectangle. You will notice you still have the rounded rectangle. This is because the Rectangle tool always uses the last settings for the tool. In the Property Inspector, set the width of the rectangle to 40 pixels and the height to 10 pixels. The result is an object that has something of a pill shape.

7. The next step is to work on making things a bit more realistic. To start, zoom in on the object with the Magnifying Glass tool. Now you can see what you are doing.

To give the object a more natural look, select the Gradient Transform tool and click once on the gradient. You will see, as shown in Figure 11-6, a couple of lines, an anchor point with a + sign, and a white dot appear around the selection.

The white dot allows you to rotate the gradient. Place the cursor over the dot and, when you see the rotate cursor, drag the dot in a counterclockwise direction. The gradient now runs from top to bottom rather than left to right. Click and drag the anchor point until it is a few pixels above the outside edge of the stroke. As you drag, the lines also move toward each other. The effect you are looking for here is one where the gradient looks like a light is shining upward. To finish, open the Align panel and center the Thumb on the stage.

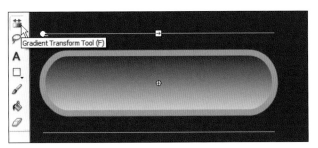

Figure 11-6. The Gradient Transform tool allows you to manipulate gradients.

8. Return to the main timeline and create a new movie clip named Slide. Select the Line tool and draw a vertical line that is 4 pixels wide and filled with a medium gray color— #999999. In the Property Inspector, set the height of the line to 170 pixels. Close the movie clip by clicking on the Scene 1 link to return to the main timeline.

   Though this may seem like a relatively simple step, in many ways it is the most critical. The reason it is being placed in a movie clip is because the height of this movie clip will determine the degree of the effect. The Thumb movie clip is going to be moving up and down the scale. We will be using ActionScript to determine the position of the Thumb on the Scale as a percentage of the Scale movie clip's height. This number will then be used to change the video.

9. Create a new movie clip named Slider. Drag the Slide movie clip from the library into the Symbol Editor and set its X and Y position in the Property Inspector to 0.

   This is an important step because if you were to simply draw the line, you wouldn't have been able to readily determine the all-important ._height property of the movie clip.

10. Select the Line tool and draw three horizontal lines just to the right of the top, middle, and bottom of the Slide movie clip.

11. Select the Text tool, click once on the stage, and enter the word Slider. Set this text in the Property Inspector to a 12-point black sans serif font and set the Text type in the Property Inspector to Dynamic Text.

12. Switch to the Selection tool. Click on the Slide movie clip and give it the instance name of slide in the Property Inspector. Click on the text and then give it the instance name of _labelField (see Figure 11-7). Click the Scene 1 link to return to the main timeline.

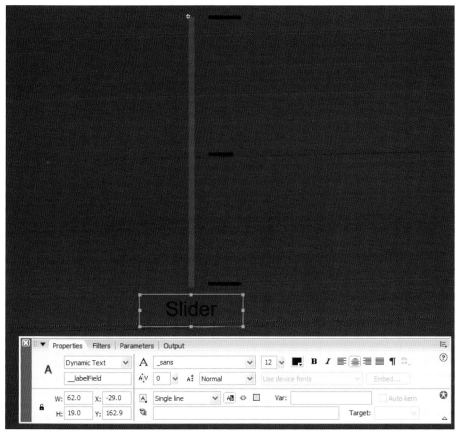

Figure 11-7. The all-important slider is ready to go to work.

"Wiring up" custom components with ActionScript

With the artwork created, you can now turn your attention to the code that makes the components work.

You will need to write two scripts in separate ActionScript documents. The first script, called `DraggableButton.as`, will create the methods and properties for the `Thumb` movie clip, which will become a Button component. The second script, called `Slider.as`, will create the methods and properties for the slider.

As you have done in earlier chapters, the two AS files will be kept in a folder in the directory for the project, and the path to each file will be used when you convert the movie clips in the library to components. The path to the folder is `Chapter 11/Exercise/ com/interactivityunlimited/controls`.

1. Open a new Flash document and select ActionScript file from the New Document dialog box. Name the file DraggableButton and save it to the controls folder. Click OK to close the dialog box and open a blank ActionScript document.

2. Click once in line 1 of the document and enter the following code:

```
import flash.geom.Rectangle;

class com.interactivityunlimited.controls.
DraggableButton extends MovieClip {
  var __data:String;
  var __message:String;
  var  ourBroadcaster:Object;

  var hitArea:MovieClip;
  var constraint:Rectangle;
  var lastSliderValue:Number;
  var isDrag:Boolean;
```

The first line imports a `Rectangle` class from the Flash geometry class. This rectangle will be used to define the area in which the button can be dragged. The second line, which is the class definition, ends with a { because all of the code you will write will contain the properties and methods of the class just defined. The brackets contain all of the items in a class and act as code block containers. If they weren't there, Flash wouldn't have a clue regarding the variables and functions (properties and methods) that are added to the `DraggableButton` class you are creating. Incidentally, `DraggableButton` is an extension of the `MovieClip` class. Simply put, this means that anything you can do a `MovieClip`, you can do to our `DraggableButton`.

The remaining lines create the variables that will be used throughout the script. The `__message` variable may strike you as a bit odd. It will attach the name of the event—the mouse is pressed or the `Thumb` is dragged—which will be transmitted to the slider, which will become a high-performance listener.

3. Press Enter/Return twice and enter the following:

```
function DraggableButton() {
  ourBroadcaster = new Object();
  AsBroadcaster.initialize(ourBroadcaster);

  constraint = new Rectangle( 0, 0, 0, 0 );
        }

  [Inspectable(type='String', defaultValue='drag', ➥
name='Event Message')]
  public function get message():String {
    return __message;
  }
```

```
public function setMessage( newMessage:String ):Void {
  __message = newMessage;
}

public function setConstraint( x, y, width, height ):Void {
  constraint = new Rectangle( x, y, width, height );
}

public function calculateSliderValue():Void {
  var sliderData:Number = Math.floor(((constraint.bottom - this._y)➡
  /constraint.bottom) * 100);

if( sliderData != lastSliderValue ) {
   ourBroadcaster.broadcastMessage( __message, sliderData );
   lastSliderValue = sliderData;
  }
 }
```

The `DraggableButton()` function, also known as the constructor for this class, is going to be called as soon as `attachMovie()` is called in the `Slider.as` file. The `Slider.as` file will be the component the movie uses, and the parameters you write for it will appear in the Component Inspector or in the Parameters area of the Property Inspector.

The first two lines set up the object to function as a broadcaster. Remember a broadcaster, as we pointed out in Chapter 9, essentially says, "Hey, something just happened!" and that message will be picked up by a listener.

The next line creates a new rectangle that is placed at the 0 point on both the x-axis and the y-axis and is 0 pixels wide and 0 pixels high. This rectangle will be used to ensure the `Thumb` movie clip in the FLA, when it is placed on the stage, is constrained to only up and down movement and that it is also constrained to the height of this rectangle.

The next code block creates the list that will appear in the Component Inspector or in the Parameters tab of the Property Inspector.

The real grunt work is done in the `setConstraint()` and `calculateSlider`➡ `Value()` functions.

The `calculateSliderValue()` function is the key. As the `Thumb` moves up and down the slider, the distance from the top to the bottom of the slider is used to calculate a percentage value—`sliderData`—that will be used to control the various effects. Let's assume the height of the slider is 100 pixels and the `Thumb` is 50 pixels above the bottom of the slider. The resulting value is 50, and that value is used to set the value of the effect. The value is then broadcast out to the listener and, because it is moving, the value is assigned to `lastSliderValue` in case we need to get the most recent slider position.

4. Press Enter/Return twice and enter the following code:

```
public function onMouseMove() {
  if( isDrag ) {
     calculateSliderValue();
   }
  }

public function onPress():Void {
    this.startDrag( true, constraint.left,  constraint.top, ➡
    constraint.right, constraint.bottom );
    isDrag = true;
  }

public function onRelease():Void {
  this.stopDrag();
  calculateSliderValue();
  isDrag = false;
}

public function onReleaseOutside():Void {
   onRelease();
}

public function addListener( theListener:Object ):Boolean {
  return ourBroadcaster.addListener( theListener );
}

public function removeListener( theListener:Object ):Boolean {
  return ourBroadcaster.removeListener( theListener );
  }
}
```

The first four functions simply treat the Thumb as a draggable button and answer the questions:

- What is the percentage value if it is being dragged?
- Where can it be dragged?
- What happens when the user stops dragging and releases the mouse button?
- What happens if the user lets go of the mouse outside of the Thumb?

The last two functions create a listener and add it to the broadcaster and, when the Thumb isn't being dragged, removes the listener.

That's it for the DraggableButton.as file. Save it to the controls folder. When you have done that, close the script.

Though we haven't used it very much in this book, there is a little button on the Actions panel that looks like a small blue check mark. This is the Check Syntax button. Clicking this button will allow you to make sure you have used the proper syntax in the code you write. If there is a mistake, a dialog box will appear and the error will also be shown in the output panel. If there are no mistakes, a dialog box will inform you of this as well.

The next step is to create the script for the slider where the Thumb will be placed.

5. Create a new ActionScript document, name it Slider.as, and save it to the controls folder. Click once on the first line of the Actions pane and enter the following:

```
class com.interactivityunlimited.controls.Slider extends MovieClip {
var __thumb:MovieClip;
var __slide:MovieClip;
var __labelField:TextField;

var __label:String;
var __message:String;
var ourBroadcaster:Object;

var lastSliderValue:Number;

[Inspectable(type='String', defaultValue='Slider', ➥
 name='Slider Label')]

public function get label():String {
  return __label;
}
public function set lLabel( newLabel:String ):Void {
  __label = newLabel;
  __labelField.text = newLabel;
}
```

Not a lot is new here. The major change is the addition of a variable named _labelField. In fact, it isn't new because that is the Instance name of the text field at the bottom of the Slider movie clip that you created earlier. When you add the components to the stage, you will see a Slider Label text input field in the Parameters. The text you enter will be used as the text named newlabel in the second-to-last line of the code.

6. Press Enter/Return twice and enter the following code:

```
[Inspectable(type='String', defaultValue='sliderEvent', ➥
 name='Slider Event')]

public function get Message():String {
  return __message;
}
```

```
      public function set Message( newMessage:String ):Void {
        __message = newMessage;
      }

      public function get Value():Number {
        return lastSliderValue;
      }

      public function sliderMoved( sliderValue:Number ):Void {
        lastSliderValue = sliderValue;
        ourBroadcaster.broadcastMessage( __message, sliderValue );
      }

              public function addListener( theListener:Object ):Boolean {
                return ourBroadcaster.addListener( theListener );
              }

              public function removeListener( theListener:Object ):Boolean {
                return ourBroadcaster.removeListener( theListener );
              }
```

Apart from the code block at the top, there isn't much new here either. The first code block will create a second parameter named `Slider Event` that is associated with this component. Again, because the user will input the text, the text input into the parameter will be used as the value for the `sliderEvent`.

7. Press Enter/Return and input this function:

```
      public function Slider() {
        ourBroadcaster = new Object();
        AsBroadcaster.initialize(ourBroadcaster);

        __labelField.text = __label;

        __thumb = this.attachMovie( "Thumb", ➥
         "__thumb", this.getNextHighestDepth() );

         __thumb._x = __slide._x;
         __thumb._y = __slide._y + __slide._height;
         __thumb.setConstraint( __slide._x, ➥
        __slide._y, 0, __slide._height );
        __thumb.message = "sliderMoved";
        __thumb.addListener( this );
       lastSliderValue = 0;
       }
      }
```

This function (again, known as the constructor) is the engine that will build the slider. The first thing it does is to assign the text entered into our `__label` property to the slider. The next code block pulls the `Thumb` movie clip out of the library and places it over the `slider` movie clip using the `getNextHighestDepth()` method.

The `getNextHighestDepth()` method is quite useful if you are placing movie clips on the stage using ActionScript. Instead of assigning a depth for each new movie clip created, you can let the software do the work. For example, assume you add a new movie clip at level 2. This method will keep track of that, and the next one created will be placed at level 3, if there is nothing on level 3, and so on.

With the `Thumb` on the stage, two things happen. The first is the horizontal position of the movie clip is used to determine the `_slide` variable's `_x` value and the `Thumb` is placed at the bottom of the slider. The `setConstraint()` method of the `DraggableButton` component object is called using the values determined from our `__slide` movie clip. Finally, a listener is added to the `Thumb` and the value for the slider is set to 0. By assigning `sliderMoved` to the `Thumb` message, we are telling the `Thumb` that we want it to broadcast an event message using this name, which is what the slider will be listening for.

Save the script to the `controls` folder and close the script.

Creating the components and adding them to the stage

Now that you have written the code that will control the ten sliders on the stage, you have to convert the movie clips to components.

1. Open your jordievision.fla file and open the library. Right-click (Windows) or Control-click (Mac) on the Thumb movie clip. Select Component Definition from the context menu to open the Component Definition dialog box shown in Figure 11-8.

   In the AS 2.0 Class field, enter com.interactivityunlimited.controls.DraggableButton. Then, click once on the icon in the Description area and select Button Icon from the pop-up list. A button icon will replace the generic icon in the dialog box. Click OK and, when the dialog box closes, the Thumb's icon in the library will have changed from a movie clip to a button.

2. Open your jordievision.fla file and open the library. Right-click (Windows) or Control-click (Mac) on the Thumb movie clip. Select Component Definition from the context menu to open the Component Definition dialog box shown in Figure 11-9.

   In the AS 2.0 Class field, enter com.interactivityunlimited.controls.DraggableButton. Then, click once on the icon in the Description area and select Generic Icon from the pop-up list. Click OK and, when the dialog box closes, the slider's icon in the library will have changed from a movie clip to the icon shown in the Component Definition dialog box.

Figure 11-8. The Thumb movie clip in the library is converted to a component.

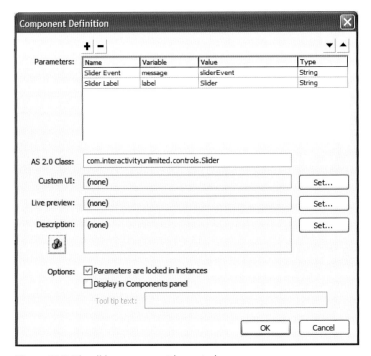

Figure 11-9. The slider component is created.

3. Click once on the Components layer to select it. Select the Text tool and click once on the interface above the Blur area. Enter the word MOVIE. Set it to a 12-point bold sans serif font and set the X position to 390 and the Y position to 7 in the Property Inspector.

4. Now you are going to add a text box that will allow you to enter the name of a video to be played. Click once more to the right of the text just entered. In the Property Inspector set the Text type to Input text, the Instance name to movieName, the Width to 155, and the Height to 19. Add the filename BreadQT.flv so that the text area will contain some text when you test the movie. You can change the text to other filenames at runtime.

   Now select the word *Movie*, cut it, select the Labeling layer, and select Edit ➤ Paste In Place. Paste another copy of the text on the Clipboard into the Labeling layer and place it under the text just added. Select the Text tool, highlight the text, and change the word to BLEND.

5. Drag a ComboBox component from the Components panel to the Components layer and place it under the Text input box you just created. This ComboBox component is going to function as a pop-down menu that will allow you to apply a blend mode to the video. Select the ComboBox and click once on the Parameters tab of the Property Inspector.

6. Double-click the data strip in the Parameters tab to open the Values dialog box shown in Figure 11-10. Click the + sign to add a value. Enter the following values:

   - normal
   - layer
   - multiply
   - screen
   - lighten
   - darken
   - difference
   - add
   - subtract
   - invert
   - alpha
   - erase
   - overlay
   - hardlight

   When you finish, click OK to close the Values dialog box.

> Be sure to follow our spelling here. These will be the actual values called by ActionScript and they must have the correct syntax to work. That includes the lowercase letter at the start of each mode.

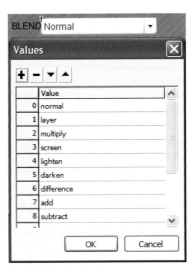

Figure 11-10.
The data values are added to the ComboBox component.

Now that you have added the data, the next task is to enter the names that will appear in the menu. It is important that you follow the order we have given because each name will be directly associated with its data counterpart. Double-click the labels strip and, when the Values dialog box opens, enter the following:

- Normal
- Layer
- Multiply
- Screen
- Lighten
- Darken
- Difference
- Add
- Subtract
- Invert
- Alpha
- Erase
- Overlay
- Hard Light

Click OK to close the Values dialog box. Select the ComboBox component on the stage and give it the instance name of blendMenu.

7. Drag two copies of the slider component to the Components layer and place them in the Blur area. Add four copies of the slider component to the Color and Glow areas of the interface as well.

8. Each of the ten sliders you just added to the interface, as shown in Figure 11-11, will need an instance name that can be accessed by ActionScript. Click once on the first slider in the Blue area and give it the Instance name of blurHorizontal in the Property Inspector. Select the next slider in the Blur area and give it the instance name of blurVertical. Moving from left to right in the Glow and Color areas, select the slider components and give them the following instance names:

- glowVert
- glowHor
- glowStrength
- glowAlpha
- colorRed
- colorGreen
- colorBlue
- colorAlpha

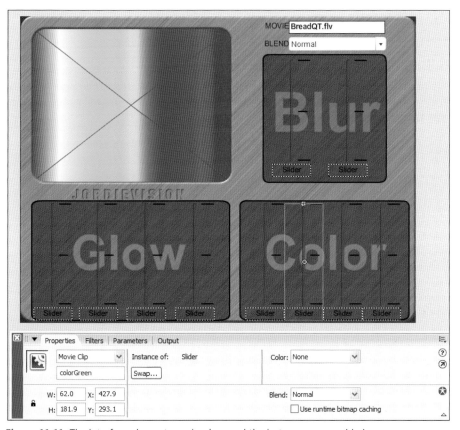

Figure 11-11. The interface elements are in place and the instance names added.

9. The final step, before you add the code to the Actions layer, is to add the parameters for each slider. These parameters are the ones you created earlier in the Slider.as document. Click on the Horizontal Blur slider to select it and click the Parameters tab in the Property Inspector. You will see the values from the Inspectable[] parameters of the Slider.as document appear in the parameters for the selected components. Use the following values for each slider component on the stage:

- Horizontal Blur: Slider Event = hor; Slider Label = Horizontal
- Vertical Blur: Slider Event = vert; Slider Label = Vertical
- Vertical Glow: Slider Event = vert; Slider Label = Vertical
- Horizontal Glow: Slider Event = hor; Slider Label = Horizontal
- Glow Strength: Slider Event = strength; Slider Label = Strength
- Glow Alpha: Slider Event = alpha; Slider Label = Alpha
- Red Color: Slider Event = red; Slider Label = Red
- Green Color: Slider Event = green; Slider Label = Green
- Blue Color: Slider Event = blue; Slider Label = Blue
- Alpha Color: Slider Event = alpha; Slider Label = Alpha

Pulling it all together with ActionScript

The interface is constructed, the components and their parameters are in place, and the time has arrived to pull it all together with ActionScript. The code you will write will target all of the components on the stage.

1. Select frame 1 of the Actions layer and open the ActionScript panel. Click once in the Script pane and enter the following code:

```
import flash.filters.*;

var movieName:TextField;
var mainVideo:MovieClip;
var colorMatrix:Array = new Array( 1, 0, 0, 0, ➡
0, 0, 1, 0, 0, 0, 0, 0, 1, 0, 0, 0, 0, 0, 1, 0 );

var blur:BlurFilter = new BlurFilter( 0, 0, 3 );
var glow:GlowFilter = new GlowFilter( 0xffff00, 0, 0,➡
 0, 2, 3, true );
var color:ColorMatrixFilter = new ColorMatrixFilter( colorMatrix );

var filterArray:Array = [color, blur, glow];
var videoScreen:Video;
var nc:NetConnection = new NetConnection();
nc.connect(null);

var ns:NetStream = new NetStream(nc);
```

The script starts off with the declaration of several variables. One that may catch your attention is the use of a color matrix array to change the values of the red, blue, and green pixels in an image. But you can also use it to change the `Alpha` value of those pixels at the same time.

The `colorMatrix` filter lets you apply a 4×5 matrix of color transformation values to an image or, in this case, a video inside a movie clip. This explains the 20 numbers that are in the list. If you were to write out the matrix it would look like this:

1,0,0,0,0

0,1,0,0,0

0,0,1,0,0

0,0,0,1,0

If you compare the numbers in the matrix to the numbers in the list, you will see they match. Though it may look complex, it is not difficult to follow it. Row 1 is the red component of the pixel color and the remaining rows are the green, blue, and alpha components. The numbers used essentially say that there is no change to start with, though later you will be changing the color using the values in the matrix. Why toss 20 numbers into a list? Do it this way and you only have to write the values once.

The really neat thing about the `colorMatrix` is it allows you to make changes to the hue, saturation, alpha, and other effects while the movie is playing. The numbers used in the matrix can be any number between 0 and 1. For example, if the first number in the red row is .5, you have just reduced the saturation of the red component of each pixel of the image.

For those of you who are sticklers for detail, or have a morbid fascination regarding minutiae, the color model used by this filter is RGBA. When the filter is applied, each color component in each pixel is multiplied by the corresponding value in the RGBA matrix. This new value is applied to each pixel in the original image

The next two variables set the parameters for the `Blur` and the `Glow` filters, and the next variable, named `color`, makes all of the numbers in the `colorMatrix` list available to the `colorMatrix` filter.

The rest of the script assigns our filters to a list in the order that will be applied to our video and creates the `NetConnection()` and `NetStream()` objects that will be used to play the video.

2. Press Enter/Return and add the following code:

```
var blendController:Object = new Object();
blendController.change = function( evt:Object ):Void {
  mainVideo.blendMode = evt.target.data[evt.target.selectedIndex];

}


function reapplyFilters():Void {
  mainVideo.filters = filterArray;
}
```

We're taking a model/view/controller (MVC) approach to controlling our filters. When you work with ActionScript, much of what you do in assigning classes and so on is virtual. That means you really can't "see" what you have done until you play the movie. The MVC approach we are using helps with that visualization.

The model is the data and, as you know, data can be anything from a series of numbers to a number of FLV files. In this case we are using a filter object, such as a blurFilter, and all of its settings, which are the filter's parameters. Essentially, this data is what the computer works with. The issue is that we, as humans, can't see data. It is an intangible.

To see what the data is doing (a blur on the x-axis for example), we have to put this stuff we call "data" into a form we understand. This is the view portion of the model/view/controller approach to controlling a filter. The view takes the data, or model, and represents it in a form that we can comprehend; hence, the view. In the case of this exercise, and the blurFilter, it is applied to a movie clip object that happens to be used to play a video. Moving one of the two Blur sliders (the controllers) changes the data because the start point for that data is 0 and the change will be applied to the video playing in the movie clip.

To start, the blendController function uses the data portion of the ComboBox component containing the blend modes as its model. The function is designed to change the blend mode to whatever data value attached to the label is selected in the ComboBox.

The second function keeps an eye on the filters and reflects the change to the filter array as the slider (controller) moves up and down. A good example would be the Blur filter. The first variable referring to it—var blur:BlurFilter = new BlurFilter(0, 0, 3);—starts by applying no horizontal or vertical blur to the image and sets the blur quality to high (3). When the slider starts moving and the blur is applied to both the horizontal and vertical axes, those values will be used as the new values in the BlurFilter and reflected in the filterArray. The values in the filterArray are then reapplied to the movie clip playing the video.

3. Press Enter/Return and add the following code:

```
var blurController:Object = new Object();
blurController.vert = function( blurValue:Number ):Void {
  blur.blurY = blurValue;
  reapplyFilters();
}

blurController.hor = function( blurValue:Number ):Void {
  blur.blurX = blurValue;
  reapplyFilters();
}

blurHorizontal.addListener( blurController );
blurVertical.addListener( blurController );
```

The first two functions capture the value of the vertical and horizontal blur sliders and apply those values to the filter object, in this case named `blur`. The `reapplyFilters()` function is then called in order to show the filter changes on our video. The last two lines of the code are what attach the sliders to the `blurController` object. In many respects, the controller object can be said to be listening to the sliders. How does it get the value for the filter? This was done earlier at the end of the `Slider.as` script.

The rest of the coding for the remaining sliders follows this very model.

4. Press Enter/Return and add the following code, which captures the value of each slider and applies the change to the video:

```
var glowController:Object = new Object();
glowController.vert = function( blurValue:Number ):Void {
  glow.blurY = blurValue;
  reapplyFilters();
}

glowController.hor = function( blurValue:Number ):Void {
  glow.blurX = blurValue;
  reapplyFilters();
}

glowController.strength = function( strengthValue:Number ):Void {
  glow.strength = strengthValue;
  reapplyFilters();
}

glowController.alpha = function( alphaValue:Number ):Void {
  glow.alpha = alphaValue / 100;
  reapplyFilters();
}

glowVert.addListener( glowController );
glowHor.addListener( glowController );
glowStrength.addListener( glowController );
glowAlpha.addListener( glowController );

var colorController:Object = new Object();
colorController.red = function( aValue:Number ):Void {
  var matrix:Array = color.matrix;
  matrix[0] = aValue/100;
  color.matrix = matrix;
  reapplyFilters();
}
```

```
colorController.green = function( aValue:Number ):Void {
  var matrix:Array = color.matrix;
  matrix[6] = aValue/100;
  color.matrix = matrix;
  reapplyFilters();
}

colorController.blue = function( aValue:Number ):Void {
  var matrix:Array = color.matrix;
  matrix[12] = aValue/100;
  color.matrix = matrix;
  reapplyFilters();
}

colorController.alpha = function( aValue:Number ):Void {
  var matrix:Array = color.matrix;
  matrix[18] = aValue/100;
  color.matrix = matrix;
  reapplyFilters();
}

colorRed.addListener( colorController );
colorGreen.addListener( colorController );
colorBlue.addListener( colorController );
colorAlpha.addListener( colorController );

reapplyFilters();
mainVideo.blendMode = "Normal";
blendMenu.selectedIndex = 0;
blendMenu.addEventListener( "change", blendController );
```

Now that all of the sliders are "wired up," the time has arrived to pay attention to the star of the show—the video.

5. Press Enter/Return and add the following:

```
mainVideo.videoScreen.attachVideo(ns);

ns.onStatus = function( evt:Object ):Void {
  if( evt.code == "NetStream.Play.Stop" ) {
    ns.seek(0);
  }
}

movieName.onChanged = function( newName:TextField ):Void {
  ns.play( newName.text );
}

ns.play( movieName.text );
```

The video is "fed" into the video object in the movie clip and the `onStatus` function simply replays the video when it finishes.

The next code block captures the text in the `Input Text` block and loads the movie entered. The final line of the code plays the video.

6. Save and test the movie (see Figure 11-12).

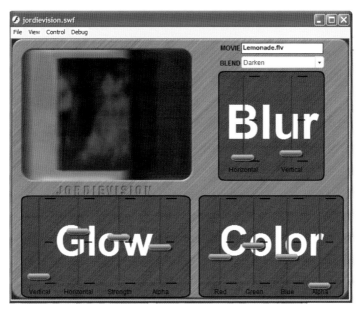

Figure 11-12. Playing with the lemonade video

Summary

In this chapter, we moved into a fairly interesting project that allowed you to apply the blend modes and three filters to a video. The purpose of the exercise was to give you a widget you could play with. Of course, the ulterior motive was to show you how to manipulate a video in a movie clip using a custom component and one—the ComboBox component—that ships with Flash Professional 8.

Though this exercise could easily be placed in the category of intermediate to advanced, you should by now have a deeper understanding and sensitivity to the power of ActionScript and how it can be creatively applied to video. The ability to programmatically apply filters and manipulate color using the `colorMatrix` feature opens up a world of possibilities to you. Still, as you can see by playing with the sliders, you can also overdo it.

In the next chapter, we explore the area of motion graphics and, hopefully, help you realize that Adobe After Effects 7 and Flash Professional are on the verge of becoming the dynamic duo of web video.

12 MOTION GRAPHICS USING ADOBE AFTER EFFECTS 7 AND FLASH PROFESSIONAL 8

When Adobe acquired Macromedia in December 2005, they also acquired Flash. Though the industry reacted to the news rather indifferently, several developers saw the integration of Flash with After Effects as a major development. At the same time that Flash becomes a viable web video creative tool, the company that produces one of the hottest video effects tools out there acquires the product. To think they will exist in separate product solitudes is a huge mistake. These two applications were made for each other and, finally, they are living under the same roof, so to speak.

After Effects 7 is the latest iteration of the application, and it sports a spiffy, easier-to-use interface; improved performance; and a number of other features that are too extensive to get into in this chapter. Instead, this chapter is designed to give you, the Flash developer or designer, an idea of some of the techniques and tools you can use when looking to incorporate video into your Flash projects.

Throughout this book, we have hinted at the possibilities. This chapter is not designed to teach you how to use After Effects but to start looking at the possibilities in front you. We are not going to claim that After Effects 7 is simple to use and master. It isn't—but it is rather important to note that the learning curve for After Effects, in many respects, matches that of Flash. It is steep to start with but once you get the fundamentals under your belt, you will discover that After Effects and Flash are quite the unbeatable creative combination.

Finally, attempting to cover the gamut of motion graphics and where After Effects 7 and Flash Professional 8 fit into the picture is a rather tall order and simply can't be done in one chapter of a book. Instead think of this chapter as a source of ideas and the start of a rather interesting journey. Download the Chapter 12 Exercise folder and let's get going.

After Effects text animation for Flash

In Chapter 8, we briefly introduced you to the animation presets. Simply put, they are "prerolled," drag-and-drop animations that result in some pretty amazing effects. The ones we used in Chapter 8 were the Drop Bounce and Rain In effects. In this exercise you will deal with a rather common design problem: fitting a text effect into a defined area of the stage rather than using the whole stage for the effect.

1. Open the `FireEscapes.fla` file in your Chapter 12 Exercise folder. The plan is to add a text animation to a Flash site dedicated to "House Hunting in New York." The image on the right side of the stage will be used in frame 1, and it is your job to create a motion graphic that fits the left side of the stage.

Obviously, using the entire stage size—550 pixels wide by 400 pixels high—for the text effect in After Effects would be like using an atom bomb to light your barbeque grill. There is far too much stage space being used for a small text area. Instead, if you select the image, you will notice in the Property Inspector that the image (see Figure 12-1) is 300 pixels wide by 400 pixels high. Subtract that width from the stage width, and you only need an area that is 250 pixels wide. The animation will leave the title at the mid-point of the area, meaning you don't need the full stage height for the animation. The final result is an animation that will fit into a stage area that is 250 pixels wide by 200 pixels high, which also tells you the dimension used for the comp in After Effects.

> Just to keep this first exercise in your "comfort zone," we will be using the Rain In effect. Also if you don't have After Effects, all is not lost. Copies of all the After Effects files created in this chapter can be found in the `After Effects` subfolder inside the Chapter 12 Exercise folder.

Figure 12-1. Use the dimensions of the blank area of the stage to determine the comp size in After Effects 7.

2. Open Adobe After Effects 7. Select Composition ➤ New Composition and create a new comp with the following properties:

- Name: House
- Lock Aspect Ratio: Deselected
- Width: 250 pixels
- Height: 200 pixels
- Pixel Aspect Ratio: Square Pixels
- Frame Rate: 24

Click OK to close the New Composition dialog box.

The settings match the dimensions determined earlier. You don't need to lock the aspect ratio because this will not result in a video file and it is a good habit to match the comp's frame rate to that of the Flash movie.

3. Select the Text tool, click once in the composition window, and enter the words House Hunting in New York. Select the text with the Text tool and, in the Character panel (see Figure 12-2), use the following settings:

- Font: Times
- Style: Bold
- Size: 30 pixels
- Color: Yellow

4. With the text still selected, select Window ➤ Paragraph and click the Center Alignment button in the Paragraph panel. Click once between the words Hunting and in. With the Shift key held down, press Enter/Return. If necessary, use your arrow keys to position your text so it looks like Figure 12-2.

There are some pretty powerful text tools in this application, and we'll be getting into them a bit later in this chapter. Though we suggest the Times font, feel free to use Times New Roman or another serif font. In the example, we used Times Bold. If you have this font or are using one containing the word *Bold* or *Heavy* in the font's name, you should leave the Style at Regular. Setting the Style to Bold will only make the words less legible and readable.

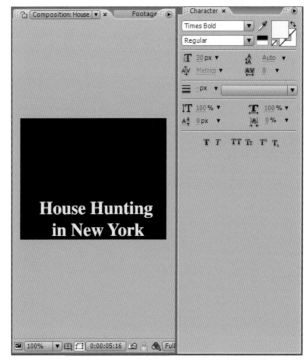

Figure 12-2. The text is formatted.

5. If it isn't open, open the Effects & Presets panel by selecting Window ➤ Effects and Presets. Twirl down the Animation Presets folder and select Text ➤ Animate In. When the Animate In presets are visible, drag the Raining Characters In preset on top of the text in the comp window.

When you drag the preset on to the text, a symbol will appear over where the text had been. When you release the mouse, the Effect Controls panel will open in the Project panel. We aren't going to play with any of the values here so you can ignore it. If you want to test the effect, click the play button in the Time Controls panel or press the spacebar. When you finish, rewind the comp to the start.

Your text block stretches quite a distance (see Figure 12-3) above the comp window. You don't need that wasted space. Here's how to fix it.

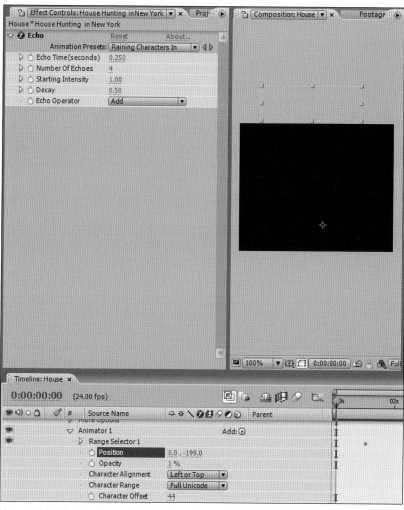

Figure 12-3. The starting position for the effect is changed.

6. Twirl down the source name in the timeline. Now twirl down Text and twirl down Animator 1. Making sure the playback head is at the start of the timeline, click and drag the second Position number. The text box moves up and down above the comp window, depending on which direction you move. Place the text box so its bottom edge is sitting on the top edge of the comp window. We found that –140.0 worked, but your number may be different.

> *The first* Position *number moves the selection right or left in the comp.*

Now that the animation's start and end points have been set, you can turn your attention to reducing the duration of the movie and speeding things up.

7. Twirl down the Range Selector 1 in the timeline. This will make the key frames accessible. If you look at the timeline, you will see the key frames are indicated by diamonds, as shown in Figure 12-4. The first key frame is at the one-second mark on the timeline and the second is around the three-second mark. This tells you the animation starts after one second and lasts for two seconds. Zoom in on the time-line by dragging the Zoom slider to the right. The timeline will change from show-ing seconds to showing frames. Click once on the first key frame and drag it to the 00:12f mark on the timeline. By dragging the first key frame to the 12f mark you have essentially extended the animation another half-second.

8. Drag the right edge of the work area bar on the timeline to the four-second mark and release the mouse. This has the effect of shortening the duration of the clip. The next step in the process is to actually trim out the extra time after the four-second mark. To do this, select Composition ➤ Trim comp to work area.

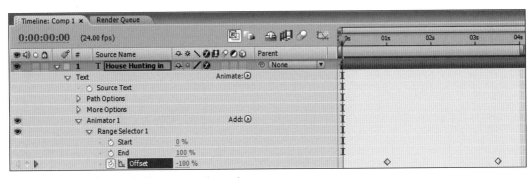

Figure 12-4. Preparing to trim the comp to the work area

9. Select File ➤ Export ➤ Macromedia Flash (swf). A dialog box will open prompting you to save the file. Navigate to the Exercise folder and give it a name—we used House—and click Save. The SWF Settings dialog box will now open. Be sure to select Ignore in the Unsupported features pop-down menu and click OK. After Effects will create the SWF and place it in the Exercise folder. At this point you can choose to save the comp as an AEP file or simply quit the application without sav-ing the changes.

> *Get into the habit of saving the AEP file. It keeps all of your settings, which means if you need to modify them, the settings are readily available.*

10. Return to your Flash document and create a new movie clip (in the completed file we named it House but you can use any name you wish). When the Symbol Editor opens, select Import ➤ Import to Stage. Locate your SWF in the import dialog box and click OK. The SWF will import to the timeline as a series of key frames.

11. Click the Scene 1 link to return to the main timeline. Add a new layer named Rain and drag the movie clip from the library to the first frame of this new layer. Position the movie clip on the stage and save and test the movie, as shown in Figure 12-5.

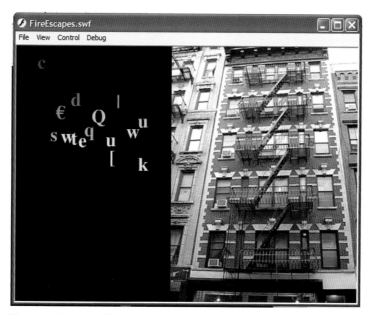

Figure 12-5. It is raining houses in New York.

Doing the "rotation" dance

If there is a Holy Grail in Flash animation it is the ability to "spin" objects in a 3D space. There are any number of methods, ranging from the simple to the complex. Most of them involve "faking" rotation by distorting the objects. Other solutions range from simply handling the animation in a third-party application such as Electric Rain's Swift 3D, to creating the animation in a 3D rendering application. If you have After Effects 7, you already have a set of 3D tools at your disposal, and you can create some rather interesting motion graphics effects using the features that ship with the application.

There is a small problem with this approach. You can't apply the effect, create the SWF, and have it spin in a movie clip as you did in the previous exercise. The object will import into Flash as nothing more than a series of key frames with no movement. This means the animation needs to be exported out of After Effects as an FLV and added to the stage using either a video object or the FLV Playback component. Knowing this, it is critical that the dimensions of the comp in After Effects match the area in the Flash movie where the animation will appear.

In this exercise we start by showing you how to use Flash to rotate an object around the vertical axis, and then we will dig into After Effects and create a rotation using the horizontal axis. There will be a bit of a twist to this: as the words spin, they change.

1. Open a new Flash document, select the Text tool, click on the stage, and enter House Hunting. In the example in the Chapter 12 Complete folder we set the text in the FlashSpin.fla file as 60 point _sans, but you can use any font and point size you wish. In the Property Inspector set the Text property to Static and then convert the text to a movie clip named House. Open the movie clip, select the text, and press Ctrl+B (PC) or Cmd+B (Mac) three times until the text looks like a bunch of pixels. Click the Scene 1 link to return to the main timeline and delete the movie clip from the stage.

> *In this exercise the text needs to be graphic, not text. This explains why you selected the text and used the keyboard command for Break Apart. This procedure converts vectors, like those used in text, into bitmaps. Just be aware that once text is broken apart it is no longer editable as text.*

2. Select the Text tool, click on the stage, and enter in New York. Set the Text property in the Property Inspector to Static. Convert the selection to a movie clip named House2, open the movie clip, and break this text apart as well. Click the Scene 1 link to return to the main timeline and delete the movie clip from the stage.

3. Open the Align panel—choose Window ➤ Align—and, as shown in Figure 12-6, align the House movie clip to the center of the stage.

4. Add a key frame at frame 10 of the timeline. Select the movie clip on the stage and open the Transform panel—choose Window ➤ Transform. Deselect Constrain in the panel and set the horizontal scale value to 5% (be sure to press Enter/Return after setting the value). This will "squash" the text. Right-click (PC) or Control-click (Mac) between the two key frames and select Create Motion Tween from the context menu.

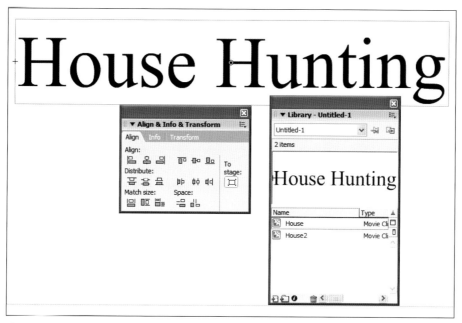

Figure 12-6. The text is ready to go for a "spin."

5. Insert a key frame in frame 11 of the timeline and select the movie clip on the stage. Select the Properties tab of the Property Inspector and click the Swap button. This will open the Swap Symbol dialog box (see Figure 12-7). Select the House2 movie clip and click OK. Notice how the movie clip appears on the stage with the same distortion as the one it replaced?

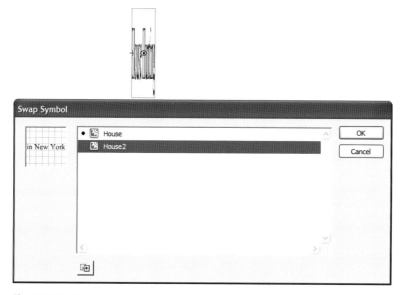

Figure 12-7. You can swap symbols at the click of a mouse.

6. Insert a key frame at frame 20 of the timeline. Select the symbol on the stage and set its horizontal scale value to 100% in the Transform panel.

7. Add key frames at frames 30 and 31. Select the movie clip on the stage in frame 30 and set its horizontal scale value to 5%. Select the object on the stage in frame 31 and swap this symbol with the House movie clip.

8. Add a key frame at frame 40 of the movie, select the symbol on the stage, and set its horizontal scale value to 100%. Add motion tweens between the key frames and then save and test the movie (see Figure 12-8).

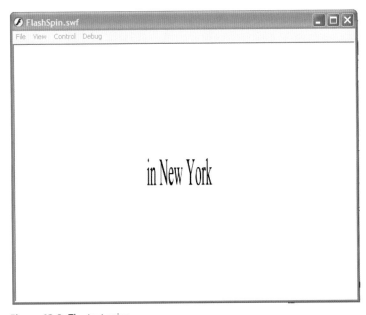

Figure 12-8. The text spins.

Going for a "spin" in After Effects 7

As you have seen, it is possible to create a spinning motion graphic in Flash, but the process is a bit convoluted, especially if you are using text. After Effects 7 contains a number of effects that handle the chores for you.

The 3D effects give you the ability to create some rather amazing motion graphics that are relatively easy to apply and manipulate. Just be aware that the workflow is a bit different with these effects. They need to be exported out of After Effects as an FLV, not a SWF. If you export the SWF you get a bunch of key frames and no motion.

> Before we get going, this exercise covers a very basic feature of the 3D capabilities of After Effects. You could add a serious amount of power and complexity in After Effects that we simply can't cover in one exercise.

1. Open the `AEFireEscapes.fla` file in your Chapter 12 Exercise folder. You will notice there is a red box on the stage. This is used to indicate where the motion graphic will be placed on the stage and will give you the dimensions of the area where the motion graphic will appear. If you select the red box and click the Properties tab of the Property Inspector you will see it is to be placed in an area that is 95 pixels high by 235 pixels wide.

If you don't have AfterEffects, skip to step 10 and use the `Spin.flv` *file located in the* `After Effects` *folder in the Chapter 12 Exercise folder.*

---

2. Open After Effects 7 and create a new composition named Spin. Set the width of this comp to 235 pixels and the height to 95 pixels. Set the frame rate to 24 fps and be sure to use Square Pixels. Click OK to close the New Composition window.

3. Select the Text tool, click once in the Comp Preview window, and enter House Hunting in New York. Click once between the words Hunting and in. With the Shift key held down, press Enter/Return. Select the text and, in the Character panel, use these settings:

   - Font: Times, Time Bold or _serif.
   - Font Style: Select Bold from the pop-down if you aren't using a font with the word *Bold* or *Heavy* in its name.
   - Color: Yellow.
   - Font size: 30 pixels.

4. Select Window ➤ Paragraph and select the Center Alignment. If necessary, position the text in the composition window as shown in Figure 12-9.

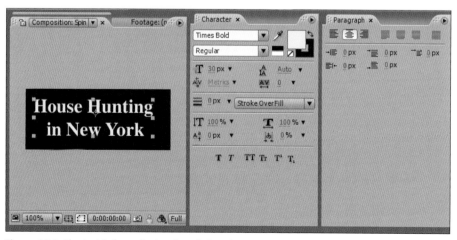

Figure 12-9. The text is formatted and ready to spin.

5. If it isn't open, open the Effects & Presets panel by selecting Window ➤ Effects & Presets. Twirl down Perspective and drag the Basic 3D effect strip onto the text in the comp window. The Effect Controls (see Figure 12-10) will appear in the Project panel. These effects will be used to control the spin of the text.

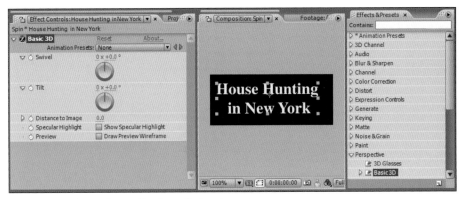

Figure 12-10. The Basic 3D effect is applied to the text.

6. Twirl down the text in the timeline and then twirl down Effects and Basic 3D. The properties that affect the spin of the text are Swivel and Tilt. Swivel will rotate the selection using the vertical axis, and Tilt does the rotation on the horizontal axis. We will be using Tilt.

7. Drag the playback head to the one-second mark on the timeline and click the stopwatch beside the Tilt property to add a key frame. A small diamond will appear on the timeline.

Now that the key frame is in place, you can concentrate on the animation.

8. Select the key frame and set the Tilt value to +45 degrees. This can be done by

- Dragging the Tilt knob in the Effect Controls panel
- Double-clicking the value in the Effect Controls panel and entering 45 as the Tilt value
- Clicking and dragging the value to the right in the Effect Controls panel
- Double-clicking the Tilt value in the timeline and entering the value
- Clicking and dragging the Tilt value in the timeline to the right

9. Add four more key frames at the times shown here and give each the following Tilt value. All you need to do is scrub the playhead to the next position on the timeline and change the setting. After Effects will automatically add the key frame:

- 2-second: 135
- 3 -second: 225
- 4-second: 0

If you click the play button in the Time Controls panel, you can preview the animation.

10. Trim the timeline to the length of the work area and select File ➤ Export ➤ Flash Video (FLV) to open the Flash 8 Video Encoder.

At this stage you can save the comp and quit After Effects.

> *Copies of the QuickTime movie—*Spin.mov*—the FLV, and the AEP file are in the After Effects folder in the Chapter 12 Exercise folder.*

11. Return to Flash, add an FLV Playback component to a new layer in the timeline, and set the contentPath to the FLV just created.

12. Save and test the movie. The text, as shown in Figure 12-11, is spinning.

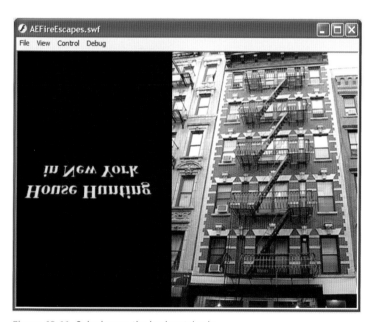

Figure 12-11. Spinning on the horizontal axis

Text in motion with the "Wiggler"

When you start using After Effects, there will come a time when you look at the presets and think, "Gosh, I am bored with these." That will be the point where you discover Adobe has a wonderful sense of humor and you start using the Wiggler. In the text options, on the timeline, the Wiggly selector can be added to a chunk of text to randomize the values of any of the properties associated with that group. That description may sound rather formal, but when it comes to adding effects, randomness can lead to some happy surprises.

Essentially you can have text bend, move, blur, spin, and so on by simply giving it some parameters for the effect. Where the randomness comes in is how the effect is applied. The parameter is the outer limit, which means the effect can be applied to any letter in the group and it will change using any value up to the parameter. For example, the phrase "New York" contains seven letters. They are in a fixed position but the parameter says the maximum distance they can move is 50 percent of the start position. When the Wiggler is applied, each letter will move any distance from 1 percent to 50 percent, meaning one letter may move a short distance while the one beside it moves to the other side of the screen.

This section will be composed of two exercises. The first will be a short one, designed to introduce you to the Wiggler. The second one will take what you have learned and create a rather complex motion graphic.

1. Open the `Wiggler1.fla` file in your Chapter 12 Exercise folder. As soon as it opens you will see it is the same House Hunting layout used earlier in this chapter. The difference is a red box is on the stage. The art director wants to have the animation appear at that size—235 pixels by 235 pixels—and with the same background color. To add some contrast the words House and York will be yellow (#FFFF60), the remaining words will be black (#000000), and the background color for the animation will be red (#FF0000).

2. Open After Effects 7 and create a new comp named House. Set the dimensions to 235 pixels wide by 235 pixels high. Set the frame rate to 24 fps and click OK to close the New Composition dialog box.

3. Adding the background color can be done in a couple of ways. The first is to select Composition ➤ Background Color (see Figure 12-12) and choose the red by clicking on the color chip in the dialog box to open the Color Picker. You can add the red by entering FF0000 at the bottom of the dialog box. This is where hex colors used in web development can be entered. This color will appear as the background color used in the comp window.

The second method is the one we are going to use because it is quite familiar to you. You can add layers to your After Effects projects. After Effects layers work in exactly the same manner as their Flash counterparts. They are stacked on top of each other, and you change their order by dragging them up or down to new positions in the timeline. Where After Effects layers and Flash layers part company is that layers in After Effects can be used for specific purposes such as a text layer that holds only text and a solid layer that can create solid color images up to 30,000×30,000 pixels in size.

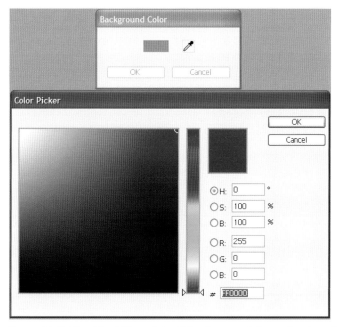

Figure 12-12. The After Effects Color Picker lets you define web color values.

4. Select Layer ➤ New ➤ Solid to open the Solid Settings dialog box shown in Figure 12-13. Set the Width and Height values to 235 and select Square Pixels from the Pixel Aspect Ratio pop-down. Click on the color chip and set the color of the solid to FF000. When you click OK a new layer named Red Solid 1 will appear on the timeline.

Figure 12-13. Adding a new solid layer to the timeline

5. Select Layer ➤ New ➤ Text and a new text layer will appear on the timeline. Enter House Hunting in New York. Click once between the words Hunting and in and, with the Shift key held down, press Enter/Return. Select the text and apply the following values in the Character panel:

■ Font: We chose Impact but you can choose any sans serif face, such as Arial or _sans.

■ Style: Style Regular or Bold, depending on the font you chose.

■ Size: 24 pixels.

■ Leading: 46 pixels.

■ Color: Black for the words Hunting in New and yellow (FFFF60) for the words House and York.

To start wiggling the words, follow these steps:

6. Twirl down the text layer and click the Animate button on the layer strip. A pop-down menu will appear and show you all of the individual properties that can be put in motion. Select All Transform Properties (see Figure 12-14) from the menu. A new animator, named Animator 1, will open in the timeline.

7. Now that you have an animator, click the Add button and choose Selector ➤ Wiggly. A new Wiggly Selector 1 item will be added to the timeline and the text properties that can be "wiggled" appear under the Wiggly selector. Now the fun starts.

■ Drag the playback head across the timeline. Notice nothing happens. This is because all of the properties are at their current default value of 0.

■ Click-drag the Position values. The value on the left moves the letters right and left. The value on the right moves the letters up and down. Drag the playback head across the timeline and the letters will move in random directions based on the values used in the Position area. Double-click the values and enter 0 for both Position values to return to the starting state of the text block.

■ Click-drag the Scale value. When you scrub the timeline, the letters seem to pulsate as they randomly approach the maximum value. Reset the value to 100%. The first value scales along the y-axis and the second one scales along the x-axis. With the Lock icon selected by default, changing one value changes the other.

■ Double-click the Rotate value and set it to 45 degrees. Scrub the timeline and the letters appear to rotate, to a maximum value of 45 degrees, to the right. Reset the Rotate value to 0. The first value determines the number of times the layer rotates.

Figure 12-14. Getting ready to wiggle some words

8. Twirl down the Wiggly selector to open the Wiggle options. They are as follows:

- Mode: This pop-down determines how the Wiggly selector should be combined with the selectors above it in the timeline. This one is really complex and we won't be touching it.

- Max Amount and Min Amount: These two options specify the range of variation. To understand how this works, assume you change the position values to 50,50. Some of the letters move off the screen while others move up and down. The Max Amount value moves the pixels down and to the right. The negative Min Amount values moves them up and to the left.

- Based on: Applies the wiggle based on characters, words, or lines of text.

- Wiggles/Second: Set this to a low value and things move slowly.

- Correlation: Controls whether the character offsets are different (0%) or all the same (100%). This essentially "tightens" the spread of the characters in the animation; smaller numbers pull the characters closer to each other.

- Temporal Phase: Changes the "timing" of each of the wiggles. The first number is the number of revolutions per second that will be applied, and the second is the degrees through which the selection will rotate.

- Spatial Phase: Moves the pattern like a wave through the text.

9. Now that you understand what the various options do, use these values for the Wiggly selector:

   - Wiggles/Second: 2.5

   - Temporal Phase: 40 degrees

   - Spatial Phase: 100 degrees

   - Max Amount: 100%

   - Min Amount: –100%

   - Position: 50,50

   - Scale: 45%

   - Rotation: 30 degrees

If you click the play button in the Time Controls or press your spacebar, you can see your animation in action. Obviously, if the viewer is going to be able to understand the text, the letters are going to have to stop their wiggling and dancing and come back into order. This is rather simple to accomplish. As you saw at the start of this exercise, if the properties are reset to 0, there is nothing to wiggle and the letters move back into their starting positions.

So let's wrap up this animation.

10. Add key frames for each of these properties at the one-second and six-second marks on the timeline.

11. Select the following key frames at the six-second mark and change their values to

    - Max Amount: 0

    - Min Amount: 0

    - Position: 0

    - Scale: 0

    - Rotation: 0

If you drag the playback head back to 0 and press the spacebar, you will see the letters frantically wiggling (see Figure 12-15) and then slow down as their values approach 0. When the playback head passes the six-second mark, the letters are back to their starting position.

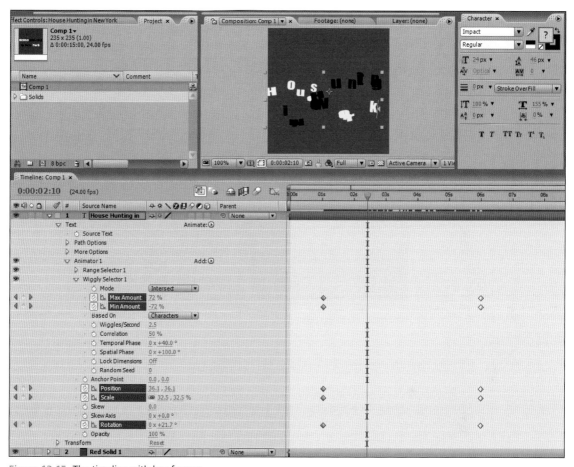

Figure 12-15. The timeline with key frames

12. Pull the work area end handle to the seven-second mark and trim the comp to fit the work area.

13. Export the file as an FLV to the Exercise folder. When you have finished creating the FLV, save the file and quit After Effects.

14. Return to the `Wiggler1.fla` file. Add a new layer named Video and delete the red box on the stage.

15. Add an FLV Playback component to the stage in the Video layer. Set its contentPath to the FLV file you just created and be sure there is no skin in the component's parameters.

16. Save and test the movie to see your wiggling text (see Figure 12-16).

Figure 12-16. Wiggling in New York

Creating a "wiggly" splash screen

In this exercise we bring video and text into play to create a "splash page" for a site devoted to motion graphics in Flash Professional 8. The plan is to use a video of flames and overlay a "wiggly" motion graphic on top of it. This exercise will introduce you to such After Effects techniques as animating on multiple layers, easing in, and easing out, which are remarkably similar to their Flash counterparts.

> *In this example the authors will be using an Artbeats video—*RF108.mov*—that can be found in the Artbeats Video Bundle obtained from the Artbeats catalog at* www.artbeats.com. *Though this material is royalty free, making it available to you through this book is not allowed through the license. If you don't have this particular clip, feel free to use any footage you may already have. The important aspect here is not the footage but how the footage is used.*

1. Open After Effects and create a new comp that is 320 by 240, uses square pixels, and has a frame rate of 24 fps.

2. Select File ➤ Import ➤ File and locate your footage. Click the Open button in the Import File dialog box and the footage will be imported into your Project panel.

3. Drag the footage from the Project panel to the timeline. Position the footage in the comp window and, once you are satisfied with the position, click the selection box under the Lock icon in the timeline to lock the layer. This ensures you don't accidentally move the video or otherwise manipulate it during the rest of the process.

4. Add a new text layer to the composition. Select the Text tool. Click once on the comp and enter the words Flash Professional 8. Use these formatting settings:

   ▧ Font: Arial or other sans serif font. In this example we use Arial Black.

   ▧ Style: Bold. If you are using a font whose name contains the word *Bold*, *Black*, or *Heavy*, leave the style at Regular. In our case we use Arial Black (Style is left at Regular).

   ▧ Size: 26 pixels

   ▧ Color: White or FFFFFF in the Color Picker.

   ▧ Alignment: Center.

5. Create a new type layer, select the Text tool, and enter the words Motion graphics on fire. Use these formatting settings:

   ▧ Font: Arial or other sans serif font. In this example we use Arial Black.

   ▧ Style: Bold. If you are using a font whose name contains the word *Bold*, *Black*, or *Heavy*, leave the style at Regular. In our case we use Arial Black (Style is left at Regular).

   ▧ Size: 18 pixels

   ▧ Color: Yellow or FFFF00 in the Color Picker.

   ▧ Alignment: Center.

6. Select the word fire (see Figure 12-17). This word is going to get a little more emphasis because of the flames in the background. Use these formatting settings for the selection:

   ▧ Font: Arial or other sans serif font. In this example we use Arial Black.

   ▧ Style: Bold. If you are using a font whose name contains the word *Bold*, *Black*, or *Heavy*, leave the style at Regular. In our case we use Arial Black (Style is left at Regular).

   ▧ Size: 24 pixels

   ▧ Color: Orange or FF6600 in the Color Picker.

   ▧ Alignment: Center.

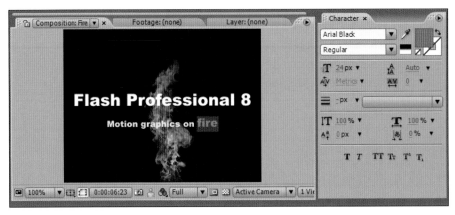

Figure 12-17. The text is in place.

With the text in place and, with apologies to Dr. Evil, "Let's get jiggy with the Wiggler."

In the previous example, you were given the opportunity to see how a wiggle can be applied to all of the text properties. In this one, you will learn how to target a property resulting in a more focused animation.

7. Twirl down the Flash Professional text layer and click the Animate button. Select Position (see Figure 12-18) from the Animate pop-down menu. This will add Animator 1 to the layer. Twirl down the Animator 1. Select the second item in the Position property and click-drag the mouse to the right to a value of -90. Click the Add button and select Selector ➤ Wiggly Selector. Press the spacebar and you will see the letters moving around.

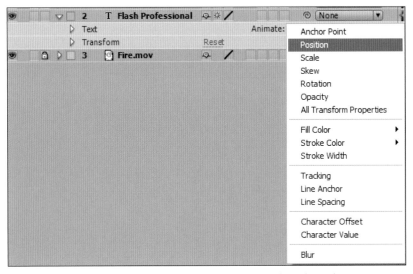

Figure 12-18. Specific properties of the object on a layer can be animated.

8. That's quite interesting because you have specified how the characters move. Let's add a bit more chaos to this animation. Click the Add button and select Property ➤ Scale, and then repeat this by selecting Property ➤ Rotation. These three geometric properties are now in one animator and can be controlled by a Wiggly selector. Change the parameters to the following values:

   ▪ Position: 0,90

   ▪ Scale: 300%

   ▪ Rotation: 1, 300 degrees

   Press the spacebar and you now have a totally different animation that is a bit chaotic.

9. Chaos is fine, but it can be a bit disorienting to the user. Let's try to bring a touch of order to the chaos. In the timeline, twirl down the Wiggly Selector 1. The Wiggles/Second value is currently 2. Let's experiment with a different value. The movie *The Matrix* is famous for a scene in which the hero dodges a hail of bullets by seemingly slowing down time itself. You can do that here as well. Reduce the Wiggles/Second value to 0.3. Set the Temporal Phase and Spatial Phase values to 0 and press the spacebar. It's "bullet time." So much for playing; let's get back to work.

10. Pull the playback head back to the 0-second mark and add key frames to the Temporal Phase and Spatial Phase values. Add another key frame for each value at the one-second mark and change both values to 2, 0.00 degrees.

You just added two revolutions to the text. Press the spacebar and the text will move into hyper-wiggle. As the playback head reaches the one-second mark, where you just inserted the key frame, the animation will slow down.

11. Move the playback head to the two-second mark and click the blank check box on the left side of the timeline for the Temporal Phase and Spatial Phase layers. Adding these two key frames will lock the slow motion in place until you are ready to start another animation.

12. Add two more key frames to the Temporal and Spatial Phase layers and change the rotation value in both to 4. Add key frames at the four-second mark to keep the animation in place. Drag the playback head to the 0 mark and press the spacebar. This time, keep an eye on the characters. If they seem to be too spread out, change the Correlation value to 75% or lower. Press the spacebar again, and you will see the letters are quite a bit closer to each other.

It would be nice if the viewer could read the text without it jittering all over the screen. As you recall from the previous exercise, the Wiggler can only animate a property if its value is greater than 0.

13. Move the playback head to the four-second mark and click the stopwatch for the Position, Scale, and Rotation layers to add key frames. Add key frames for these layers at the five-second mark and change the Scale value to 100% and the Position and Rotation values to 0.

14. Select each of the new key frames at the five-second mark and press Shift+F9. This is the command for Ease In. You can tell an Ease In has been applied because the key frame in the timeline switches from its diamond shape to an arrow shape. Press the spacebar to preview the animation.

In the previous exercise you let After Effects figure out how to slow down the animation and bring the letters back into line. It was rather smooth, but the real issue is not the smoothness. If things are randomly jittering and wiggling, they don't all slow down at the same rate.

When you throw a ball in the air, it doesn't move upward from your hand at a uniform speed. As it leaves your hand it accelerates. Somewhere around the middle of its travels upward, it will have a uniform speed but shortly after that gravity gets hold of it and the upward motion decelerates to 0. The initial toss is an Ease In—acceleration decreases to a uniform speed—and once gravity gets hold of it, that is the Ease Out point—deceleration to 0.

Easing the animation in essentially says to After Effects, "Here's where I want to start and here's where I want to end. Make it appear real." In this case the animation for each letter would appear to slow down as it approaches the key frame at frame 5. It is only as the playback head approaches that key frame that the letters will randomly approach the final position.

15. That takes care of the first text block. Save the project and let's turn our attention to the remaining text.

> There are a couple of ways to apply an Ease In or Ease Out. The first is to select the key frame and press Shift+F9 (Ease In) or Ctrl+Shift+F9 (PC) or Cmd+Shift+F9 (Mac) for Ease Out (see Figure 12-19). The other method is to right-click (PC) or Cmd-click (Mac) on a key frame to open the context menu. When the menu opens, select KeyFrame Assistant and select Ease In or Ease Out from the submenu that appears.

16. Twirl up the text layer you have been working on to give yourself more room on the timeline and twirl down the second text layer. Click on the layer name and press the S key to open the Scale property. Change the Scale amount to about 80%.

17. Select Animate ➤ Property ➤ Position. Then select Animate ➤ Property ➤ Rotation. Select the Animator 1 and add a Wiggly selector. With the Wiggly selector added, change the Position value to 0, 100 and the Rotation value to 0, 40 degrees. Press the spacebar.

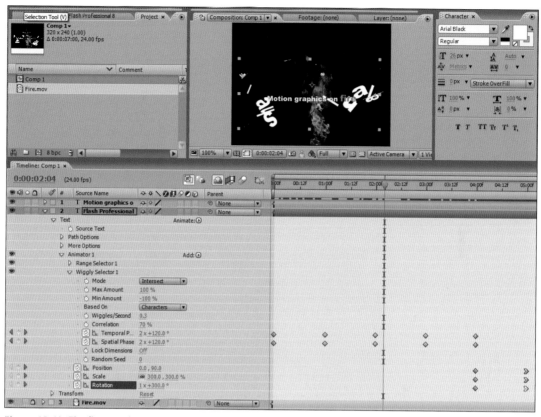

Figure 12-19. The first text layer is animated. Note the Ease In icon on the timeline.

The whole line of text appears to be on some sort of sugar high and is jumping all over the screen. This is not exactly what was planned. You want the Wiggler to randomize the values but not push them into continuous motion. Let's use the Wiggler to move the letter and rotate them, but let's smooth out the animation from its current frantic "break dance" to a smooth waltz across the dance floor.

18. Twirl down the Wiggly selector and set its Wiggles/Second value to 0.

19. Drag the playback head to the six-second mark on the timeline and add a key frame to the Position and Rotation values in the Animator 1 layer.

20. Drag the playback head back to the five-second mark and change the Position and Rotation values in the Animator 1 to 0. Press Shift+Ctrl+F9 (PC) or Shift+Cmd+F9 (Mac) to select Ease Out for the animation in the Position and Rotation layers. Instead of the entire line bouncing around, we want the viewer's eye to focus on the word fire.

21. Drag the playback head to the five-second mark of the timeline. Click once on the text in the comp window and look for the Range selector icon. It is a vertical gray line with a small arrow to the left of it on the left edge of the bounding box. When you find it, drag the arrow to the left edge of the letter f in the word fire.

The Range selector (see Figure 12-20) is a neat feature. In the case of this animation you only need the word fire moving. Placing the Range selector to the left of the word will only animate the characters and/or words to the right of the Selector. Even though a Wiggler is in play, this gives you total control over the animation.

Figure 12-20. The Range selector, circled in red, lets you control what moves and what doesn't.v

22. Press the spacebar to preview your animation (see Figure 12-21). Not a bad job at all. Congratulations.

23. Save the project.

Figure 12-21. The word fire is in motion.

Rendering video from After Effects

Throughout this chapter we have been directly exporting an FLV file out of After Effects. There will be times where you may need a digital video instead. Here's how you do that:

1. Click once on the comp window and select Composition ➤ Add to Render Queue. This will highlight the Render Queue panel under the timeline.

The Render Queue panel (see Figure 12-21) is split into two distinct areas. At the top is where the project will be rendered to a digital video, and the bottom half is where you set what type of video will be produced and the compression to be applied to the video. You can see the default format and compression values by twirling down the Render Settings and the Output Module.

The Render Settings are acceptable. Let's change the Output Module to create a QuickTime movie instead of the default AVI.

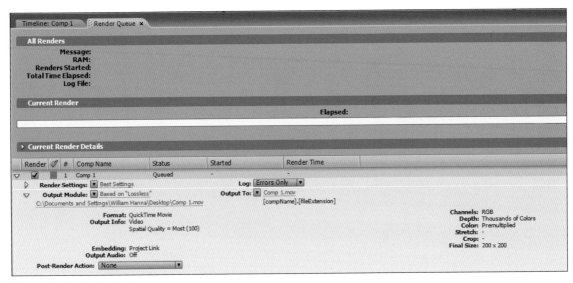

Figure 12-22. The Render Queue panel

2. Twirl up the Render Settings to collapse them. Click the Lossless link in the Output Module to open the Output Module Settings dialog box.

3. Click once on the Format pop-down and select QuickTime Movie. In the Embed Options pop-down, select None. You don't need a link to this project to be added to the video.

4. Click the Format Options button to open the list of codecs in the Compression Settings dialog box that can be applied to the video.

> *Exercise some caution here because if this video is destined for conversion to an FLV file, you will be applying double compression to the video both here and in the Flash 8 Video Encoder, which results in rather poor quality.*

5. This file is going to pay a visit to the Flash 8 Video Encoder, so select Video in the Compression type pop-down menu and click OK to return to the Output Module Settings dialog box. It is a lossless compressor, so no information will be lost when the video is created.

6. With this particular project there will be no need for a change in file size and there is no audio track, so feel free to click OK. This will close the dialog box and return you to the Render Queue panel.

If you do have an audio track in your After Effects project, don't just assume it will be added when you create the video. If you leave the Audio Output *check box deselected (see Figure 12-23), your soundtrack won't be added to the final output.*

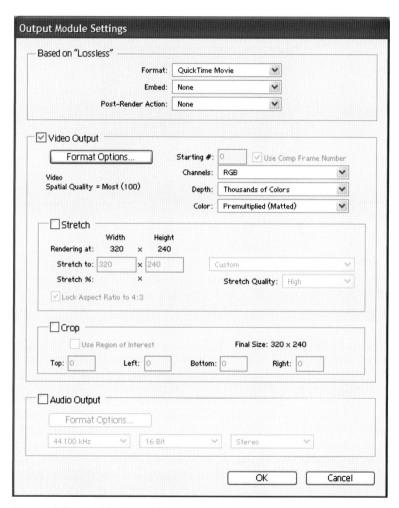

Figure 12-23. The video is ready for output.

7. Click the link in the Output To area. This allows you to name the file (Comp 1 is so boring!) and determine which folder on your computer will be the final location of the rendered video. When the Output Movie To dialog box opens, navigate to the folder where the MOV file is to be saved, name the movie Fire.mov, and click the Save button.

8. At this point you are ready to "lock and load" the video. Click the Render button in the Render Queue panel. You will be shown the progress of the render process and, when it finishes, you will hear a chime.

9. Save the project and quit After Effects.

10. Preview your movie in the QuickTime player, as shown in Figure 12-24.

Figure 12-24. Smokin' in QuickTime!

Summary

We hope, through this brief overview, that you have a sense of some of the animation capabilities of After Effects and how it can support your needs in Flash. Whether it's a text animation that has to fit into a specific location in a Flash movie or a splash page, After Effects is an indispensable tool when it comes to Flash video.

Throughout this book you have created a number of animations using the Effects & Presets panel to create a title sequence. You have also explored, briefly, how a 3D animation can be applied in After Effects. You should also now be aware of the power of the animation selectors in After Effects. We showed you two ways of putting text into motion using a Wiggler. One was fairly simple, and the other one not only expanded the use of this function but also showed you how to create a QuickTime video in After Effects. That video can then either be exported out as an FLV file or as a digital video for later conversion to an FLV through the Flash 8 Video Encoder.

This has been quite an exploration. We started with the creation of a simple FLV file, meandered through video creation in iMovie and Movie Maker, and then started exploring the creative aspects of Flash video, ranging from creating and using alpha channel video to some rather amazing creative uses of Flash video, such as masking and filters. You have explored how to create a video wall, use a web camera, choose and play multiple videos, and even created your own personal FLV tool.

That is a lot of ground and, in many respects, we have just scratched the surface of the power of Flash video on the Internet. Over the coming months and years, as Adobe makes the integration of its tools even tighter with Flash, the creative possibilities available to you will explode. That should be an immense amount of fun.

Speaking of fun… as we tell anybody who will listen, the amount of fun you can have with Flash video should be illegal. We'll see you in jail.

INDEX

W

X

Y

Z

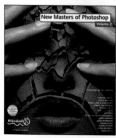
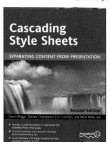

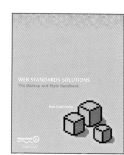

friendsofed.com/forums

Join the friends of ED forums to find out more about our books, discover useful technology tips and tricks, or get a helping hand on a challenging project. *Designer to Designer*™ is what it's all about—our community sharing ideas and inspiring each other. In the friends of ED forums, you'll find a wide range of topics to discuss, so look around, find a forum, and dive right in!

- **Books and Information**

  Chat about friends of ED books, gossip about the community, or even tell us some bad jokes!

- **Flash**

  Discuss design issues, ActionScript, dynamic content, and video and sound.

- **Web Design**

  From front-end frustrations to back-end blight, share your problems and your knowledge here.

- **Site Check**

  Show off your work or get new ideas.

- **Digital Imagery**

  Create eye candy with Photoshop, Fireworks, Illustrator, and FreeHand.

- **ArchivED**

  Browse through an archive of old questions and answers.

HOW TO PARTICIPATE

Go to the friends of ED forums at **www.friendsofed.com/forums**.